Introducing Daoism

Introducing Daoism
religious tradition,
historical survey.

Livia Kohn trac
antiquity, following
day. She explores
tradition in the wor
early forms of self-c

Each chapter int
in Daoism, and Da(
and doctrine, medit

Introducing Dao
and examines its ac
and study of Daois:
tradition today, this
learning more abou

Illustrated throu
pronunciation guid
understanding and

Livia Kohn is Prof(
For her current acti

World Religions series

Edited by Damien Keown and Charles S. Prebish

This exciting series introduces students to the major world religious traditions. Each religion is explored in a lively and clear fashion by experienced teachers and leading scholars in the field of world religions. Up-to-date scholarship is presented in a student-friendly fashion, covering history, core beliefs, sacred texts, key figures, religious practice and culture, and key contemporary issues. To aid learning and revision, each text includes illustrations, summaries, explanations of key terms, and further reading.

Introducing Daoism
Livia Kohn

Introducing Judaism
Eliezer Segal

Introducing Buddhism
Charles S. Prebish and Damien Keown

Introducing Christianity
James R. Adair

Introducing Hinduism
Hillary P. Rodrigues

Introducing Japanese Religion
Robert Ellwood

Forthcoming:

Introducing American Religions
Introducing Chinese Religions
Introducing Islam
Introducing New Religious Movements
Introducing Tibetan Buddhism

Introducing Daoism

Livia Kohn

Routledge
Taylor & Francis Group
LONDON AND NEW YORK

First published 2009
by Routledge
2 Park Square, Milton Park, Abingdon, Oxon OX14 4RN

Simultaneously published in the USA and Canada
by Routledge
270 Madison Ave, New York, NY 10016

Routledge is an imprint of the Taylor & Francis Group, an informa business

© 2009 Livia Kohn

Typeset in Jenson and Tahoma by
HWA Text and Data Management, London
Printed and bound in Great Britain by
TJ International, Padstow, Cornwall

British Library Cataloguing in Publication Data
A catalogue record for this book is available from the British Library

Library of Congress Cataloging-in-Publication Data
Kohn, Livia, 1956–
   Introducing Daoism / Livia Kohn.
      p. cm. – (World religions)
   Includes index.
   1. Taoism. I. Title.
   BL1920.K63 2008
   299.5´14–dc22   2008010152

ISBN10: 0–415–43997–3 (hbk)
ISBN10: 0–415–43998–1 (pbk)

ISBN13: 978–0–415–43997–8 (hbk)
ISBN13: 978–0–415–43998–5 (pbk)

Contents

Illustrations

Dynastic chart

Sui	581–618
Tang	618–907
Empress Wu	690–705
Five Dynasties	907–960
Liao	916–1125
Song	960–1279
Northern	960–1126
Southern	1126–1279
Mongol-Yuan	1260–1368
Ming	1368–1644
Manchu-Qing	1644–1911
Republic (Taiwan)	1911–
People's Republic	1949–

Pronunciation guide

The transliteration used in this book is Pinyin, the official form of transcribing Chinese used in mainland China. Although Pinyin is most commonly used today, older works and some recent studies still make use of the traditional Wade-Giles system. Generally, vowels are very close in both systems, with the one exception that Wade-Giles uses the "ü" with umlaut while Pinyin for the most part does not, especially after the vowels "j" and "ch." The pronunciation is "ü" in either case.

Consonants differ more significantly. Whereas Pinyin conforms to standard English usage, in Wade-Giles all aspirated consonants (written with an apostrophe) are pronounced as original (T' = T, P' = P), while nonaspirated ones are pronounced softly (T = D, P = B), thus the traditional transliteration "Taoism" and the more modern "Daoism." In addition, "J" in Wade-Giles is "R" in Pinyin, and pronounced like a deep, growling "R." Finally, the various "tch" and "dse" sounds differ:

PY	WG	English	Example
x	hs	soft sh	Xu = Hsü = Shü
j	ch	soft dch	Juan = chüan = dchüen
q	ch'	sharp tch	Qi = ch'i = tchee
zh	ch	soft dch	Zhang = Chang = Dchang
ch	ch'	sharp tch	Cheng = Ch'eng = Tcheng
zhi	chih	soft dch-rr	
chi	ch'ih	sharp tch-rr	
zi	tzu	soft dse	Laozi = Lao-tzu = Laodse
ci	tz'u	sharp tse	
si	ssu	hissing sse	

Acknowledgments

We are indebted to the people and archives listed below for permission to reproduce photographs or original illustrative material. Every effort has been made to trace copyright-holders. Any omissions brought to our attention will be remedied in future editions.

Bridgeman Art Library:

An oracle bone of the Shang dynasty
Portrait of Confucius
The Three Pure Ones
The three gods Fu Lu Shou

www.wudangquan.net:

A Daoist practicing the sword

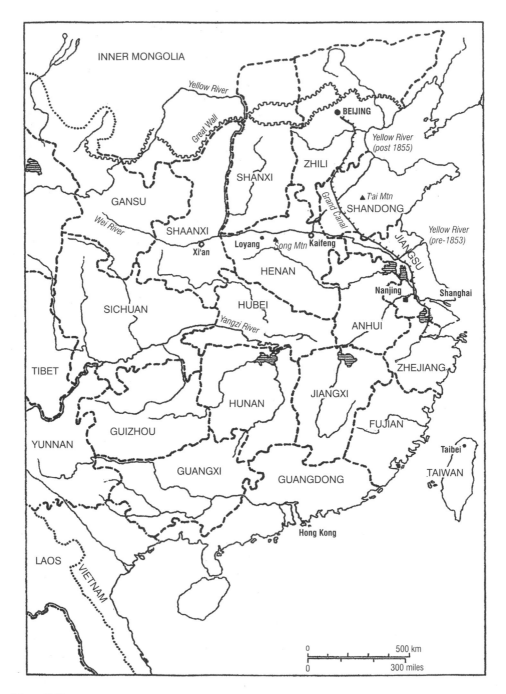

Map of China

Introduction

Background to Daoism

In this chapter

Daoism forms an integral part of Chinese culture and has not only contributed considerably to its shaping and development, but is also deeply embedded in it. In the time before even the first traces of Daoism appear on the historical horizon – usually associated with the philosopher Laozi, dated to around 500 B.C.E. – various cultural perceptions and religious practices were established that have had a lasting effect on Daoist philosophy, cosmology, ritual, and religious cultivation ever since. The four most notable ones form the contents of this chapter.

Main topics covered

- Shang ancestors and divination
- The *Yijing*
- Philosophical Schools
- Confucianism

Shang ancestors and divination

The Shang dynasty (*c.* 1600–1028 B.C.E.) is the earliest Chinese state documented in writing as well as archaeological finds – its predecessor, the Xia dynasty (*c.* 2100–1600 B.C.E.), and its contemporary, the western culture in Sichuan, are only known from excavated tombs and artifacts. Ruling the central area of China with a capital in what is today Henan, the Shang state worked through an extensive administrative bureaucracy, constituted by the king as central ruler, his relatives, local aristocrats, and educated upper-class officials.

Shang ancestors

The dominant belief of the dynasty was that the otherworld was similarly organized as the Shang bureaucracy. Populated by nature deities such as sun, moon, rain, and thunder as well as a plethora of ancestors – most importantly those of the ruling house and its original founder, known as Shangdi or Highest Ruler – the realm beyond had a major impact on all events and occurrences on earth. Ancestors not only served as intermediaries to the great nature deities but also influenced events on earth by bestowing either blessings or curses on human actions.

As a result, all actions involving the ruler, from the most mundane to the most decisive, had to be submitted to the ancestors' inspection and were either supported or rejected. All events likely to occur were posted to the ancestors for their prediction and guidance. Different ancestors, moreover, were responsible for different areas of life. They received regular offerings based on a complex ritual schedule that followed a calendar consisting of a ten-day week and twelve-year cycle. Both are still in use in China today, notably for fortune-telling purposes.[1]

Ancestor worship and divination

The key religious activity of the Shang dynasty involved ancestral sacrifices and divination. Ancestral sacrifices consisted of regular offerings of food and drink in special ritual vessels, usually cast from bronze. They came in all shapes and sizes and were richly ornamented with supernatural figures and intricate patterns. These vessels are the famous Shang bronzes, exhibited in numerous museums around the world, and the object of more or less skilled forgeries since the Song dynasty.

Divination, unlike fortune-telling from palms, playing cards, or dreams, is the reading of divine guidance through secondary signs. A well-known Western example is the auguries of ancient Rome, where the flight pattern of birds was interpreted to foretell the success or failure of an upcoming battle. Shang rulers employed the so-called oracle bones. Discovered by accident by local farmers in Henan in the 1920s, the bones were first taken to be dragon bones and ground up as potent aphrodisiacs. Once identified by archaeologists, they were brought to museums and gradually their writing, the earliest form of Chinese characters, was deciphered and has since been called the oracle-bone script.

Oracle bones

Oracle bones were originally carapaces of turtles, seen as symbols of the cosmos with their square base (earth) and round top (heaven). Later, when China ran out of turtles and even could not import more from Vietnam, shoulder blades of cattle were used. Trained technicians drilled holes into them at specific spots, then heated them over a

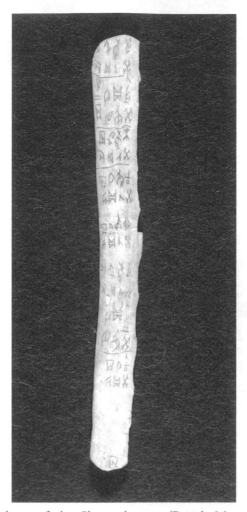

Figure 0.1 An oracle bone of the Shang dynasty (British Museum, London, UK/The Bridgeman Art Library.)

fire. As a result, in the drilled area the bone would crack. The cracks were interpreted by professional diviners to mean either yes or no. Even today the character for divination is the image of a crack: ⼘ . Both question and answer were recorded by scribes, leaving a good record of the concerns and tendencies of the ancient Chinese. Questions could be both simple and more complicated, including the outcome of warfare, the birth of son or daughter, the relief for the king's toothache. Over the years, the bones were reused, so that many have inscriptions on both sides.

While it is clear that oracle-bone divination was a very involved ritual that required various specialists, scholars are divided with regard to its exact nature. Was the divination in essence a bureaucratic and rather rational method of learning the ancestors' intention (e.g. David Keightley)? Or was it a more ecstatic and shamanic rite that involved direct contact with the otherworld and was undertaken to the accompaniment of music and dance, and possibly with the help of alcoholic drinks and psychedelic drugs (e.g. Chang Kwang-chih)? Similarly it is not clear whether the bronze vessels, undoubtedly used to present offerings to the ancestors, were mere vessels for food and drink or, through their animal designs and intricate patterns, represented the divine conveyance of shamanic priests in their excursion to the heavens. Both methods, the rational divination according to signs and the ecstatic/ shamanic way of connecting to the gods have continued actively in Chinese culture, so history does not provide an answer.

Impact on Daoism

Daoists incorporated a heavy dose of Shang religion into their beliefs and practices. The Daoist otherworld is hierarchically organized and populated by nature deities and ancestors, joined in due course by pure divine emanations of the Dao and lofty spirit immortals; regular rituals to these various deities are essential to maintain harmony in the cosmos. The gods have to be appeased to prevent disasters but they can also be enticed to give guidance to human beings; communication with them is a bureaucratic act that involves the written language, no longer in the form of oracle-bone inscriptions but through petitions, contracts, mandates, and other formal documents. Daoist priests are intermediaries of the divine realm and occupy official positions in the otherworld; equipped with special passports and sacred passwords, they can – like shamans – travel into the spheres beyond.

The Yijing

Another early feature of Chinese culture that exerted a strong impact on Daoism is the *Yijing* or *Book of Changes*. Historically it supplanted Shang oracle-bone divination when the dynasty changed to the Zhou (1028–221 B.C.E.).

Belief in Heaven

Without giving up on nature gods and ancestors, the Zhou put their dominant faith in Heaven (*tian*). Unlike the Highest Ruler of the Shang, this was not a former human being and thus not guided by personal whims and moods. Rather, Heaven was a process, an abstract representation of the cycles and patterns of nature, a nonhuman force that interacted closely with the human world in a nonpersonal way.

For example, if people behaved in a morally upright way and the ruler did well, Heaven responded by creating harmony through appropriate weather patterns, fertility, and general wellness. It thereby showed its approval and granted the dynasty the right to rule, known as the "Mandate of Heaven." On the other hand, if people behaved badly and the government mismanaged the realm, Heaven showed its displeasure by sending along floods, droughts, earthquakes, locust plagues, epidemics, and the like. These were signs that the ruling dynasty had forfeited its Mandate and that it was time for a change. In Zhou thinking, Heaven thus represented the sum-total of human and natural activities, matching their impulses with appropriate responses.

The notion that humanity and nature/Heaven existed in a close, if not immediate, relationship has remained central to Chinese thinking, and even in 1976 it was very clear to all Chinese that the massive earthquake in August was a harbinger of the death of Chairman Mao in September – both equally signifying upheaval and major change. Daoists adopted this thinking, and the entire complex of Daoist ethics revolves around it (see Chapter 6).

Textual history

The *Yijing*, then, is a divination manual that – rather than providing yes/no answers as the oracle bones did – helps people determine the inherent tendencies in the course of Heaven and aids them in making good decisions through formal judgments and advice. Compiled into a coherent book by Confucius around 500 B.C.E., its system claims to go back to prehistory when a mythical ruler named Fu Xi discerned its original symbols from constellations in the stars. King Wen, the mastermind behind the Zhou conquest, supposedly first standardized its basic judgments.

Named one of the Six Classics by Confucius, the *Yijing* became part of literati training and was adopted by the Chinese upper classes. Many used it to gain personal readings on official careers and family concerns; some studied it in more detail and wrote commentaries and interpretations. In recent years, the text has also made inroads in the West, where translations have multiplied – some highly specialized such as, for example, a women's version called *The Kuan-yin Book of Changes*. Numerous people all over the world still explore the ancient classic for spiritual advice, use it for divination, and trust in its workings.

The eight trigrams

The system of the *Yijing* is based on the two cosmic forces yin and yang, which are symbolized by written lines: an unbroken line indicates yang, while a broken line shows yin. The two lines, like the binary pattern at the base of computing, are combined two by two into four symbols: double yang, yang over yin, double yin, and yin over yang. Next the lines are combined into eight symbols of three lines each, known as trigrams and linked symbolically with cosmic phenomena. The eight trigrams (*bagua*) are as follows:

heaven (*qian*, creative)	☰	earth (*kun*, receptive)	☷
fire (*li*, clinging)	☲	water (*kan*, abysmal)	☵
wind (*sun*, gentle)	☴	lake (*dui*, joyous)	☱
thunder (*zhen*, arousing)	☳	mountain (*gen*, still)	☶

These trigrams are still in wide use today. For example, they signify the Eight Corners of the house or room in fengshui and are commonly found on mirrors and other protective devices. In Daoist cosmology, they have played an important role in signifying different cosmic directions and dimensions. For example, they were arranged in two different patterns, laid out on a geographical grid, that represented the state before creation or "Former Heaven" (*xiantian*) and the forces of the universe

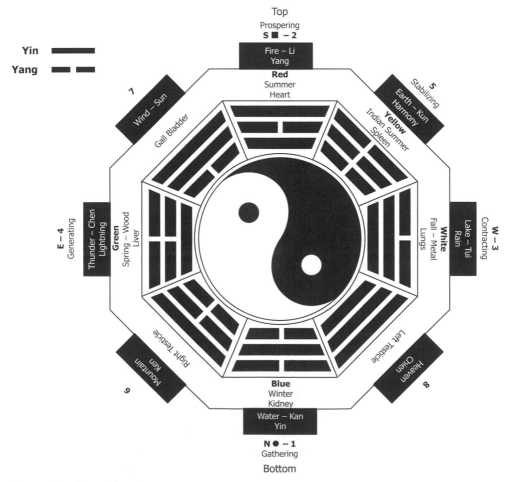

Figure 0.2   The eight trigrams

after creation or "Later Heaven" (*houtian*), states that also apply to the human body as pre- and postnatal.

Thus, before creation or birth in this body, Heaven (*qian*) is due south, while Earth (*kun*) is due north, Fire (*li*) and Water (*kan*) are to the east and west. In the course of creation, described as the union of Heaven and Earth, *kun* desires to join with *qian* and moves south. After connecting with *qian*, it establishes itself in the southwest. Similarly, Heaven, in an effort to merge with Earth, begins to move north and eventually comes to reside in the northwest. Fire and Water in the meantime rotate by ninety degrees and end up on the north–south axis. As Fire is established in the south and Water in the north, they match the set-up of the five phases that governs the world as we know it.

Hexagrams and judgments

In the *Yijing* proper, the trigrams are further used as building blocks for the so-called hexagrams, which consist of two-by-two combinations of trigrams into figures consisting of six lines. The sixty-four hexagrams make up the main body of the book. Each hexagram comes with an explanation of the image, a judgment, an explanation of the judgment, and a fortune for each individual line. For example, Hexagram no. 5, *xu* ("waiting") consists of the trigrams *kan* and *qian* or "water" over "heaven." Its image explanation runs:

> Clouds rise up to the heaven, the image of waiting. Thus the superior man eats and drinks, is joyous and of good cheer.

This presents the current situation in its essence. The text then provides a "judgment" which gives advice:

> Waiting. If you are sincere, you have light and success. Perseverance brings good fortune; it furthers one to cross the great water. (Wilhelm, *I Ching*, 24–25)

As this shows, the text gives general advice, often couched in rather ambiguous and vague terms. It reflects the reality of Zhou-dynasty life, where family relations were important, travel and communication were hard, the key relationship was with the lord or great man, and inner sincerity was valued highly. It is accessible today through commentaries, both traditional and modern, and often has to be read with a good dose of intuition and personal feeling.

Divination methods

There are two methods of obtaining a hexagram-fortune from the *Yijing*, both leading to an answer for a specific question one has in mind. The first, more traditional method is complicated. It involves the use of fifty milfoil stalks (long stems of a plant). First, one stalk is put aside, then the remaining forty-nine are divided into two piles. Four stalks are then counted off between each finger until there remain either one, two, three, or none. These remaining numbers are interpreted according to yin and yang – 1 = strong yang, 2 = strong yin; 3 = weak yang, 0 = weak yin – and the resulting line is written down, adding a little cross on the side if the line is strong. This is repeated five more times to obtain six lines total. The lines are written down from the bottom to the top. The resulting hexagram can then be looked up in the book. Every line that has a cross next to it, moreover, can be changed into its opposite, again beginning from the bottom and working upward. In this way further hexagrams are obtained to indicate later developments.

The second method to obtain a hexagram is a great deal easier and more popular today. It involves three identical coins, in which head is designated yang and tail means yin. Yang, moreover, counts 3, while yin counts 2. Throwing the three coins at any one time will result a total count of 6, 7, 8, or 9. These translate into lines: 9 = strong yang, 6 = strong yin, 7 = weak yang, and 8 = weak yin. Again, the line is written down, the throwing of coins repeated, and the hexagram obtained.

Role in Daoism

Daoists as much as other Chinese literati have used the *Yijing* for millennia to give guidance and to support them in their decision making. In alchemy, moreover, Daoists have used the hexagrams to symbolize the waxing and waning of yin and yang through the seasons, placing them in a series of twelve hexagrams that each show either an increase or decrease in yang lines:

This sequence shows the increase of yang between the winter and summer solstices – the latter located in the center of the line and symbolized by the six-yang hexagram "heaven" – followed by the increase of yin as the year once again moves toward winter. The system allows a subtle patterning of seasonal change which in turn creates the optimal conditions for the concoction of an elixir or the growth of the immortal embryo. Besides applying the *Yijing* in its originally intended mode as a divination manual, Daoists also employ its symbols to express subtle cosmological and internal transformations. In cosmological and alchemical treatises, the trigrams show the directions and dimensions of the universe while the hexagrams signify subtle stages and times of cultivation.

Philosophical schools

The Zhou dynasty ruled China for almost a millennium, from 1028 to 221 B.C.E. However, it did not maintain power steadily or without challenge for this entire period, but underwent various changes and transformations. One change occurred in 771 B.C.E., when the dynasty was attacked by Central Asian tribes and had to move its capital east to what is today Luoyang. Another major change occurred in the fifth century (479 B.C.E.), when it lost all but the most elementary ritual powers and a number of independent states or dukedoms emerged that in fact shaped the politics of the country. Historians have called this latter phase of Zhou rule the Warring States period, since the various states were not satisfied with the land and populace they controlled, but strove to enlarge their sphere of influence and made war with increasing frequency.

The Iron Age

One reason why war was more of an option than before is that around 500 B.C.E., China was undergoing tremendous economic and political changes. The arrival of iron-age technology created better ploughshares, wagon axles, and weapons. It not only caused an increase in food production which resulted in massive population growth but also led to greater mobility and wealth among the people, inspiring them to strive for more power, land, and goods. Rather than fighting for this by engaging in combat among select troops and feudal leaders, local lords began to set large infantry armies against each other, disrupting agricultural cycles and causing devastation in vast sections of the country. The overall result was a time of great unrest and transition which left many people yearning for the peace and stability of old.

Philosophical tendencies

It was also a time of great learning and increased literacy as the cumbersome writing of the oracle-bone script had given way to more manageable characters, known as the greater and lesser seal scripts, which are still used in chops today. Literacy and learning, moreover led to the arising of several philosophical schools. They all had in common that they bemoaned the current state of affairs, looked backward to the good times of antiquity, and proposed various social and individual measures that would lead not only to overall harmony but also to greater success in rulership, conquest, and population retention. Besides the theoretical and cosmological speculation typical of Western philosophy, Chinese philosophers thus also engaged in political doctrines and proposed practical methods for the recovery of long-lost harmony.

Six schools

The earliest document of Daoism, Laozi's *Daode jing*, dates from this time and has to be read in this context. Daoism forms one of six philosophical schools of ancient China, two of which have left no serious imprint on the Chinese religious scene. They are the Mohists (named after Master Mo, *c.* 479–438) who preached universal love and equal goodness towards all; and the Logicians who insisted that all ills could be cured if one only rectified language to be perfectly logical: "A white horse is not a horse" is one of their standard sayings, insisting that everyone use the correct term and thus, by rectifying his or her mind, contribute to the harmony of the world.

The remaining three schools have remained present in Chinese thinking; they have variously impacted Daoism in the course of its history. They are Confucianism, Legalism, and Yin-Yang cosmology. Especially the latter has become the foundation of much of Daoist thought and cosmic patterning (see Chapter 4).

Legalism

Legalism was first formulated by the philosopher Xunzi (*c.* 300–230) in the third century B.C.E. Reflecting Warring States reality, he assumed that people's nature is originally evil and that everyone is set only on personal profit, no matter what the cost to others. Life accordingly is a battle for limited resources and the bottom line is "every man for himself." To make social harmony possible, there have to be strict rules and enforceable laws joined by punishments that will make everyone sit up and listen.

The Legalists served as advisers to the First Emperor (Shihuang) of China, whose dynastic name Qin gave us the name "China." The unifier of the warring states in 221 B.C.E., he is best known for building sumptuous palaces, the Great Wall, and the Terracotta Army. Standardizing measures, wheel sizes, coins, and the Chinese script, he created a new political entity on Chinese soil, advancing the kingdom of the Zhou to the status of empire. He also ruled with strict laws and executed ruthless punishments to the point where soon after his death in 210 B.C.E. the populace rose in rebellion and brought about a new dynasty, the Han.

Beyond aiding greatly in the unification of China, the Legalists are responsible for codifying Chinese law. They created a long-lasting system of mutual responsibility, dividing all neighborhoods and villages into groups of five families who would be punished or rewarded summarily for the deeds of any one of them. They made widespread use of the death penalty, also for entire clans and household groups; of physical punishments, from flogging through locking into the cangue – a square board locked around the person's neck – to dismemberment; and of forced labor and exile, usually in the far reaches of the Chinese empire where the climate was harsh, the food was rough, and no one knew the finer sides of culture. Prisons were run by Confucian trained magistrates but were only used to keep criminals out of circulation while they awaited trial. After trial and sentencing, also run by the magistrate, the culprit would be executed, sent away, or flogged. The system was harsh and relentless, with minimal chances of escape.

Daoists have always been radically opposed to the Legalist position and relegated their drastic punishments to the hells and underworld prisons. Still, Daoist organizations and monasteries had to work in an environment that was dominated by Chinese law, and time and again they adopted strict rules and measures even within their groups.

Confucianism

Confucianism has provided the social conscience not only of China but also of Daoism. Its five virtues (benevolence, righteousness, wisdom, propriety, and honesty) are the leading light of all Chinese ethics and form an important goal of Daoist cultivation. Its emphasis on family values and loyalty to the ruler, its political vision of harmony and Great Peace have continued to inspire Daoists – who were not, as commonly thought, apolitical and detached, but who developed a complex political philosophy and took an active interest in running the government at various times in history. Vice versa, Daoist mystical thought and cultivation practices have exerted a strong influence on Confucianism, especially in the Song and late imperial periods.

Basic tenets

At the root of the teaching is Confucius (552–479 B.C.E.) with his sayings as documented in the *Lunyu* (Analects). Following him, and matching the dominant

Figure 0.3   Confucius (Bibliothèque Nationale, Paris, France/The Bridgeman Art Library.)

trend of Warring States philosophy, Confucians look back to the Golden Age of the past. Unlike Legalists who see people as inherently evil and establish harsh laws, and unlike Daoists who find people naturally good and suggest perfect alignment with natural spontaneity, Confucians understand that people can be either good or evil and should be taught to do the right thing. The right thing, then, is the correct understanding of social hierarchies and the practice of morality and social awareness.

Without denying the value of all-encompassing nature, of cosmological alignment with Heaven, of laws, and of ancestral advice, Confucianism focuses on ritual formality (*li*) as its key method of bringing the world back to the Golden Age. Representing the image of a ritual vessel, the word *li* means "to arrange in order" and designates ways of how people in society should best interact in a well-ordered fashion. In practice it means three things: interpersonal politeness, governmental organization, and religious devotion.

Etiquette and politeness

First, among personal relationships *li* means etiquette, politeness, and good social behavior. It manifests in respecting the social boundaries, notably the five relationships (ruler-minister, father-son, husband-wife, older-younger brother, friend-friend), honoring one's elders and caring for one's juniors. The key virtues here are benevolence (*ren*), a general sense of consideration and kindness, and filial piety (*xiao*), the devotion of the younger toward their seniors.

Reciprocity is essential. A senior person has to be generous, giving, and gentle toward the younger generation, while a junior person needs to behave with respect, circumspection, and obedience. If both sides fulfill their roles, society and by extension the world will function with utmost harmony; if one side fails, the other is released from its obligation and revolution can occur. Flexibility is equally important. Everyone living in a Confucian society (nowadays especially Singapore, Taiwan, Korea, and Japan) has to know how to work in all different roles and positions, since no one can always be senior or junior at all times. Comparable to Immanuel Kant's concept of "the unenforceable" – a level of social control between legal sanctions and personal restraint – the system works by evoking shame and embarrassment, social ostracism and loss of face. There are no formal punishments for failure to work within the rules, yet the moral structure is pervasive and has worked effectively for millennia.

> The Master said: Guide them by edicts, keep them in line with punishments, and the common people will stay out of trouble but will have no sense of shame. Guide them by virtue, keep them in line with *li*, and they will, besides having a sense of shame, reform themselves. (*Lunyu* 2.3)

Institutional correctness

On a second level, *li* is applied to public organizations and government institutions. Each agency has to know exactly what to do and when to do it and has to be able to sit back and do nothing at certain times as much as it needs to be forceful and vigorous on occasion. Timing – the realm of the cosmologists – is very important. In ancient China, where politics were intricately linked with the will of Heaven and the ancestors, numerous government offices dealt with divination, astronomy, calendar science, and the like. Officials in these agencies had to have a clear definition of their role and had to be able to advance and retire in the right measure and at the right moment.

Their key virtues are righteousness or social responsibility (*yi*) and loyalty to the ruler (*zhong*). Government is centralized and hierarchical, but its open flow of administration – matching the naturalistic vision of Dao – depends on the proper functioning of individual officials. Guidelines and rules abound, formulated early in the *Liji* (Book of Rites), but again there are no serious laws involved, the most dire punishment being release from office.

Ritual propriety

Third and last, *li* also means religious ritual, the practices used to communicate with the ancestors, the various gods of earth and nature, and with Heaven. In the ideal Confucian system, every Chinese family takes care of their ancestors, every household worships a stove god, every village a village god, and every town a city god – all to maintain the proper order within the larger cosmic realm seen as the direct continuation of life on earth. In addition, the ruler and his officials present regular seasonal sacrifices to Heaven and Earth, reporting activities and ensuring the proper blessings in the form of right weather and good fortune. The ritual aspect of Confucianism is not as well known but it has pervaded traditional Chinese society and is still present in popular stove and village gods as well as the great Altar to Heaven, one of the main Beijing tourist attractions in the south of the city.

Learning

To become adapt in the complexity of society and religious worship, people should study, especially history and literature as contained in the Six Classics (the *Books of Changes, Rites, Songs, Music,* and *History,* as well as the *Spring and Autumn Annals*). They should also practice the six arts of the gentleman: poetry, calligraphy, numbers, music (lute), archery, and charioteering. Some are inherently more apt to learn and become ideal Confucian gentlemen (*junzi*) than others, but there is hope for everyone. Learning, moreover, is not a burden but a pleasure, an exciting adventure of becoming increasingly aware of oneself and the social intricacies in one's surroundings, an ongoing effort at creating the ideal human being in the ideal human society.

Connection to Daoism

Daoists do not quite share this enthusiasm for learning – they tend to be more in favor of unlearning and forgetting with the goal of reaching a more natural state of mind – but they appreciate the social awareness and cosmic harmony proposed by Confucians. Plus, not only did the *Daode jing* arise in a dialogue with Confucian thought, but throughout history Daoists have lived and breathed Confucian society all around them. The need for proper social graces, the unfolding of essential virtues, and the vision of a well-integrated and harmonious society have pervaded Daoism from the very beginning, making Confucianism another important factor in the background of the tradition.

Key points you need to know

- Daoism is deeply embedded in Chinese culture and has incorporated several important elements that are present in Chinese history even before the beginnings of Daoism.
- From Chinese religion as known already from Shang dynasty documents and artifacts, Daoism has inherited its belief in a bureaucratically organized otherworld, its veneration of ancestors, its emphasis on the written language in ritual, and possibly its shamanic/ecstatic tendencies.
- The *Yijing* or *Book of Changes* is important as a divination manual but also plays a key role in Daoist cosmological speculation and alchemy.
- Daoists do not share the urge to punish with Legalists but have had to live in a society dominated by Legalist-inspired laws and have created similar rules and organizations within their tradition.
- Confucianism focuses on ritual formality (*li*) as its key method, sees society as hierarchically structured, emphasizes life-long learning, and proposes a set of virtues that have played an important role in Daoist communities and practice.

Discussion questions

1. What is divination and what are some of its main methods in China and the West?
2. How does the *Yijing* work?
3. What are some key points of difference between Legalists and Confucians?

Note

1   The twelve-year cycle, based on the time it takes for the planet Jupiter to circle the sun,
    is familiar in the West through zodiac charts. For more details on the calendar, see
    Chapter 4.

Further reading

Allan, Sarah. 1991. *The Shape of the Turtle: Myth, Art, and Cosmos in Early China*.
    Albany, NY: State University of New York Press.
Chang, Kwang-chih. 1980. *Shang Civilization*. New Haven, CT: Yale University
    Press.
Eno, Robert. 1990. *The Confucian Creation of Heaven: Philosophy and the Defense of
    Ritual Mastery*. Albany, NY: State University of New York Press.
Graham, A. C. 1989. *Disputers of the Tao: Philosophical Argument in Ancient China*.
    La Salle, IL: Open Court Publishing Company.
Keightley, David N. 1978. *Sources of Shang History: The Oracle Bone Inscriptions
    of Bronze Age China*. Berkeley and Los Angeles, CA: University of California
    Press.
Wilhelm, Richard. 1950. *The I Ching or Book of Changes*, Bollingen Series XIX.
    Princeton, NJ: Princeton University Press.

Part I

Foundations

1 *The Dao that can't be told*

In this chapter

The earliest and best known text of Daoism is the *Daode jing* (Book of Dao and Virtue), found in various ancient manuscripts and translated innumerable times into other languages. The work is associated with the philosopher Laozi, allegedly a contemporary of Confucius who later grew into the Highest Lord Lao, a major deity of the religion still worshiped widely today. The text also establishes major fundamental tenets of Daoist worldview, such as Dao, yin-yang, simplicity, forgetting, sage, and nonaction. It has received numerous commentaries in China and was translated over 300 times into English alone, including some rather off-beat versions, such as "The Tao of Meow." It has also played an important role in the ritual practice of religious Daoists.

Main topics covered

- The text of the *Daode jing*
- The Dao
- Creation and decline
- The sage
- Interpreting the *Daode jing*
- Lord Lao
- Ritual applications

The text of the Daode jing

The *Daode jing* or – as it was known in early China – the *Laozi* is a short text in about 5,000 characters, commonly divided into eighty-one chapters and two parts, one on Dao (Chapters 1–37), and one on De or virtue (Chapters 38–81). It is written in verse – not a rhyming, steady, rhythmic kind of verse, but a stylized prose that has strong parallels and regular patterns – and contains sections of description

Figure 1.1 Laozi, the Old Master and alleged author of the *Daode jing*

contrasted with tight punch lines. Many of its lines are terse, almost aphoristic in nature; the text reads more as a collection of sayings than a philosophical discourse. It has survived in several key editions.

> True words are not beautiful;
> Beautiful words are not true.
> A good man does not argue;
> He who argues is not a good man.
> The wise do not have extensive knowledge;
> Those of knowledge tend not to be wise.
> The sage does not collect things for himself,
> Yet the more the does for others, the more he gains,
> The more he gives to other, the more he possesses.
> Just as the way of Heaven is to benefit all and not do harm,
> So the way of the sage is to act but not compete. (Chapter 81)

Manuscript editions

Opening a tomb of the southern Chu culture in Guodian (Hubei) in August of 1993, the local archaeological team unearthed 804 bamboo slips containing roughly 16,000 characters of text. The materials, dated to around 300 B.C.E., contain parts of five ancient philosophical works, including fragments of Confucian and other texts. Among them are thirty-three passages that can be matched with thirty-one chapters of the *Daode jing*, but with lines in different places, and considerable variation in characters from the standard, transmitted edition.

Generally, the fragments are concerned with self-cultivation and its application to questions of rulership and the pacification of the state. Polemical attacks against Confucian principles as useless or even harmful are not found; instead, negative attitudes and emotions are criticized. The Guodian find of this so-called "Bamboo Laozi" tells us that in the late fourth century the text existed in rudimentary form, and consisted of a collection of sayings not yet edited into a coherent presentation. It shows that gradually a set of ideas and practices was growing that would eventually develop into something more specifically Daoist.

From about 150 years later we next have the Mawangdui version, named after a place in Hunan where three tombs were excavated in 1973 that had been closed in 168 B.C.E. Housing the local ruler of the area, his wife, and eldest son, they contained a veritable treasure trove of finds: food stuffs, garments, miniature servants, and various artworks as well as a number of medical and philosophical manuscripts. The texts were written on silk and for the most part dealt with cosmology and longevity techniques, such as breathing, exercises, and sexual practices. Among them were two copies of the *Daode jing*, the so-called silk manuscripts.

Unlike the earlier "Bamboo-Laozi," the Mawangdui silk text contains a complete version of the *Daode jing* that differs little from the transmitted edition in eighty-one chapters. There are some character variants which have helped clarify some interpretive points, and the two parts are in reversed order, i.e. the text begins with the section on De or virtue, then adds the section on Dao. The manuscripts are important because they show that the *Daode jing* existed in its complete form in the early Han dynasty and that it was considered essential enough to be placed in someone's grave.

Following this, we have what is known as the standard, transmitted edition of the text, which goes back to the third century C.E. At this time the erudite Wang Bi (226–249) edited the text and wrote a commentary on it that Chinese since then have considered inspired. It has shaped the reception of the text's worldview until today and forms the basis of practically all Western translations.

Authorship

The *Daode jing* is commonly associated with an old sage known as Laozi, the Old Master. According to introductions to the text, he was a sixth-century official of the Zhou dynasty who had both eminent knowledge of the rites and strong reclusive tendencies. Confucius heard of him and went to learn his teaching. Despite being rebuffed he came away with such a deep impression that he compared Laozi to a dragon. Later, so the story continues, when Laozi felt that the dynasty was declining, he left China for the western lands and on the road transmitted his ideas to the border guard Yin Xi who compiled them into the *Daode jing*.

The first source that reports this story and connects the thinker with the text is Sima Qian's *Shiji* (Historical Records), dated to 104 B.C.E. Admitting uncertainty and referring to several figures who might have been Laozi, he focuses predominantly on an archivist at the royal Zhou court by the name of Lao Dan, but mentions several other personages, such as the recluse Laolaizi, and establishes a connection to the up-and–coming Li family, providing Laozi with a surname.

Legend development

A. C. Graham, analyzing this first biography of Laozi, locates its source among originally Confucian stories, written to provide Confucius with a respected archivist as a teacher and to show his unwavering eagerness to learn. Following this, several polemical moves led to the composite legend of Laozi. First, the sage was linked to the growing collection of aphorisms and philosophical sayings which grew into a coherent text around 250 B.C.E. and thus elevated to a senior "Daoist" thinker. Next, after the First Emperor unified the empire, he was identified with the Grand Astrologer Dan who, in 374, had predicted the supremacy of Qin – an identification that recommended Daoist advisers to the new emperor. Third, the story established a claim of extended longevity for Laozi, useful in view of the First Emperor's immortality aspirations.

The story about Laozi's departure for the west, next, was added to explain why the Old Master, although long-lived, was no longer around to advise the First Emperor in person. Under the Han, moreover, when the Daoists' link with the toppled Qin dynasty became a liability, Laozi was resettled to Bozhou (Henan) near the Han rulers' place of origin. Adopted by the Li clan, he obtained a family name, while his descendants served the Han as loyal subjects. In the following centuries Laozi continued to rise in the esteem of his countrymen, to eventually become a major Daoist deity by the name of Highest Lord Lao (Taishang Laojun).

The Dao

The key concept of the *Daode jing* and of all Daoism is the Dao, the underlying cosmic power which creates the universe, supports culture and the state, saves the good and punishes the wicked. Literally "the way," Dao refers to the way things develop naturally, the way nature moves along and living beings grow and decline in accordance with cosmic laws.

Definition

The *Daode jing* begins with the words: "The Dao that can be told is not eternal Dao." Still, it is possible to create a working definition. Benjamin Schwartz describes it as "organic order," organic in the sense that – unlike its later personification in Lord Lao – it is not willful, not a conscious, active creator or personal entity but an organic process that just moves along. But beyond this, Dao is also order – clearly manifest in the rhythmic changes and patterned processes of the natural world. As such, it is predictable in its developments and can be discerned and described. Its patterns are what the Chinese call "self-so" or "nature," the spontaneous and observable way things are naturally. Yet, while Dao is nature, it is also more than nature – its deepest essence, the inner quality that makes things what they are. It is governed by laws of nature, yet it is also these laws itself.

In other words, it is possible to explain the nature of Dao in terms of a twofold structure: "eternal Dao" and "the Dao that can be told." One is the mysterious, ineffable Dao at the center of the cosmos; the other is Dao at the periphery, visible and tangible in the natural cycles of the known world.

Eternal and peripheral

The eternal Dao is described in the *Daode jing* as invisible, inaudible, and subtle. "Infinite and boundless, it cannot be named; it belongs to where there are no beings; . . . it is altogether vague and obscure" (Chapter 14). This Dao, although the ground and inherent power of the human being, is entirely beyond ordinary perception. Beyond all knowing and analysis, it cannot be grasped. The human body, senses, and intellect are not equipped to deal with it. The only way a person can ever get in touch with it is by forgetting and transcending ordinary human faculties, by becoming subtler and finer and more potent, more like Dao itself.

The Dao at the periphery, on the other hand, is characterized as the give and take of various pairs of complementary opposites, as the natural ebb and flow of things as they rise and fall, come and go, grow and decline, emerge and die. The *Daode jing* speaks about it in terms of clearly visible patterns of nature and society and points out various concrete activities of alignment. It shows how things develop in alternating movements of yin and yang, how they always move in one direction or the other: up or down, toward lightness or heaviness, brightness or darkness, life or death. Nature is a continuous flow of becoming that ranges between latent and manifest, circular and linear, back and forth – part of and supported by the ineffable Dao at the center.

Flowing with Dao

Dao is always good. Bad times, bad things, bad people, all forms of evil happen when things move against the flow of Dao. That does not mean that there is no room for recession, decline, or death. All these things are there, but not considered evil. Rather, they are a necessary part in the ongoing flux of life in which everything is relative and related to everything else. Yin and yang are interdependent and relative forces that always move together and in alteration, and neither of them is evil. Thus, for example, decline as such is not evil but part of the natural rhythm of things. It can become evil when it is violently forced upon nature or society at a time of growth. Similarly, growth, unlike what modern societies think, is not necessarily always good. It can become evil, when massive expansion is pushed forward at a time of rest or reduction. It is essential, therefore, to know the patterns of Dao – either personally or politically – and learn to adapt to its rhythms.

Nonaction and naturalness

The way to be with Dao is through nonaction (*wuwei*) and naturalness (*ziran*). This does not mean doing nothing, becoming like a vegetable, or being totally spontaneous without any planning whatsoever. Rather, it means letting go of egotistic concerns – what Daoists call "passions and desires" – in favor of finding a sense of where life, nature, and the world are headed. It means to abstain from forceful and interfering measures that cause tensions and disruption in favor of gentleness, adaptation, and ease. Then one can attain success, contentment, and long life. As the text says:

> Act on things and you will ruin them.
> Grasp for things and you will lose them.
> Therefore the sage acts with nonaction and has no ruin,
> Lets go of grasping and has no loss. (Chapter 64)

In traditional China this idea was mainly applied in politics, but over the years people have also found it helpful in ordinary life. An example for a modern application is given by Liu Xiaogan in a discussion of "naturalness" as understood in China today (in Kohn and LaFargue 1998). He presents the case of a farmer who is about to modernize his farm. If the farmer looks around and finds many modern methods being applied, understands the rationale behind them and their advantages for everyone concerned, and if he has both the time to investigate the new methods and the money to make the investment, then the time is right and things in all likelihood will proceed smoothly. On the other hand, if he is forced into modernization and pushes against the natural flow, he will come to harm. Finding the best way to live in the world is thus a key focus of Daoist thought – through alignment with the cosmic flow in the ancient philosophy, aided by veneration of the gods and appropriate rituals in the later religion.

Creation and decline

While Dao exists continuously and is always present in all that is, the original development of the world proceeded in several stages. The text notes that at the root of creation Dao rested in deep chaos (Chapter 42). Next, it evolved into the One, a concentrated state cosmic unity that is full of creative potential and often described in *Yijing* terms as the Great Ultimate (Taiji). The One then brought forth "the Two," the two energies yin and yang, which in turn merged in harmony to create the next level of existence, "the Three" (yin-yang combined), from which the myriad beings came forth. From original oneness, the world thus continued to move into ever greater states of distinction and differentiation.

Human beings

A similar development takes place within human beings. The oneness of primordial creation is the original endowment that all living beings receive from Dao. It appears in the fulfilled state of the embryo and the infant, a state of undifferentiation and wholeness. As people grow up and engage in active life, however, this oneness is lost. The dualism of yin and yang comes to dominate mind and world. As a result, everything people see happening around them is perceived as depending on the interaction of opposites.

As yin and yang change into each other at their peak, so all opposites in the world alternate. Whatever is yin can only maintain its yin-nature until it reaches its pinnacle. Then it reverts back to yang, and vice versa. For people's activities, this means that the straightforward pursuit of a goal does not always lead there. Rather, the text advises, to grow one should first shrink; to strengthen one should first weaken; to gain one should first give; and to hold on one should first let go (Chapter 36).

Cultural decline

The active presence of yin and yang in human life and mind leads to varying attitudes and modes of behavior in the world. Eventually their increasingly sophisticated interaction brings about cultural and psychological complexity. Gradually the Golden

Age of an intact, harmonious, and simple society declines. The Dao becomes weaker and seems to be lost completely. The most obvious manifestation of this loss is the sensory involvement of people with the things around them, their increasing dependence on outside objects, which eventually will do them harm. Thus the text says:

> The five colors blind people's eyes;
> The five tones deafen their ears.
> The five flavors spoil their palate;
> Excitement and hunting madden their minds;
> Goods hard to get do harm to their ways. (Chapter 12)

The multiplicity of sensory inputs and cultural attainments cripples people's instinctive nature: not only their eyes and ears but also their spontaneously good moral characters. Originally people are full of propriety and compassion; they naturally know how to be truly and wholly in the world. As these things are lost, formal moral codes and social rules, documented especially in the so-called Confucian virtues, rise to the fore. A conscious knowledge of right and wrong replaces spontaneous intuition; a culturally enforced practice of filial piety substitutes for natural caring (Chapter 18). As a result, human beings impose their conceptions and wills on nature instead of following it along. All official rules and personal guidelines to correct behavior can do little to patch up the deficiency of Dao. Instead of the organic order of Dao, disorder and confusion prevail in the world.

The sage

The person who emerges as the hero in this situation, who will bring the world back into balance, is the perfect human being or sage (*shengren*). He or she can be any individual, man or woman, from any social stratum – in fact Daoist literature often presents simpleminded wood-gatherers or fishermen as true sages. In the *Daode jing*, however, the sage is ideally the ruler. He stands at the apex of human society and mediates between Heaven and Earth like a sacred shaman-king. The sage has realized the original Dao; in his mind he is like Heaven and Earth. Because of his exposed position in society, he has the power to impart purity and harmony to others. Wherever the sage goes, all around him partakes of cosmic oneness. There are no disasters or misfortunes.

Simplicity and nonaction

The way in which the sage achieves his perfection is through a return to simplicity. Sages, and essentially all people, should lead a simple life on the outside and develop a pure mind within. They should give up learning and all conscious efforts at making the world a better place, placing the efforts into "embracing the One," reaching for "highest weakness," becoming "like infants," and being "pure in wisdom" (Chapter 10). By flowing with Dao, they realize their true inherent nature and achieve lasting satisfaction.

The sage as ruler, moreover, naturally leads the country to a full recovery of cosmic harmony. Once he has attained the One and has concentrated his cosmic energy, Dao will radiate through him. To bring peace and purity to the people, he deals with society by acting in nonaction. Without ever imposing his personal patterns and wishes on the flow of nature, he attains the perfect way of being in the world and follows the natural course of things as they come and go. Without acting willfully or driven by any specific purpose, he recognizes the signs of the cosmos and moves along with it in intuitive harmony. Such government brings peace. On the other hand, any active management of worldly affairs leads to failure and harm. As the text says:

> Those who would take over the earth
> And shape it to their will
> Never, I notice, succeed. . . .
> At no time in the world will a man who is sage
> Over-reach himself,
> Over-spend himself,
> Over-rate himself. (Chapter 29)

Nonintervention is thus the key to good government, to a harmonious and peaceful world. This nonintervention also includes an attitude of nonviolence – it propagates a freely moving, open and relaxed life in the world. Nonaction is the perfect way to keep the world flourishing and people happy.

Ideal community

The sage is at one with the entire world because he has become one with Dao. The radiance of his Dao causes the people to recover their original purity and their harmony with the rhythm of the universe. Society gives up sophistication, culture, and luxury. Ritual propriety and formal moral codes are no longer needed. The ideal life of plainness and simplicity develops naturally. People once again live in small communities, take care of their simple needs, and happily refrain from venturing into the unknown. As the text describes it, there will be small communities with few people. They may have all sorts of devices and implements, but they will not use them. They will be content where they are and not search for different places or fancier goods, eschewing carriages and wagons, armor and weapons.

> Although a neighboring state may be visible,
> Although one may hear its cocks crow and its dogs bark,
> Yet the people grow old and die
> Without ever visiting there. (Chapter 80)

This ideal state of a harmonious society, where people lead a life of simplicity, later continues in the ideal of Great Peace, a key concept in the Daoist religion. It proposes universal perfection through alignment with the rhythm of yin and yang, an open network of government and administration, and the practice of seclusion, meditation, and quietude.

Interpreting the Daode jing

The *Daode jing* can be read as a religious, political, military, or naturalistic treatise, dealing with psychology, the natural world, or society. Even if one decides on one particular reading, contradictions abound: while there is an obvious relation of Dao to the absolute of mystics in general, it is not clear whether it is immanent or transcendent; while there may be a naturalistic philosophy in the text that could be linked with modern Western science, it still shows a high concern for government policy and advice on human activity. Similarly, the text contains both a strong rejection of all value-judgments and clear preferences for one member of the opposite pairs that it poses (softness over hardness, femininity over masculinity, etc.). Sorting out these various positions and their interrelation has been the task of commentators and translators for many centuries.

Commentaries

Each reader of a classic, and particularly one as multifaceted as the *Daode jing*, creates his or her own understanding of the work. Some engage with the text to such a degree that they decide to write down their vision and interpret it in a formal commentary. Each commentator accordingly engages with the text on terms of his own time, culture, and experience, recreating it in a new way and reinterpreting its sayings and key concepts. Commentaries – and also to a lesser degree translations – serve to develop a sense of contemporality so that the text can be received by people as meaningful in their own time and becomes relevant to their world. They hope to render the text into a more current language while circling around its obscurities, lessening its paradoxes, and reducing its originality.

The *Daode jing* is a particularly attractive object for commentaries and translations, because of its short phrases, its obscure philosophical statements, and its compelling metaphors. Unlike more historically embedded works, it speaks to people beyond time and culture; unlike more strictly philosophical texts, it is short in phrasing and natural in language.

Major types

There are three major types of commentaries to the *Daode jing*. One type focuses on philology, examining the exact nature of the language, phrasing, and punctuation of the text, and looking at variants and possible readings of words. Thus, for example, the very first chapter has the lines: "Nonbeing names the origin of Heaven and Earth; Being names the mother of all things." By combining the characters "nonbeing/being" and "names," this can also be read: "The nameless is the origin of Heaven and Earth; the named is the mother of all things." Philological commentaries thus establish clarity of language through detailed linguistic analysis or by finding similar phrases and expressions in contemporaneous documents.

Another type of commentary relates the *Daode jing* to longevity and cultivation practices. The best known among them is by Heshang gong, a legendary figure who supposedly lived in the Former Han dynasty. He connects numerous passages and phrases with physical cultivation. For example, he reads the phrase "valley spirit" in chapter 6 as "nurture the spirits," then identifies these "spirits" as the vital energetic powers residing in the five inner organs. He also reads the phrase "mysterious female" as "mystery and female" and connects the two terms to Heaven and Earth and the absorption of their energies through nose and mouth. Later commentators worked along similar lines and in their turn found the rationale for various cultivation practices, such as inner alchemical transformation and embryo respiration in the lines of the *Daode jing*.

The third major type of commentary engages the text with in-depth philosophical speculation. The most important is by Wang Bi whose work also set the standard edition of the text. He relates Dao to nonbeing (*wu*), the underlying ground of existence, its source and ultimate end. Nonbeing is at the root of all and needs to be activated in a return to emptiness and spontaneity, achieved through the practice of nonaction, a decrease in desires and growth of humility and tranquility. Other works of this type tend to relate the *Daode jing* to Buddhist and Confucian concepts, engaging in process metaphysics and social speculation, respectively.

Recently, modern Chinese thinkers have developed their own vision of the *Daode jing*, seeing it as an antidote to environmental damage, government interference, and the increasing preoccupation with materialist goals. In typical commentary fashion, this reading once again connects the ancient classic with concerns of the current age, keeping the book and its ideas relevant and vital.

English translations

The *Daode jing* has received about 300 translations into English. The first, by Protestant missionaries in the late nineteenth century, tried to relate it to Western concepts of God and found it badly lacking. Early twentieth-century readings were more open to its views and strove to understand it in its own terms. By the mid-twentieth century, scholars like Joseph Needham and Holmes Welch saw in its philosophy a powerful alternative to Western mechanistic thinking and a possible antidote to current American problems. The book became the harbinger of alternative freedom, an escapist manual that lauded spontaneity, going with the flow, and letting things be.

Translations of the text differ widely. This is partly because of the terse, aphoristic nature of the text which often leaves out pronouns and grammatical particles. In addition, language in ancient China was not yet standardized so that different characters that had the same sound (homophones) were sometimes used for the same word, creating potential confusion. Also, often key words had a wide range of meaning, leaving it to the reader or translator to make a more or less informed decision. And, finally, uncertainties about syntax abound due to the fact that ancient Chinese is uninflected, i.e. has no specific grammatical endings for gender, plural, or past tense.

Each translation thus reflects the preferences and concerns of the translator, and although there are large numbers of them already, publishers are still eager to put out yet another – a testimony to the timelessness of the book and to a constant need for new readings.

Kinds of renditions

Like commentaries, so translations come in several kinds. One kind strives to stick as closely as possible to the original. It attempts to do a word-for-word rendition, hoping to capture the feelings of the text as it presents itself in the original language. The strongest example of this type is the *Daode jing* rendition by Stephen Addiss and Stanley Lombardo. The first line, for example, reads: "Dao called Dao is not Dao." The phrasing is adept and conveys the terseness and potency of the original diction.

Another kind of translation, exemplified in the works by Arthur Waley, Wing-tsit Chan, and Michael LaFargue, works to elucidate the historical context and social reality of the original. It remains close to the text but does not save on nouns or prepositions to clarify certain phrases or statements. It uses footnotes to amplify and explain the text and hopes to give an accurate reading of the text within its own cultural framework.

A third type of translation serves to make the text relevant to the modern age. Making ample use of pronouns, articles, and other grammatical helpers, this type also takes images and concepts and translates them into present-day reality. Thus, for example, the historically-minded Wing-tsit Chan translates Chapter 46:

> When Dao prevails in the world, galloping steeds are turned back to the fields.
> When Dao does not prevail, war horses thrive in the suburbs.

The contemporary adaptation by Stephen Mitchell, on the other hand, has:

> When a country is good, factories make trucks and tractors.
> When it is bad, warheads are stockpiled outside the cities.

Though the text is still the same, the translation has gone a long way beyond the mere rendition of words and phrases into the realm of culture and reinterpretation.

Recreations

In addition to these translations, there are also some recreations of the *Daode jing*, undertaken by writers who are fascinated by the text but who do not actually know Chinese. Their work tends to be highly poetic and is often very enticing, and in some cases even exotic. An enjoyable example follows the tradition of Benjamin Hoff's *The Tao of Pooh* (1982). It is *The Tao of Meow*, a *Daode jing* by and for cats by Waldo Japussy (1990). Part of Chapter 2 reads:

> The Wise Cat spends most of his day asleep.
> He knows that if he waits, all things will come to him.
> He does not have to set things in motion,
> Just lie in wait until# they appear.

A more serious translation, for people, that also belongs into this group is Witter Bynner's *The Way of Life* (1944). Based on various translations of the original, it is beautifully written and carries a deep meaning. A more recent example of the same type is Wayne W. Dyer's *Chang Your Thoughts – Change Your Life* (2007), in which he encourages people to adopt the teachings of the text in their lives today, changing from fear to curiosity, from control to trust, and from entitlement to humility. He rephrases *wuwei* as "noninterference" and explains the idea of knowing when to stop as: "When your cup is full, stop pouring." Beyond the written renditions, the poetic power of the text has also inspired musical versions, as for example one by The Tao Alchemical Company which set parts of Witter Bynner's text to country-blues. Even in modern America, therefore, the *Daode jing* is still actively consulted and praised in song.

Lord Lao

Just as the text has remained active and undergone numerous transformations, so did its alleged author continue to grow over the ages. After Laozi's first biography in the *Shiji* described above, the Old Master rose to fill three major new roles – as immortal, cosmic deity, and the savior of humankind.

Figure 1.2 Lord Lao, the supreme deity

Han developments

Three main Han-dynasty groups contributed to this process in its earliest stages. First, there were individual seekers of long life and immortality, the so-called magical practitioners (*fangshi*). They adopted Laozi as their patriarch and idealized him as an immortal, a particularly gifted human being who, by his own initiative and efforts, had attained the purity and power of the celestials.

Second, the political elite, the imperial family and court officials, saw in Laozi the personification of Dao and worshiped him as a representative of their ideal of cosmic and political unity alongside the Yellow Emperor (Huangdi) and the Buddha. Laozi here was known as the Highest Lord Lao and became the object of formal imperial sacrifices.

Third, popular religious cults, millenarian in nature and expecting the end of the world, identified Laozi as the god who had continuously manifested himself through the ages and saved the world time and again. He would, they believed, come again as the messiah of the new age of Great Peace. Also called Lord Lao or, in some groups, Yellow Lord Lao (Huanglao jun), this deified Laozi was like the personification of

Figure 1.3 Laozi as master of qigong

cosmic harmony worshiped by the court but equipped with tremendous revolutionary power. As a messiah, he could overturn the present and reorganize the world, leading the faithful to a new state of heavenly bliss in this very life on earth.

The growth of the God

As Daoism continued to flourish in the middle ages (300–500 c.e.), Lord Lao fulfilled new roles. He was visualized in meditation, identified with the Buddha, represented in statues, and encountered in trances as the giver of revelations. With the integration of the various Daoist schools into one organized system in the sixth century, his life story developed into a complex, integrated myth and he became the third and most popular member of the Daoist trinity. Next, the emperors of the Tang dynasty (618–907), belonging to a family named Li, claimed descent from him and recorded many numinous appearances of his divine form, through which he showed approval of their rule. He unfailingly protected the land and gave succor to the faithful.

Under the Song (960–1280), Lord Lao received continued imperial honors, but was replaced as protector of the state by the Dark Warrior. To maintain the claim to his central position, Daoists wrote extensive hagiographies of him that traced his cosmic life from the beginning of creation to miracles wrought in the eleventh century. At the same time, newly emerging Daoist sects venerated him as the giver of revelations and popular talismans. The Yuan dynasty (1280–1368), under Mongol rule, saw first a major elevation, then the downfall of organized Daoism. Taking Lord Lao along, this development resulted in an overall decrease in his importance, both politically and in the cult. Nevertheless, in the following dynasties he remained the central deity of the two leading Daoist schools, Celestial Masters and Complete Perfection, and appeared in vernacular literature as a wondrous immortal and valiant fighter for the good. To the present day, statues of Lord Lao stand in Daoist monasteries, the main locations of his exploits are honored as holy places, and tales of his life are told in books and picture stories.

Ritual applications

As Laozi grew into a god, so the *Daode jing* evolved into a holy book. Already in the second century B.C.E., it was considered a sacred text that should be recited to the greater benefit of self and state. By the second century C.E., it was the central text of the Celestial Masters, the earliest communal Daoist organization, who recited it both as a devotional exercise and for its magical effect. To ensure the proper efficacy of this recitation, practitioners had to be morally pure. Accordingly the Celestial Masters also used the text also as the inspiration for certain behavioral rules, outlined in conjunction with a commentary of the early third century. They provide both general behavioral guidance based on the philosophy of the *Daode jing* (such as practicing nonaction, cultivating softness and weakness, and lessening desires) and a set of concrete regulations and temporal taboos.

In the fifth century, recitation of the *Daode jing* was widely practiced among Daoist schools and linked closely with the attainment of immortality. For example, Yin Xi, the Guardian of the Pass, recited the *Daode jing* 10,000 times over a period of three years. As a result, he gained eternal life and the state of no death. According to his biography, he "attained inner sincerity in his essence and pervasion in his meditation so that he could pervade the mystery."

That this practice and its effect was not merely part of mythology is evidenced in the *Zhen'gao* (Declarations of the Perfected, DZ 1016), a record of Daoist teachings and practices dated to around the year 500. According to this, a certain Old Lord instructed three members of the Zhou family, the father and two sons, to recite the *Daode jing*. The father and elder brother succeeded in reciting the text 10,000 times and flew off as celestials. The younger brother, however, only reached 9,733 times and did not attain immortality.

Ritual meditation

In addition, the *Daode jing* also stood at the center of a ritualized meditation. According to a fifth-century text that served as a preface to the text, the *Daode zhenjing xujue* (Introductory Explanations to the *Daode jing*), Laozi gave detailed instructions on how to properly venerate the scripture. Adepts should purify themselves thoroughly and enter a special meditation chamber, where they burn incense, straighten their robes, bow to the ten directions, and actively visualize Laozi and his major assistants.

Only in the venerable presence of these personages is the *Daode jing* to be opened. Its recitation must further be preceded by a formal prayer, in which the adept calls down the Lord of the Niwan Palace, the central representative of the gods and resident in the central palace of the head. As the deity approaches, the room undergoes mysterious changes: a radiance as of seven jewels spreads, doors and windows open spontaneously. A link of light to the higher spheres is thus established, through which the practitioner floats up and away into the purple empyrean. Finding himself among the stars, he has the sun and moon at his sides and approaches divine immortals to gain immortality for himself – and not only for himself but also for his ancestors of seven generations.

After this invocation, when the adept has placed himself firmly among the celestials, he proceeds with the ritual. The text says,

> Finish the recitation, then click your teeth and swallow your saliva thirty-six times. Visualize the green dragon to your left, the white tiger to your right, the red bird in front of you, and the dark warrior at your back.
>
> Your feet stand between the eight trigrams, the divine turtle and the thirty-six masters bow to you. In front, you see the seventeen stars, while your five inner organs give forth five radiant energies and a divine pattern streams across your body.
>
> On three sides you are joined by an attendant, each having a retinue of a thousand carriages and 10,000 horsemen. Eight thousand jade maidens and jade lads of heaven and earth stand guard for you. (Section 5)

Clicking the teeth and swallowing saliva are part of the standard Daoist meditation ritual, symbolic forms of announcing one's communication with the deities and opening the energy channels within. The adept is instructed to place himself in the cosmic center by seeing himself surrounded by the heraldic animals of the four directions, representing constellations in the sky, and placing his feet firmly on the eight trigrams of the *Yijing*. Everyone bows to him, and he is fully established among the stars. His body has become a pure constellation of light and energy patterns. Then he sees himself supported by attendants, one on each side and behind him, who in turn, as in an imperial procession, are joined by thousands of followers and servants. Now that the celestial position of the meditator at the center of the cosmos is firmly established, he can recite the *Daode jing* in its truest environment and to its greatest effect.

Later developments

Over the following centuries, the *Daode jing* continued to be actively used both in meditation and liturgy. It played an important role in the formal ordination of priests, representing a level of advanced lay followers who were preparing to leave the householder's life but had not yet done so. Their progress was divided into two stages. First he or she – women being treated as equals in the priestly system – learned basic meditation and recitation techniques, worshiped Laozi and Yin Xi as their major patriarchs, and observed ten precepts that included the five universal rules (and also Buddhist precepts) against killing, stealing, lying, sexual misconduct, and intoxication, together with a set of guidelines to help practitioners to live in harmony with their families and their communities.

Second, they took additional precepts and received more detailed instructions on the *Daode jing*, undergoing an ordination ceremony that named them Preceptors of Eminent Mystery and bestowed upon them a variety of exegetical, devotional, and technical materials linked with the text. They included early commentaries on the *Daode jing*, technical interpretations of the text, philosophical and mystical exegeses, practical manuals on *Daode jing* meditation and ritual, and formal hagiographies of Laozi and Yin Xi. The importance of the *Daode jing* as a sacred scripture in priestly and monastic ordination still continues. To the present day followers chant the text in monasteries of the Complete Perfection school, whose ordinands receive it at first initiation together with a set of ten precepts and guidelines for self-cultivation. The text and its alleged author, moreover, have guided seekers of self-cultivation, inspiring numerous meditation techniques as well as recent qigong methods.

Key points you need to know

- The *Daode jing* is the oldest transmitted text of Daoism; it consists of two main parts and eighty-one sections or chapters; it is written in verse, often aphoristic.
- The alleged author of the text was Laozi, the Old Master, a legendary figure whose biography dates from around 100 B.C.E.; he was later divinized and still plays an important role in the Daoist religion as Lord Lao.
- Dao at its core is ineffable and inaccessible by human perception or intellect; on its periphery it can be observed in the workings of natural rhythms, described in terms of yin and yang.

- There was a Golden Age in prehistory which declined with the arrival of culture and technology; by acting naturally in accordance with one's Dao-given nature one can return to this state of purity and simplicity.
- To do so, one should live a simple life, reduce sensory input, make the mind tranquil, and follow the natural course of things in nonaction.
- The person who realizes this fully is called the sage; he is ideally the ruler of the country, in which role he can spread the harmony of Dao everywhere.
- Commentaries to the *Daode jing* have interpreted it in terms of philology, philosophy, and spiritual cultivations; they reach from the early centuries B.C.E. to the present day.
- Translations of the text are exceedingly numerous; they can be literal, historical, or spiritual in nature.
- The text has also played an important part in Daoist ritual through recitation, meditation, and ritual transmission as part of priestly ordination.

Discussion questions

1. Do concepts like Dao and related ideas have relevance in the modern world? If so, what might that relevance be?
2. What other figures in human history can you think of whose historical existence was overlaid by layers of legends? Who might even have been made into gods? How does this process work?
3. Is it legitimate to take an ancient text of out its historical context, reinterpret its phrases and concepts, and use it in a completely new way from its original intention?

Further reading

Chan, Alan. 1991. *Two Visions of the Way: A Study of the Wang Pi and the Ho-shang-kung Commentaries on the Laozi.* Albany, NY: State University of New York Press.

Chan, Alan. 2000. "The *Daode jing* and Its Tradition." In *Daoism Handbook*, edited by Livia Kohn, 1–29. Leiden: E. Brill.

Hansen, Chad. 1992. *A Daoist Theory of Chinese Thought: A Philosophical Interpretation.* New York: Oxford University Press.

Henricks, Robert. 1989. *Lao-Tzu: Te-Dao ching.* New York: Ballantine.

Henricks, Robert. 2000. *Lau Tzu's Dao Te Ching: A Translation of the Startling New Documents Found at Guodian.* New York: Columbia University Press.

Kohn, Livia and Michael LaFargue, eds. 1998. *Lao-tzu and the Dao-te-ching*. Albany, NY: State University of New York Press.

Kohn, Livia. 1998. *God of the Dao: Lord Lao in History and Myth*. Ann Arbor, MI: University of Michigan, Center for Chinese Studies.

LaFargue, Michael. 1992. *The Tao of the Tao-te-ching*. Albany, NY: State University of New York Press.

Schwartz, Benjamin. 1985. *The World of Thought in Ancient China*. Cambridge, MA: Harvard University Press.

2 At ease in perfect happiness

In this chapter

The second major text of Daoism is the *Zhuangzi*, named after the philosopher Zhuang Zhou and compiled in the third century B.C.E. Written in prose, the work contains various developments of early Daoist thought, but focuses mostly on a vision of ecstatic freedom in the midst of ordinary life, expressed as "perfect happiness" or "free and easy wandering." It outlines a number of different methods – from intellectual to meditative – that lead to this desirable state and tells many stories illustrating its realities. Over the centuries, the *Zhuangzi* has been the subject of select commentaries and interpretations; it has also exerted a great influence on ecstatic poetry of the middle ages and on the uniquely Chinese development of Chan (Zen) Buddhism.

Main topics covered

- The *Zhuangzi*
- The world of Zhuang Zhou
- The ideal life
- Poetic adaptations
- The Zen connection

The Zhuangzi

The *Zhuangzi* takes its name from a minor government servant by the name of Zhuang Zhou (*c.* 370–290 B.C.E.). Highly erudite, he found officialdom useless and withdrew to dedicate himself to his speculations, teaching his ideas to disciples and inspiring them to write his teachings down. The same *Shiji* chapter that discusses the legendary Laozi mentions that Zhuangzi was famous for his way with words. The literary mastery of the text is undisputed, and many consider it the first document of Chinese fiction.

The *Zhuangzi* emerged from the same political environment as the *Daode jing* but has a different focus in that it is more concerned with mental attitudes and condemns active political involvement. Zhuang Zhou found that the ongoing arguments among the different philosophical schools were futile and would not lead to serious improvements. He concluded that "right" and "wrong" were highly volatile categories, that all viewpoints were relative, and that the mind and its perception tended to be fallacious and one-sided. As a result, he makes a strong case for the cultivation of nondual perception and a way of life that is free from constraints – mental, personal, and social. To attain harmony in life one need not become a sage; it is sufficient to free one's mind and flow along smoothly with the course of Dao.

Editions

This philosophy – besides certain other early "Daoist" trends – makes up the bulk of the book, which consists of thirty-three chapters and is divided into three parts: Inner Chapters (1–7), Outer Chapters (8–22), and Miscellaneous Chapters (23–33). This tripartite division was established by the main commentator of the text, Guo Xiang (252–312), who lived in the same era as Wang Bi, the principal editor of the *Daode jing*. Both men were part of an intellectual movement known as "Profound Learning" (sometimes also called Dark Learning or "Neo-Daoism"). Growing in reaction to the strong Confucian control of intellectual life, this movement focused on a search for a spiritual dimension of life through the recovery and reinterpretation of less political classics, including Daoist philosophers and the *Yijing*.

According to Guo Xiang's postface to his edition (recovered in a manuscript in Japan), the *Zhuangzi* he received consisted of fifty-two chapters, many of which had extraneous materials and fanciful stories he found unworthy of Zhuang Zhou. He duly proceeded to eliminate these parts, which dealt with magic, exorcism, dream interpretation, ecstatic journeys, medical lore, and natural transformations. He then set out to streamline the rest into parts and chapters he found suitable. As a result, with the exception of very few fragments, the earlier version of the *Zhuangzi* is lost and our current edition, and with it the main orientation of its worldview, are the result of Guo Xiang's revision.

Early Daoist strands

Still, it is likely that the existing text contains materials from the third and second centuries B.C.E. In particular it has information from four distinct strands of Daoist worldview and practice. There is first the school of Zhuang Zhou himself, which is documented in the Inner Chapters (also considered the oldest) and in chapters 16–27 and 32 of the later parts of the book. Then, as analyzed by A. C. Graham, there are the strands of the so-called primitivists (Chapters 8–10), the syncretists (Chapters 11–15, 33), and the hedonists (Chapters 28–31).

The primitivist chapters express a worldview very similar to that of the *Daode jing*, but are more radical in their demand for simplicity and the return to an uncomplicated life. They condemn all forms of culture as evil and destructive, and see the ideal society strictly in terms of the *Daode jing* when it talks about the small community of people who eschew all cultural and technological advances and live a simple life. Their idea is to keep people in one place as much as possible, to have them maintain a simple outlook on life and inner contentment by limiting their horizons of experience.

The primitivists, sometimes also called anarchists, hate all government and idealize the time before the arrival of iron-age technology. They suggest that when there were fewer people, no communications, no governments, and no infantry-fought wars, life was simple, easy, and good. They are, in one word, the proponents of a movement back to the Stone Age and away from everything "modern" society has to offer. Their vision is not the same as that of the *Daode jing*, which still advises ways of working with the present rather than rejecting it altogether, but it is built on the same fundamental ideas of simplicity, nonaction, and small, controlled social units. Later this primitivist strand in Daoism was continued in the ideal of the anti-social hermit who preferred his lonely hut and simple food to a comfortable and well-appointed life in society. This figure has appeared variously throughout Chinese history and is still present today, as Bill Porter has demonstrated in his book *The Road to Heaven* (1993).

Hedonists and syncretists

The hedonist strand in the *Zhuangzi* is diametrically opposite to the primitivist vision. It promotes ease and leisure, a life of no constraints and no restrictions, an attitude of giving in to desires and serving only one's own happiness and satisfaction. The underlying idea here is: "What is good for me is good for the universe." The reasoning behind it is that if the individual is part of Dao, then whatever he or she feels and wants is also part of Dao, and therefore all one's personal desires are expressions of the greater cosmic goodness and have to be satisfied without fail.

The hedonist strand is closely associated with a philosopher named Yang Zhu (ca. 440–360 B.C.E.), who also merits a chapter in the *Liezi* (Book of Master Lie), a text that was lost early and reconstituted in the second century C.E. Like the primitivists, hedonists radicalize one aspect of the teaching of the *Daode jing*, but pick a different one: the idea that all and everything belongs inherently and inextricably to Dao. They refuse to acknowledge the difference between inner purity and potential forms of disharmony caused by desires and a sensory overload. Instead, they accept every aspect of life as positive. The result is a certain ruthlessness when it comes to making personal sacrifices – Yang Zhu would not give up even a nail on his finger to save the world – and a freewheeling, happy-go-lucky attitude toward life.

Hedonist ideas have continued in Daoism in the figure of the eccentric poet and social dropout, drunk and in disregard of social conventions. They are also apparent in certain later figures, such as the Eight Immortals, who are well known for their ease in life, their eccentric leisure activities, and their happy laughter at everything and with everyone.

The syncretist sections of the *Zhuangzi*, finally, demonstrate the integration of more formalized forms of cosmology and worldview into the basic understanding of Dao. Already the *Daode jing* made a distinction between Dao as the creative, ineffable center and its manifestation in the visible world. Now the latter aspect of Dao is formulated in more technical detail and outlined in recognizable patterns. The rhythm of yin and yang, already present in the *Daode jing*, is further subdivided into five subtler phases and explained in complex cosmological correlations that also take into account observations of the natural world, the movements of the stars, and the hexagrams of the *Yijing*. Also, the ideas of other thinkers of the time merged into the system, allowing for social hierarchies and enforced regulations as part of Dao. This dimension of ancient Daoist thought became dominant under the Han dynasty, when cosmology was formalized and adopted as a governing tool. It also became the basis of much later Daoism.

Beyond these three strands, which each came to played its own part in the Daoist religion, the dominant mode of the *Zhuangzi* is the vision associated with Zhuang Zhou himself. Its overall outlook, as well as its technical terms and metaphors, have pervaded both Daoism and Chinese literature ever since.

The world of Zhuang Zhou

Zhuangzi rejects any entity or essence beyond natural life. For him, everything exists the way it is just because it is, in perfect spontaneity or naturalness (*ziran*). There is no principle or agency at the origin of life. There is only the underlying current, the continuous and all-encompassing flow of Dao. As Guo Xiang explains in his commentary:

> What existed before there were beings? If I say yin and yang were first, then that means yin and yang are beings, too. What, then, was before them? I may say nature was first. But nature is only the natural way of beings. I may say perfect Dao was first. But perfect Dao is perfect nonbeing. Since it is nonbeing, how can it be before anything else? So, what existed before there were beings? There must always be another being thing without end. Thus I understand that beings are what they are by nature; they are not caused by anything else.

> There is thus no ultimate cause to make things what they are. The universe exists by itself and of itself; it is existence just as it is. Nothing can be added to or subtracted from it; it is entirely sufficient upon itself.

People, like everything else, are part of the universal flow, of the spontaneous Dao and nature. Like all other entities, they arise and pass away, always in motion and constantly changing. Like all existing things, they have their particular inborn characteristics – their genetic make-up – and the position they are born in – their social circumstances and opportunities. These two, called inner nature and destiny (*xingming*), make people be who they are in life. They are inescapable just as the natural characteristic of change is in everything that is. Through them, Dao determines the particular way of being of the entire cosmos as much as of each individual.

The ideal way of being in the world, then, is to live as fully as possible in accordance with this personal Dao, the inner quality that determines the way people are. There is no point in trying to be something else. Nobody can ever comprehend what life is like for beings of a totally different size and dimension. The frog in the well has no concept of what it is like to live in an ocean. The little sparrow will never know what it is like to soar as a mighty eagle. Thus, freedom and ease in life do not come from wishing to attain one single goal that is the same for all – a high social position, advanced career, or scholarly erudition, for example – but from realizing who one is and where one stands in the world and doing what one does best to the fullest of one's ability.

Making all things equal

The problem with all this is that, despite their inborn Dao qualities, people develop consciousness and try to place themselves in relation to others and the world. They create ideals that do not match their inborn character or social standing, thus developing strife and fostering dissatisfaction. A good deal of Zhuangzi's presentation accordingly focuses on how to overcome this consciously imposed limitation and return to perfect happiness.

One way he suggests is to work with the conscious mind, to use critical awareness and analysis to realize just to what degree our perception is unreliable, how our evaluation of life and death, good and bad, desirable and undesirable depend on mental dualism and the faculty of divisive discrimination. It means realizing our tendency to split identity into many different "I"s by comparing ourselves with others and by making deliberate choices. There is an "I" that is richer than the next man, another "I" that is not as smart as someone else. There is an "I" that thinks it will live on and on, and there is yet another "I" that knows perfectly well it will die. There is a division into this and that, into past and future, into mine and other. All these need to be recognized for what they are: artificial constructs that impede connection to spontaneity and happiness.

Overcoming this inherent tendency of the mind is called "making all things equal." It means achieving an open perception though conscious questioning. How do we know that we know? How do we come to perceive that reality is what we think it is? What evidence is there that waking and dreaming are not the same thing? How do we know that life is not a great pain and death a wonderful rest? What, really, is this "I?" There are many stories illustrating this feature of insecurity and questioning in the text, but the most poignant is the so-called Butterfly Dream:

> Once in the past, Zhuang Zhou dreamt that he was a butterfly, flitting and fluttering around, content with himself and doing what he pleased. He didn't know he was Zhuang Zhou. Suddenly he woke up. There he was, solid and clearly Zhuang Zhou. But he did not know whether, in fact, he was Zhuang Zhou who had dreamt he was a butterfly, or a butterfly now dreaming he was Zhuang Zhou. Between Zhuang Zhou and a butterfly there must be some distinction! These are the different transformations of beings. (Chapter 2)

There is, therefore, no way of really knowing for sure who we are, where we come from, and where we are going. It is best to remain fully in the present with immediate attention and detached emotions, allowing the world to flow along through us, with us, and in us.

Mind fasting and oblivion

Beyond the conscious examination and elimination of categories, Zhuangzi proposes several other methods to achieve perfect happiness. One is a practice called "fasting of the mind;" it activates *qi* or vital energy, the subtle flowing force that connects all existence, over and above sensory perception. To do so:

> Firmly concentrate your will, and you will no longer hear with your ears. Instead, use your mind to perceive sound. Then go beyond this and use your *qi* for hearing. Plain, ordinary hearing stops with the ears, the mind stops with representations, but *qi* is utterly empty and matches all things. In pure emptiness of *qi*, Dao can assemble. The attainment of this state of open emptiness is "fasting of the mind." (Chapter 4)

Another way to reach the unified and untrammeled mind is to practice "sitting in oblivion." This indicates a state of complete forgetfulness of self and other, high and low, life and death – the full attainment of utter immediacy – reached through a seven-stage progress toward the ideal mind. Zhuangzi says:

> Practice concentration for three days, and you can put the world out of your mind. Then go on for seven days, and you abandon all things. Once all things are gone from your perception, keep on practicing. After nine more days you can put all life out of your mind. Once you have reached this, you attain a level of clarity like the early morning sun.
>
> After that, you move on to see your singularity in the cosmos. Once you get there, you can reach a state of neither past nor present. Eventually you transcend

even this and attain utmost freedom by going beyond life and death. Now the end of life is no longer death for you; the beginning of life is no longer life. (Chapter 6)

The ideal life

The ideal life for Zhuangzi is a way of being in the world that transcends mental categories, emotional involvement, and bodily concerns. Developing a welcoming attitude toward all transformations and resting in the process of Heaven, the ideal person, the perfected or realized one (*zhenren*), is free from feelings and at one with Dao, completely spontaneous and at ease with all that happens, living with a sense of strong immediacy that precludes thinking, evaluating, and critical mentation. As the text says:

> The perfected of old did not know how to delight in life, nor did they know how to loathe death. They came to be without pleasure and went back to nonbeing [death] without refusal. They came in an instant, went in an instant, and that was all. They never forgot where they began; they never pursued where they would end up. They received life and enjoyed it. But then they forgot about it and returned it [to nonbeing] when the time came. . . .
>
> Therefore, in the perfected people of old, all liking was unified into one and all disliking was unified into one. Their being at-one was unified and their not being at-one was unified. When they were at-one, they acted as the companion of Heaven. When they were not at-one, they acted as the companion of humanity. Heaven and humanity not fighting each other within – this is the perfected! (Chapter 6)

The ideal way of being in the world for Zhuangzi is, therefore, to be oblivious of conscious distinctions and evaluations, free from all liking and disliking, hope and fear, and to join Heaven and Earth in open-ended transformations.

Superior skills

One who has reached this state can truly perfect his inner nature and will exhibit superior skills. The *Zhuangzi* illustrates this in various cases of ordinary craftsmen who have mastered more than just their trade. One example is Butcher Ding who cuts up oxen with the same knife for years. He never has to sharpen it because he goes along with the natural structure of the ox's body (Chapter 3).

Other examples include a boatman who runs a ferry across the gulf and a swimmer who instinctively moves with the waves. Both have a knack for the right way to handle themselves because they do not conceptualize their particular situations but act in the immediacy of life (Chapter 19). Another swimmer, interviewed about his phenomenal diving skills by Confucius, says he stays afloat without difficulty because he has managed to make himself completely at home in the water – in complete harmony with his inner nature and fate. He does not consciously know anything about swimming but moves naturally in the water because this is his nature (Chapter 19)

Yet another skilled craftsman at one with Dao is Woodworker Qing. When he carves a bell stand, he concentrates on it to the exclusion of all else. He calms his mind and empties it of all outside considerations, fasting for several days. Eventually he reaches the point when:

> I am so still I forget I have four limbs and a form and body. By that time, the ruler and his court no longer exist for me. My skill is concentrated and all outside distractions fade away. (Chapter 19)

Only in such a state of oneness with his task does he finally go to search the right material and begin to carve the bell stand.

The point of these stories is that Dao will work in all situations of life and raise them from clumsy attempts at a good performance to the perfection of naturalness or spontaneity. Naturalness is complete as and when the self is lost. The utter oblivion of the trance-like immersion in Dao, of the ecstatic flight in free and easy wandering, is the key to ultimate realization – not only of Dao but also of the individual with his particular skills and in his particular life. Everyone, therefore, was originally and can again become perfected.

Poetic adaptations

Soon after its compilation the *Zhuangzi*, in both language and vision, began to inspire ecstatic poetry. In particular, it joined with shamanic songs of south China which, as documented in the *Chuci* (Songs of Chu), detail the ecstatic travels of the shaman through various heavens to complete dissolution in the center of the universe. Making use of both, Zhuangzi's vision of untrammeled freedom and the ecstatic journey of the shaman, the aristocrat, wine merchant, and official Sima Xiangru (179–117 B.C.E.) created his *Daren fu* (Rhapsody of the Great Man) to eulogize Emperor Wu in his aspirations to immortality.

His protagonist, like the seeker in the *Zhuangzi*, yearns for the transcendent reality of the spirit and deplores the ordinary world of dust. Like the ancient shaman, he masters the world and ecstatically soars into the Great Void. The poem begins:

> In this world there is a Great Man, living in the middle continent.
> His abode extends over ten thousand miles, yet is too small for a short sojourn.
> Grieved at the world's unpleasant state, he easily rises and soars away.
> He rides a pure rainbow streaming down, mounts cloudy ether and floats upward.

In full control over the universe and with a strong sense of majesty, the Great Man sets out to arrange things according to his pleasure. He equips a magnificent chariot, drawn by radiant dragon steeds; he summons stars and deities for his entourage, commanding the powers that be. Thus set up, he embarks on a triumphant circuit throughout the universe, sure of his honored reception everywhere. Inspecting the entire world in all directions, he eventually proceeds upward, always having gods and spirits do as he bids. The River God dances for him while celestial maidens play their zithers; other deities, who do not quite obey so readily, are chastised and punished.

No place is too far or too exalted for him to reach; nothing stops him from taking what is his by right. Eventually he reaches Kunlun and visits the ruler of immortals, the Queen Mother of the West. Turning toward the north, the direction of all origins, he samples the drug of immortality. Then he enters the Dark Pass and goes through the Cold Gate. His senses work no more, he vanishes from the world, spiraling upward into the cosmic emptiness beyond all.

The poet here translates the *Zhuangzi* vision of overcoming ego-based limitations into a majestic journey through Heaven and Earth that culminates in the complete loss of personal identity as part of the cosmic void. The Great Man is the perfected of old as well as the ruler; he is also the shaman on his ecstatic journey into the realm beyond. He is a vivid representation of how ultimate freedom can and should feel.

Freedom and escape

A later adaptation of this theme appears in Ruan Ji's (210–263 c.e.) *Daren xiansheng zhuan* (Biography of Master Great Man), which imitates the earlier poem yet also develops the ideal. One of a group of eccentric outsiders known as the Seven Sages of the Bamboo Grove, Ruan Ji privatizes the Great Man: he is free within, not outwardly recognizable as the emperor. No one knows where he lives; ornaments and beauty come naturally to him; he is utterly free in his heart.

Ruan Ji's escapist attitude was typical of the politically unstable and insecure time of the third century c.e. His friends and fellow poets induced ecstatic experiences through music, wine, and drugs, especially the notorious Cold Food Powder which created psychedelic states and made the body feel very hot, causing people to take off their clothes and jump into pools. When back in their ordinary selves, they wrote poetry of freedom and escape, applying the *Zhuangzi* concept of free and easy wandering in the sense of getting away from it all and continuing the text's tradition in their desperate search for a better world within. Thus Ruan Ji says:

> Heat and cold don't harm me; nothing stirs me up.
> Sadness and worry have no hold on me.
> Pure *qi* at rest. I float on mist,

Leap into heaven, pass through all with no restraint.
To and fro, subtle and wondrous, the way never slants –
My delights and happiness are not of this world.

Ruan Ji's version of the Great Man's journey is an outburst of his desperate and never-ending yearning for the true world of "loneliness and vastness," for complete freedom from all mundane involvement by soaring up and away. He yearns for otherworldly heavens as much as for peace of mind and a quiet life on earth. No longer a circuit, the journey in his vision has become linear; it leads away and only away. Strange sights and creatures on the way are merely appreciated in relation to the protagonist's happiness and thus in terms of the distance already placed between him and his sufferings. Neither perfected, sage, or ruler, the Great Man is a creature entirely of the beyond.

The virtue of wine

Another poet who yearned to leave all behind was Liu Ling (d. 265 c.e.), famous for walking around naked in his house. When visitors confronted him with this odd behavior, he supposedly said: "I take Heaven and Earth for my pillars and roof, and the rooms of my house for my pants and coat. And now, what are you gentlemen doing in my pants?" His other call to fame is his *Jiude song* or "Ode to the Virtue of Wine," drinking being his major vehicle for the Great Man's attainment of higher spheres.

This too picks up on the *Zhuangzi*, which says that when a drunken man falls from a carriage, he will do himself no harm. Immersed in utter forgetfulness, he did not know he was riding, he does not know he has fallen: unworried and serene, he can stay whole where others would suffer grievous harm (Chapter 19). But while the *Zhuangzi* uses drunkenness as a metaphor for the perfection of forgetfulness, Liu Ling takes it literally. His ideal, hedonistically inspired, is the happy-go-lucky immortal, potbellied and bearded, with a wine flask or gourd, who has in his own way found ease in perfect happiness. His poem says:

There is Master Great Man –
He takes Heaven and Earth as a single morning,
A thousand years as one short moment.
The sun and the moon are windows for him,
The Eight Wilds are his garden.
He travels without wheels or tracks,
Sojourns without house or hearth.
He makes Heaven his curtain and Earth his seat,
Indulges in what he pleases.
Stopping, he grasps his wine-cup and maintains his goblet;
Moving, he carries a casket and holds a jar in his hand.

His only obligation is toward wine,
And of this he knows abundance. (*Wenxuan* 47)

The Zen connection

Beyond its influence on ecstatic poetry and the ideal of the happy-go-lucky immortal, the *Zhuangzi* is also a major forerunner of Chinese Chan (Zen) Buddhism. Developed in the sixth century as a movement against the formal hierarchies, ritual preoccupations, and increasing social obligations of monastic institutions, Chan represents a way to recover purity of mind and meditative attainments in the direct following of the Buddha. Highly iconoclastic, Chan rejects celestial saviors and buddhas and denies the value of scriptures. Instead, it promotes direct experience, intense personal contact with a meditation master, and hard manual labor as training for enlightenment.

It joins the *Zhuangzi* in emphasizing that there is nothing beyond the world as we know it; that the Dao (or Buddha-nature) is in everything that exists (even excrement); that all practice has to be in the present only; and that there is nothing to venerate, especially not the saints and sages of old. Just as the *Zhuangzi* calls the works of past masters the more "chaff and dregs of old" (Chapter 13), so Chan master Linji (d. 866), the founder of Rinzai Zen, says:

> What are you seeking in the realms of changing dependence? The Three Vehicles and Twelve Divisions of the teaching all are just so much old paper to mop up messes. The Buddha is an illusion; the patriarchs are old monks. (*Record of Lin Chi*, 10)

Another common point is the emphasis in Chan on the perfect "human," the true individual and realized being who is just himself, without standing, position, and rank, an ideal that closely matches the *Zhuangzi* vision of the perfected – in its original form and not as the Great Man. Also, like Zhuangzi, Chan masters tend to actively dislike philosophical abstracts and keep pulling people into the bodily here and now, using frequent shouts and hits to shake them out of preconceptions. This, of course, is to get them into a state of immediacy and away from conscious categories and evaluations – just as Zhuangzi focused on making all things equal. Thus the *Xixin ming* (On Resting the Mind), a seventh-century Chan document, says:

> Don't think much, don't know much! Much knowledge means deep involvement; it is much better to rest the will. A head full of worries means many failures; how much better just to guard the One? (*Transmission of the Lamp*, 30)

The Chan version of this guarding of the personal Dao within, then, continues the thought of Zhuangzi yet also develops it. It places it in a monastic setting and structures it with regulated meditation practice – a new version of the fasting of the mind with specific techniques and clearly defined stages. Chan also expands the earlier vision in that it sees the Dao in the Buddhist context of emptiness and the perfection of wisdom; it transforms Daoist thought through its understanding of body and mind as conditioned over many lifetimes through the law of karma and retribution. While Chan, therefore, will never be anything but Buddhist, it still owes a great deal to the philosophy and vision of Zhuangzi and can be counted among the most important heirs of the ancient Daoist text.

Key points you need to know

- The text *Zhuangzi* consists of thirty-three prose chapters that also contain materials from other early Daoist strands: primitivist (back to the Stone Age), hedonist (what is good for me is good for the universe), and syncretist (cosmology can define the Dao in the world).
- The philosophy of Zhuangzi himself focuses on perfect happiness or free and easy wandering, the state of utmost spontaneity that is reached when one fully realizes one's inner nature and destiny as given by Dao and stops trying to evaluate and judge things or strive for unsuitable situations beyond one's reach.
- To achieve this mental state, one should detach from society and practice making all things equal, fasting the mind, and sitting in oblivion.
- The end result will be a life as the perfected, unhindered by concepts and completely at ease in the world, plus exceedingly skillful at all tasks and inviolate to natural harm and hurt.
- The vision of Zhuangzi developed in poetry in the figure of the Great Man who ecstatically travels to the otherworld and dissolves into the cosmic emptiness of Great Nonbeing.
- It also served as a model for the worldview of Chan Buddhism, which combined it with monastic meditation practice and placed it into the context of the perfection of wisdom and the law of karma and retribution.

Discussion questions

1. Is Zhuangzi's vision of a perfect life in a perfect state of mind and complete harmony with the world too good to be true? Or could it have relevance for us today?
2. Is Zhuangzi's thought a form of mysticism? Is "free and easy wandering" a kind of mystical union? If so, how?

3. Do poets and Chan Buddhists betray Zhuangzi by using his ideas and metaphors in their own context? Or is the adaptation of ancient thought a legitimate thing to do?

Further reading

Allinson, Robert E. 1990. *Chuang-Tzu for Spiritual Transformation*. Albany, NY: State University of New York Press.

Graham, A. C. 1982. *Chuang-tzu: Textual Notes to a Partial Translation*. London: University of London.

Holzman, Donald. 1976. *Poetry and Politics: The Life and Works of Juan Chi (210–263)*. Cambridge: Cambridge University Press.

Knaul, Livia. 1985. "The Winged Life: Kuo Hsiang's Mystical Philosophy." *Journal of Chinese Studies* 2.1: 17–41.

Knaul, Livia. 1986. "Chuang-tzu and the Chinese Ancestry of Ch'an Buddhism." *Journal of Chinese Philosophy* 13.3: 411–28.

Mair, Victor H., ed. 1983. *Experimental Essays on Chuang-tzu*. Honolulu, HI: University of Hawai'i Press.

Mair, Victor H. 1994. *Chuang Tzu*. New York: Bantam.

Mair, Victor. 2000. "The *Zhuangzi* and Its Impact." In *Daoism Handbook*, edited by Livia Kohn, 30–52. Leiden: E. Brill.

Watson, Burton. 1968. *The Complete Works of Chuang-tzu*. New York: Columbia University Press.

Wu, Kuang-ming. 1990. *The Butterfly as Companion: Meditations on the First Three Chapters of the Chuang-tzu*. New York: Crossroads Publications.

3 *From health to immortality*

In this chapter

Cultivating the body is a key aspect of Daoist practice. The body is understood to consist of *qi* or cosmic vital energy, the material aspect of Dao. Everyone gets a certain type and amount of *qi* at birth and uses it during life. By cultivating and enhancing *qi* – through breath control, healing exercises, sexual hygiene, diets, and meditations – one can not only remain healthy but live longer and open oneself to the pervasion of Dao. An important practice is guiding the *qi* consciously around the body, first documented in an inscription of the fourth century B.C.E., then formulated in more detail in the "Inward Training" chapter of the *Guanzi*. The first outlines of breathing and physical exercises, medical at this stage but later integrated into Daoist practice, stem from the early Han dynasty. At this time, these methods were also used for the attainment of transcendence and acquisition of magical powers, notably by the so-called magical practitioners and immortals, important forerunners of Daoist saints and masters.

Main topics covered

- Body energetics
- Qi cultivation
- Healing exercises
- Magical practitioners and immortals

Body energetics

The cultivation and transformation of the body feature centrally in Daoism in all its different schools. The body is Dao in its concrete, manifest, and individual form, made up of *qi*, the cosmic energy that pervades all. The concrete aspect of Dao, *qi* is the material force of the universe, the basic stuff of nature. In ancient sources it is associated with mist, fog, and moving clouds. The character appears in Shang oracle bones as consisting of two parts: an image of someone eating and grain in a pot. Combined, these parts signal an energetic quality that nourishes, warms, transforms, and rises. Qi, therefore, is contained in the foods we eat and the air we breathe. But more subtly it is also the life force in the human body and as such forms the basis of all physical vitality.

By extension, *qi* also denotes anything perceptible but intangible: atmosphere, smoke, aroma, vapor, a sense of intuition, foreboding, or even ghosts. There is only one *qi*, just as there is only one Dao. But it, too, appears on different levels of subtlety and in different modes. At the center, there is primordial, prenatal, true, or perfect *qi*; at the periphery, there is postnatal or earthly *qi*. Like the measurable Dao, the latter is in constant motion and classified according to categories such as temperature, density, speed of flow, and impact on human life.

Qi is the basic material of all that exists. Already the *Zhuangzi* says: "Human life is the accumulation of *qi*; death is its dispersal." It animates life and furnishes the functional power of events; its quality and movement determine human health. Everyone receives a basic amount of *qi* from nature and needs to sustain it throughout life. To do so, people draw postnatal *qi* into the body from air and food, as well as from other people through sexual, emotional, and social interaction. But they also lose *qi* through breathing bad air, overburdening their bodies with food and drink, getting involved in negative emotions, or engaging in excessive sexual or social interactions.

Forms of flow

If kept in good shape, *qi* is in a state of proper or upright *qi* (*zhengqi*). As such it flows freely, creates harmony in the body and a balanced state of being in the person. This personal health is further matched by health in nature, defined as regular weather patterns and the absence of disasters. It is also present as health in society in the peaceful coexistence among families, clans, villages, and states. This harmony on all levels, the cosmic presence of a steady and pleasant flow of *qi*, is what the Chinese call the state of Great Peace (*taiping*), a state venerated by Confucians and Daoists alike.

The opposite of this balanced state is wayward *qi* (*xieqi*), also called deviant, pathogenic, heteropathic, or even evil *qi*. This is *qi* that has lost the harmonious pattern of flow and no longer supports the dynamic forces of change. Whereas upright *qi* moves in a steady, harmonious rhythm and effects daily renewal, helping health and long life, wayward *qi* is disorderly and dysfunctional, creating change that violates the normal order. When it becomes dominant, the *qi*-flow can turn upon itself and deplete the body's resources. The person no longer operates as part of a universal system and is not in tune with the basic life force around him or her.

Wayward *qi* appears when *qi* begins to move either too fast or too slow, is excessive or depleted, or creates rushes or obstructions. It can become excessive through outside influences such as too much heat or cold or internal irregularities such as strong emotions or over stimulation. It is in depletion when its flow has become tense due to nervousness or anxiety or when its volume and density have decreased due to serious prolonged illness. However, most commonly it means that the *qi* activity level is lower, that its flow is not quite up to standard, that there is less concentration in one or the other body part. In the same vein, perfection of *qi* means its optimal functioning in the body, while control of *qi* means the power to guide the energetic process to one or the other part.

Qi *cultivation*

A great deal of Daoist practice accordingly aims at controlling and guiding *qi* in the body. The earliest known reference to such practice is an inscription on a dodecagonal jade block of the Zhou dynasty that dates from the mid-fourth century B.C.E. The original function of the block remains uncertain, but the inscription in forty-five characters clearly refers to *qi*-practice. It reads:

> To guide the *qi*, allow it to enter deeply [by inhaling] and collect it [in the mouth]. As it collects, it will expand. Once expanded, it will sink down. When it sinks down, it comes to rest. After it has come to rest, it becomes stable.
>
> When the *qi* is stable, it begins to sprout. From sprouting, it begins to grow. As it grows, it can be pulled back upwards. When it is pulled upwards, it reaches the crown of the head.
>
> It then touches above at the crown of the head and below at the base of the spine. Who practices like this will attain long life. Who goes against this will die.

The practice described here has played an important role in healing and Daoist exercises since the middle ages. People inhale deeply and allow the breath to enter both the chest and the mouth. There they mix it with saliva, another potent form of *qi* in the body. Moving the tongue around their mouth, they gather the saliva and gain a sense of fullness, then swallow it, allowing the *qi* to sink down. They feel it moving deep into their abdomen, where they let it settle in the central area of gravity, known in Chinese medicine as the Ocean of *Qi* and in Daoism as the cinnabar or elixir field (*dantian*). There the *qi* rests and becomes stable.

As adepts repeat this practice, the *qi* accumulates and becomes stronger. Eventually it does not remain in the lower abdomen but begins to spread through the body or, as the text says, it "sprouts." Once this is felt, adepts can consciously guide it upwards – a technique that usually involves mentally pushing it down to the pelvic floor and then moving it gradually up along the spine, both in close coordination with deep breathing. Not only like the modern qigong and inner alchemical practice of the Microcosmic Orbit, this is also the pattern of circulation recommended in several medical manuscripts unearthed from Mawangdui (where also the first complete edition of the *Daode jing* was found) and dated to before 168 B.C.E. One of these, moreover, describes a related practice called the Buttock Pull, a tightening of the pelvic muscles and the perineum:

> Rise at dawn, sit upright, straighten the spine, and open the buttocks. Suck in the anus and press it down. This is cultivating *qi*. When eating and drinking, to relax the buttocks, straighten the spine, suck in the anus, and let the *qi* pass through. This is moving the fluid. (*Tianxia* 7)

Moving all the way up the back, the *qi* eventually reaches the top of the head. When the entire passage between the head and the pelvic floor is opened, the Penetrating Vessel is activated, the first energy line in the human embryo, the central channel to connect people to the Dao. With this line open, long life can be attained and one can reach for transcendence.

Inward training

Also dating from the fourth century, and possibly even earlier than the *Daode jing* in its formulation of body cultivation and self-realization, is the *Neiye* (Inward Training). It forms a chapter of the *Guanzi* (Works of Master Guan), a Han-dynasty collection that contains a large variety of materials, some even considered Legalist. The *Neiye* chapter has 1,622 characters, i.e. is about one third as long as the *Daode jing*. Like the latter, it is written in a style of semi-verse and echoes its description of Dao and the ideal state of a return to purity and simplicity. Unlike the *Daode jing*, however, it also provides practice instructions and gives a detailed account on how to work with *qi* to the greater benefit of self and society.

The text begins by noting how vital essence (*jing*), a concentrated from of *qi*, is essential to all life: creating the five grains on earth and coagulating into the stars in the sky. Bright and dark, vast and lofty, it is like Dao and cannot be halted by force or controlled by rational thinking and speech. However, and this is the key point of the text and a fundamental Daoist notion, it can be secured by virtue or inner power (*de*) and brought into the self with the help of awareness or intention (*yi*), the gentle conscious force that guides the *qi* through the body.

As adepts, moreover, bring the *qi* into themselves, they are filled with its power and achieve the complete balance of upright *qi* in body and mind. They reach a level of simplicity that allows them to let go of things and be free from sensory overloads and find a state of serenity and repose beyond the emotions of joy and anger, sadness, fear, and worry. They walk through life in harmony with all, untouched by danger and harm, their bodies unimpaired. At peace in themselves and in alignment with the world, they reach a level of physical health that keeps them fit and active well into old age. From there they reach beyond ordinary life to gain a sense of cosmic freedom that allows them to "hold up the Great Circle [of the heavens] and tread firmly over the Great Square [of the earth]."

Adepts, as described in "Inward Training", are like the perfected of the *Zhuangzi* in their calm repose and cosmic dimension; they are like the sage of the *Daode jing* in their deep, nonacting quietude and their alignment with the natural transformations. And like these ideal figures of the early philosophers, they bring about social change:

> With a well-ordered mind within you,
> Well-ordered words issue forth from your mouth,
> And well-ordered tasks are imposed upon others.
> Then all under Heaven will be well ordered. (*Neiye* 10)

Unlike the other early texts, though, "Inward Training" provides a practice outline that is firmly based in the body. It recommends physical control and moderation as a starting point: it is best to stop eating before one is full, to limit fasting and abstention, to refrain from indulging in leisure, and to let go of planning and worry. Next, adepts should "align the four limbs," which means they take up a stable sitting posture with the spine straight. Once seated comfortably, they begin by breathing deeply and consciously, regulating the breath and practicing single-minded focus for the attainment of a tranquil mind, also described as the "cultivated," "stable," "excellent", or "well-ordered" mind. This well-ordered mind, in turn, allows *qi* to flow harmoniously through the body and Dao to pervade one's life. Then one can live in peace and reach longevity.

Healing exercises

The same fundamental vision is further detailed and linked to physical exercises in several medical manuscripts unearthed at Mawangdui. Among a total of forty-five works, fifteen texts focus specifically on medicine and body cultivation. For the most part, they deal with technical questions, such as the diagnosis of disorders and the use of moxibustion on points of the major meridians. Five texts among them, one included in two editions, clearly represent an early stage of the meridian and diagnostic system as it became dominant later and was standardized in medical classics. Three contain herbal and magical recipes; one specializes in childbirth.

Body cultivation is the subject of six texts. Two deal almost solely with sexual hygiene, discussing the best times and frequency of sexual intercourse as well as herbal remedies for impotence and weakness. Two others touch on sexual techniques but for the most part provide information on how to improve health through breathing techniques, dietetics, and drugs. The last two echo earlier materials in that they focus on breathing and exercises. The *Quegu shiqi* (Eliminating Grains and Eating *Qi*) covers ways of fasting by means of breathing exercises. The text repeatedly contrasts "those who eat *qi*" with "those who eat grain" and explains this in cosmological terms.

The *Daoyin tu* (Exercise Chart), finally, focuses on healing exercises to enhance *qi*-flow and health that are known as *daoyin*, lit. "guide [the *qi*] and stretch [the body]." Beyond that, moreover, there is also the *Yinshu* (Stretch Book), excavated from a separate tomb, which provides the most detailed outline of early body practices yet.

The exercise chart

The *Daoyin tu* was discovered partly soaked in water and already broken into fragments. After careful examination, archaeologists restored it to its original size of 53 cm high and 110 cm wide (1 ft. 9 in. by 3 ft. 8 in.). It contains drawings of forty-four figures showing specific exercise poses, arranged in four horizontal rows of eleven items each. The figures were originally accompanied by captions naming or explaining the moves, but these have been lost for the most part, just as the text itself was untitled in the original and received its name from modern scholars.

A key representation of early body cultivation, the chart shows figures of different sex and age, variously clothed or bare-chested, in different postures and from a variety

Figure 3.1 The Mawangdui "Exercise Chart"

of angles. Both younger and older figures as well as men and women are present. The majority are fully dressed in knee-length kimono-style robes over bulging pants and pointy shoes, some with belts, some without, but a few also wear a mere hip-wrap or loin-cloth. The garments closely resemble the dress shown in Han-dynasty brick figures and funerary art and are not unlike the uniforms of the famous terracotta soldiers. The same holds true for their hairstyle. Most have their hair either tied up in various kinds of knots or wear a cap, again representing Han standard.

The majority of figures appear in standing poses, but four are kneeling or sitting – and all of these have surviving captions. One is sitting on the floor while hugging his knees into the chest "to alleviate ham pain." another is kneeling "to relieve knee discomfort." Two others are in rather awkward looking positions with knees slightly bent and arms extended – one "to stretch the neck," the other "to enhance *qi*-flow in the eight extraordinary meridians." Beyond these, all figures are depicted on their two feet, bending and stretching their torsos, arms, or legs, and showing various forms of mild exercise. None seem to be engaged in vigorous movements, wide stances, or athletic poses.

Both the variety of figures and the mix of poses preclude the possibility that the *Daoyin tu* shows an integrated sequence. It is much more likely that the chart presents different modes of body movements for specific conditions or ailments, such as swellings, abdominal problems, deafness, fevers, blockages, internal heat, warm ailments, and muscle tension.

Captions

In addition, a number of surviving captions make it clear that aside from manipulating *qi* through movement, breathing was a key aspect of healing exercises. As a related manuscript, the *Shiwen* (Ten Questions), notes: "Breathing must be deep and long, so that pure *qi* is easily held" and stale *qi* can be thoroughly cleansed. "Stale *qi* is that of old age; pure *qi* is that of longevity. He who is skilled at cultivating *qi* lets the stale *qi* disperse at night and the new, pure *qi* gather at dawn, thereby allowing it to penetrate all nine orifices and six viscera of the body." Having gained *qi* through breathing deeply, at the right times, and in the right manner, practitioners – following similar methods as outlined in the inscription and in "Inward Training" – circulate it through the body, hold it for some time, move it mentally to certain regions, and guide it purposely to relieve ailments and open energetic blockages. They also used it to stimulate or calm the body, depending on the need. For example, before going to sleep, one might practice "dusk breathing by breathing deeply, long and slow, causing the ears to not hear; thus becoming tranquil, go to bed."

Physical exercises as based on the medical tradition were thus intimately connected with the more spiritual endeavors of body cultivators. Integrating both into their daily life, adepts could hope to achieve the ideal mental balance of the ancient masters and maintain health and vigor well into old age – thereby developing an ideal of physical, mental, and spiritual wholeness that has remained a dominant feature of Daoism.

The *Stretch Book*

Further details on the practice of healing exercises appears in a manuscript found at Zhangjiashan, also in Hunan, in a tomb that was closed in 186 B.C.E. The text, entitled *Yinshu*, divides into three parts: a general introduction on seasonal health regimens; a series of about a hundred exercises, divided into three sections; and a conclusion on the etiology of disease and ways of prevention.

The first part on seasonal health regimens discusses hygiene, diet, sleep, and movement as well as adequate times for sexual intercourse. It is ascribed to Pengzu, a famous immortal of antiquity, said to have lived over 800 years. It says, for instance:

> Spring days. After rising in the morning, pass water, wash and rinse, clean and click the teeth. Loosen the hair, stroll to the lower end of the hall to meet the purest of dew and receive the essence of Heaven, and drink one cup of water. These are the means to increase accord. Enter the chamber [for sex] between evening until greater midnight [1 a.m.]. More would harm the *qi*.

Following a general outline of daily routines, the middle part of the *Yinshu* provides concrete practice instructions, describing and naming specific moves. For example:

> "Bend and Gaze" is: interlace the fingers at the back and bend forward, then turn the head to look at your heels.
>   "Dragon Flourish" is: step one leg forward with bent knee while stretching the other leg back, then interlace the fingers, place them on the knee, and look up.

Medical Use

After presenting forty exercises of this type, the text focuses on their medical uses. It often repeats instructions outlined earlier and in some cases prescribes a combination of them. For example, the lunge called "Dragon Flourish" is good for relieving tense muscles. Another kind of lunge helps with *qi*-disruptions in the muscles and intestines: move the left foot forward and the right leg back, then twist by bending the right arm at the elbow and looking back over the left shoulder. After three repetitions on both sides, one is to maintain the lunge position while raising one arm at a time and then both arms up as far as one can (each three times), bending the back and opening the torso. The idea seems to be that by stretching arms and legs one can open blockages in the extremities while the twisting of the abdominal area aids the intestines.

In addition, the *Yinshu*, like the *Daoyin tu*, also presents various breathing techniques, notably exhalations with *chui* (closed mouth, vigorous), *xu* (open mouth, gentle), and *hu* (round lips, blowing) to strengthen the body and to harmonize *qi*-flow. Going beyond the *Daoyin tu*, on the other hand, it outlines exercises in various positions, such as seated, kneeling, or lying down. For example, to alleviate lower back pain, one should lie on one's back and rock the painful area back and forth 300 times – if possible with knees bent into the chest. After this, one should lift the legs up straight to ninety degrees, point the toes, and – with hands holding on to the mat – vigorously lift and lower the buttocks three times.

Social Context

Following this detailed outline of concrete exercises, the *Yinshu* summarizes them in a list of twenty-four brief mnemonic statements. After this, in its third part, it places the practice into a larger social and cultural context. It notes that the most important factors in causing diseases are climatic excesses:

> People get sick because of heat, dampness, wind, cold, rain, or dew as well as because of [a dysfunction] in opening and closing the pores, a disharmony in eating and drinking, and the inability to adapt their rising and resting to the changes in cold and heat.

This harks back to the seasonal regimen in the beginning of the text, restating the importance of climatic and temporal awareness. The proper way of treating the body, however, as the text points out next, is accessible mainly to "noble people" of the upper classes, who fall ill because of uncontrolled emotions such as anger and joy (which overload yin and yang *qi*). "Base people," whose conditions tend to be caused by excessive labor, hunger, and thirst, on the contrary, have no opportunity to learn the necessary breathing exercises and therefore contract numerous diseases and die early.

This, as much as the fact that the manuscripts were found in the tombs of local rulers, makes it clear that healing exercises and spiritual endeavors in ancient China were the domain of the aristocracy. They provide a means to alleviate physical discomforts, extend natural longevity, and secure greater peace in life – with the overarching background goal of creating a more harmonious integrated society and the state of Great Peace. Yet at the same time, the very existence of the texts with their detailed instructions shows that the practices were public knowledge and accessible to anyone with enough interest and financial means to obtain them. Not esoteric and hidden away among hermits, some Daoist predecessors thus engaged in spiritual undertakings while yet maintaining close ties to society and acute political awareness.

Magical practitioners and immortals

Beyond these socially active and health conscious aristocrats, however, there was also a segment of the Han population that endeavored to go far beyond healing, wholeness, and long life. Magical practitioners (*fangshi*) and immortals (*xian*) prided themselves on having reached a state beyond the limitations of this world. Not unlike the Great Man, they pursued transcendence and ascent to the divine realm at the origins of the universe. To attain this, they lived in separation from society, engaged in techniques of physical and spiritual control, had their minds set on interaction with the spirit world, and acquired magical powers as they advanced in training.

This training usually involved a variety of longevity techniques – breathing exercises, diet control, healing exercises, sexual hygiene, absorption of solar energies, and meditations. Like hermits in other parts of the world, Han seekers undertook these practices with great seriousness. They lived in the wilderness, dressed in garments of leaves or deer skins, fasted by living on pure *qi* or ate raw food they found in the woods. Symbolically associated with birds in the lightness of their bodies and their ability to fly, they came to understand the workings of Dao and could exert control over natural phenomena and divine agents. Close to nature, they also attained extended longevity and continuous vigor and were believed to reach one of several paradises known as Penglai (in the eastern sea) and Kunlun (in the western mountains), imagined as luscious mountains surrounded by extensive bodies of water.

Magical practitioners and immortals were both important forerunners of Daoist masters and saints to come. Although the two kinds of ancient practitioners had much in common – living as hermits, engaging in body cultivation and *qi*-control, pursuing spiritual endeavors, and attaining magical powers – they were not the same.

Social Relevance

Magical practitioners tended to return to society where they used their magical powers in the service of others to exert control over natural phenomena and divine agents. They predicted fortunes and performed astrological divinations, analyzed weather patterns and made rain, healed diseases and exorcised demons, communicated with the dead and conjured up spirits, advised on military strategy and provided magical weaponry. The also worked on the concoction of alchemical elixirs, often on the basis of precious metals and cinnabar, that would transform people instantaneously into immortals.

Immortals, on the contrary, followed in the footsteps of Zhuangzi's perfected and, once withdrawn from society, completely dedicated themselves to the otherworld. At home both in the world and in the heavens, they accepted life and death as a single flow, took neither too seriously and made the best of all they met, exhibiting a happy attitude and playful way of being. Perfected companions of Dao, they fulfilled their potential, becoming fully human and thus superhuman. Calm and uninvolved, they could take action in just the right way, performing the most outstanding feats with ease and no particular effort, yet ultimately remained detached and separate from the human world.

Ways of attainment

The way to reaching immortality and attaining magical powers is an extension of physical and spiritual practices described earlier. It works along the same lines because in Chinese thought healing, long life, and immortality form three stages along the same continuum of the *qi*-household of the human body.

This *qi*-household in ordinary people is upset as they interact with the world on the basis of passions and desires, sensory exchanges, and intellectual distinctions. Soon they lose their primordial *qi*, begin to get sick and move toward death. Healing, then, is the stabilization of *qi* with medical means such as drugs, herbs, acupuncture, rest, and so on, moving it from a level of severe imbalance to a more harmonious state. Long life and *qi*-cultivation, next, come in as and when people have become aware of their situation and decide to heal themselves. Attaining a basic state of good health and mental calmness, they increase their primordial *qi* to and even above the level they had at birth. They thereby ensure not only that they fulfill their natural life expectancy but may even reach increased old age and vigor, as well as find a greater sense of peace and oneness with Dao.

Immortality, third, raises the practices to a yet higher level. To attain it, people have to transform all their *qi* into primordial *qi* and proceed to increasingly refine it to ever subtler levels. This finer *qi* will eventually turn into pure spirit, with which practitioners increasingly identify to become immortals or spirit-people. The practice that leads there involves intensive meditation and trance training as well as more radical forms of diet, healing exercises, and the mental guiding of *qi*. Immortality implies the overcoming of the natural tendencies of the body and its transformation into a different kind of energetic constellation. The result is a bypassing of death (the end of the body has no impact on the continuation of the spirit-person), the attainment of magical powers, and a residence in the paradises of Penglai or Kunlun. It also involves a deepened sense of oneness with Dao, an experience of floating along with cosmic changes, and the ability to command gods and demons to do as one pleases.

Immortals' tales

The wondrous feats of the immortals were first recorded in a Han-dynasty collection called *Liexian zhuan* (Immortals' Biographies). According to this, typical immortals

Figure 3.2 Chisongzi, Master Redpine

have attained superior youth and vigor as well as a close connection to the otherworld by transforming their *qi* through breath, nutrition, and sexual interaction. They live for centuries, if not millennia, and continue to flit between this and the other world at will, controlling the gods and natural phenomena as they please.

The first figure in the collection is Chisongzi (Master Redpine). He served as the Master of Rain in the government of the mythical emperor Shennong (Divine Farmer), who is credited with establishing agriculture and medicinal lore. Eschewing all natural nourishment, he lived only on liquid jade, an alchemical agent. He could step into fire without being burnt and to move about freely with the wind and the rain. Traveling to Kunlun at his leisure, he courted another mythical emperor's daughter, and together they moved off into the immortal realm.

Another famous character is Master Anqi who used to sell drugs on the shore of the Eastern Sea and was believed to be over 1,000 years old. A magical practitioner of sorts, he agreed to meet with the First Emperor of the Qin dynasty, talking with him for three days and three nights and receiving enormous amounts of gold and jewels. However, he was also a true immortal in that he did not hang on to these riches but left them in the village together with a letter to the emperor. He said that he considered himself sufficiently rewarded with a pair of red jade slippers, then added: "In a few years, come to look for me on the paradise island of Penglai!" He vanished into the blue yonder and has not been seen since.

Women Immortals

Maonü, the Hairy Lady, represents a different kind of immortal. She served as lady-in-waiting under the First Emperor and fled to the mountains at the end of his reign. There she met the hermit Guchun (Springvalley), who taught her how to live on pine needles. As a result of this diet, she became immune from cold and hunger, and her body became so light that it seemed to fly. She stayed in the mountains for several centuries, when she was discovered and hunted down. A few days of eating a normal diet caused her to age and die.

A yet different figure is the wine seller Nü Ji, who once hosted an immortal in her shop and received a sacred book in return. She unrolled the book and found that it described ways to immortality through sexual practices. Without delay, she studied the materials and set up a separate room for the practice. She invited young men to sample her delicious wine and spend the night with her. As she practiced the techniques, she grew increasingly younger and more vigorous. When her immortal instructor returned after thirty or so years, she followed him and ascended to heaven.

The *Liexian zhuan* contains over ninety such tales, some more likely than others, some placed more in the distant past and among the courts of emperors, others connected to local legends of the Han dynasty and relating tales of ordinary folk. All show how techniques of *qi*-manipulation changed the person from ordinary existence to a life of magic and took them far off into the immortal realms. The stories express the extreme dimension of Daoist body transformation, which reaches all the way from the fundamental attainment of good health through extended longevity and enhanced vigor to the realization of supernatural states and the transcendence of immortals.

Key points you need to know

- The body is the foundation of Daoist cultivation. It consists of *qi*, which is given by nature and can be either proper or wayward, deficient or excessive, wasted or enhanced.
- The earliest documented form of *qi* cultivation is guiding it through the body in a combination of deep breathing and visualization. Described also in "Inward Training," it allows people to come closer to Dao and create harmony in and around themselves.
- Healing exercises are the physical component of Daoist body cultivation. Not unlike Indian yoga, they serve to heal diseases, enhance vitality, and create a sense of connection to Dao.

- All these practices can also lead further to a state of ultimate transcendence, called immortality. Immortals overcome natural patterns, live forever, move freely through Heaven and Earth, and execute various magical feats.
- They are similar to magical practitioners, but the latter use their skills in service for society and may or may not eventually ascend to the paradises. Many immortals' tales recount stories of their wondrous feats.

Discussion questions

1. How can we best understand *qi*? How does it work: in the body, in nature, in human interaction?
2. Are physical exercises, combined with breathing and mental awareness, helpful to human health? What other systems are there that may be similar to Chinese healing exercises?
3. Are there similar tales like those of the immortals in other cultures? What can immortals compare to?

Further reading

DeWoskin, Kenneth J. 1983. *Doctors, Diviners, and Magicians of Ancient China*. New York: Columbia University Press.

Engelhardt, Ute. 2000. "Longevity Techniques and Chinese Medicine." In *Daoism Handbook*, edited by Livia Kohn, 74–108. Leiden: E. Brill.

Harper, Donald. 1998. *Early Chinese Medical Manuscripts: The Mawangdui Medical Manuscripts*, Wellcome Asian Medical Monographs. London: Kegan Paul.

Kohn, Livia. 2005. *Health and Long Life: The Chinese Way*. Cambridge, MA: Three Pines Press.

Kohn, Livia. 2008. *Chinese Healing Exercises: Coming Home to the Body*. Honolulu, HI: University of Hawai'i Press.

Lo, Vivienne. 2000. "Crossing the *Neiguan*, "Inner Pass": A *Nei/Wai* "Inner/Outer" Distinction in Early Chinese Medicine." *East Asian Science, Technology, and Medicine* 17: 15–65.

Lo, Vivienne. 2008. *Healing Arts in Early China*. Leiden: E. Brill.

Loewe, Michael. 1979. *Ways to Paradise: The Chinese Quest for Immortality*. London: George Allen and Unwin.

Roth, Harold D. 1999. *Original Tao: Inward Training and the Foundations of Taoist Mysticism*. New York: Columbia University Press.

4 Cosmos, gods, and governance

In this chapter

In addition to Shang ancestor worship and divination, the philosophy of Dao, Zhuangzi's ecstatic wandering, and personal body cultivation, the foundations of Daoism also rest on Han-dynasty cosmology. This cosmology structures the universe in patterns of correspondences, dividing all existence into the two complementary forces yin and yang, then detailing this organization with the help of the so-called five phases, energetic stages that are symbolized by five physical entities, such as wood and fire. Another important cosmological system of lasting influence is the Chinese calendar with its ten stems (signs for the ten-day week under the Shang) and twelve branches (zodiac animals).

The Han vision of the cosmos, furthermore, included a plethora of deities: celestial gods, starry constellations, nature deities, mythical sage rulers, divine ancestors, as well as various ghosts, demons, specters, and hobgoblins. Creating order in the universe accordingly meant matching the cosmic phases and pacifying the various gods and demons, aligning self and society in a larger context that included everything from the stars through the gods to the lowly creatures of earth. The vision of ultimate harmony, then, was described in terms of Great Peace, a state of complete openness and pervasion of all.

Main topics covered

- Yin and yang
- The five phases
- The Chinese calendar
- Deities, demons, and divine rulers
- The ideal of Great Peace

Yin and Yang

The most fundamental cosmological division in traditional China is into the two complementary forces yin and yang, commonly presented in the well-known circle with two black and white curved halves, plus a white dot in the black section and a black dot in the white section. The image shows the balance and yet interlocking nature of yin and yang, the fluidity of their interchange.

The system of yin and yang is based on correlative thinking, a basic pattern of the human mind that plays a role in all cultures. For example, to build the plural of *shoe*, we add the letter "s" to get *shoes*. The same applies to cat/cats, stone/stones, road/roads. But then we learn that this correlative pattern when applied to the word *foot* is wrong and instead of *foots* we use another pattern and go from *foot* to *feet*, then apply the same to get goose/geese, and so on. In all cases, the organization of language is based on a simple pattern that is correlated and repeated in different concrete cases.

The correlative system of understanding also comes into play in a more general understanding of reality. For example, the image of the human body may be applied to politics, so that the mind in relation to the body is understood as similar to the ruler's relation to his subjects. Or, vice versa, the workings of a motor engine may be used as a way to understand the functioning of the body, creating an understanding that all the different bodily parts work together like building blocs of a complex machine. In all these cases, similarities and differences between patterns are recognized and reality is understood in terms of the interaction of different aspects that impact on each other. In a further step, the correlation pattern itself creates a specific vision of reality and new realities are formed on the basis of further associations. These patterns tend to work particularly within a given culture and among people who share a common paradigm. Over time, the paradigms shift, allowing for new correlations and models to take over.

Application

Yang and yin originated from geographical observation, indicating the sunny and shady sides of a hill. From there they acquired a series of associations: bright and dark, light and heavy, strong and weak, above and below, heaven and earth, ruler and minister, male and female, and so on.

In concrete application, moreover, they indicate different kinds of action:

yang	active	birth	impulse	move	change	expansion
yin	structive	completion	response	rest	nurture	contraction

These characteristics were in turn associated with items in daily life:

yang	heaven	spring	summer	day	big	ruler	man
yin	earth	fall	winter	night	small	minister	woman

father	life	unfold	noble	marriage	soldiers	speech	give
mother	death	stagnate	common	funeral	laborers	silence	receive

It may at first glance seem that yang is "better" than yin. In the Chinese view, however, neither is better, stronger, brighter, or more preferable, and the two forces do not represent good and evil. On the contrary, the yin aspect of things is just as important as the yang, because one cannot be without the other. They are not opposites but complementary phases of *qi*-flow, one bringing forth the other in close mutual interdependence.

The five phases

The yin-yang system provides the working basis for understanding the patterns of Dao in the world and for seeing the concrete manifestations of qi-flow in the course of ordinary life. It is made more complex by a subdivision into five phases:

minor yang – major yang – yin/yang – minor yin – major yin.

In other words, the rhythmic pattern of rise and decline in the structure of energetic exchange is finely tuned. It is best explained in terms of the original meaning of the terms yin and yang, by taking the rise and dips of hills and valleys as a metaphor. When one begins to climb a hill, as one first comes out of the valley, the sun hits just a little and there is slight warmth and light: yang in its minor phase. As one ascends further, the sun gets brighter, the views are broader, there is a feeling of expanse: the major phase of yang. Reaching the top, there is a balance between yin and yang, where neither one nor the other dominates: yin-yang in balance. Continuing the walk, it is not possible to go up any more, so the descent begins. There is again less light, views are more restricted, a cooling sets in: the phase of minor yin. Eventually ones reaches the bottom of the valley, with its greater darkness, coolness, and shadiness: yin in its major phase. However long the sojourn at the bottom may seem, there is no other way but to go up again: one energetic phase forever moves into the next without stopping.

The Chinese further linked this phase system with five organic substances that symbolize the different stages:

minor yang	major yang	yin-yang	minor yin	major yin
wood	fire	earth	metal	water

These are known as the "five phases" or "five agents" (*wuxing*). They are often also referred to as the "five elements," because they have a superficial similarity with the Greek or Indian elements – water, fire, earth, and air. However, properly speaking the appellation "element" is incorrect since they do not refer to solid substances and firm, unchanging building blocks of the world. Instead, these five indicate phase energetics and dynamic stages in a constant rhythm of transformation.

The five materials

Historically, the five phases underwent several stages of development. In the *Shujing* (Book of History), a record dating from about 800 B.C.E., they appear as the "five materials" and are concrete substances, resources used for human livelihood. They are, at this stage, not understood as *qi* – which is found in sunshine, shade, moonlight, vapors, and other atmospheric conditions – but substances that people actually use. As such, they should be treated with care and used with moderation and wisdom. They are offered to the gods on the altars of soil and grain; they have to be guarded by rulers to ensure their continued productivity without excess or deficiency.

In their natural rhythm, the five materials produce each other continuously in a harmonious cycle. Thus, water comes about through rainfall. It makes things grow, so that there is lush vegetation and wood arises. Wood dries and becomes fuel for fire, which burns and creates ashes. Ashes become earth, and earth over long periods of consolidation grows metals in its depths. Metals in the depths of mountains, moreover, attract clouds and stimulate rainfall, thus closing this so-called productive cycle.

At the same time, however, the five materials also serve as a system of mutual control or checks, keeping things in their proper order. Thus, water can extinguish fire, fire can melt metal, metal can cut wood, wood can contain earth, earth can dam water, and water can again extinguish fire. Here the inherently dynamic nature of the five materials is not used to increase productivity, but to set boundaries and limit potential excesses. This is known as the controlling or conquest cycle. In all cases, the

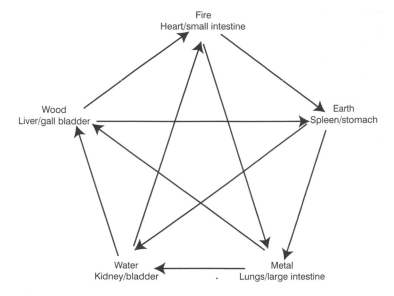

Figure 4.1 The five phases

early vision emphasizes that although the five materials are substances for human use, they are not merely innate objects but contain dynamic powers that can be turned both to production or control.

The five powers

Expanding this early model, the cosmologist Zou Yan (*c.* 350–270 B.C.E.) next created the concept of the "five powers" or "five virtues" by focusing on the potency inherent in the materials, such as wood's power to grow and be lush and fire's power to flame and rise. He then correlated these abstract powers with the political dynamics of succeeding dynasties, linking his own Zhou dynasty with the phase fire. He predicted that – following the controlling cycle of the five materials – it would be overcome by a new ruler under the symbolic power of the phase water.

Later cosmologists developed this into a great, encompassing scheme of dynastic succession and cosmological patterning so that, by the Han dynasty, the five energetic phases were associated not only with colors, but also with directions, seasons, musical tones, and with various functions in the human body, such as yin organs, yang organs, senses, emotions, and flavors. The basic chart, at the root of Chinese cosmology, the diagnostic and analytical foundation of Chinese medicine, and the essential framework of Daoism – is as follows:

yin/yang	phase	direct.	color	season	organ1	organ2	emotion	sense
mi yang	wood	east	green	spring	liver	gall	anger	eyes
ma yang	fire	south	red	summer	heart	small int.	exc. joy	tongue
yin-yang	earth	center	yellow		spleen	stomach	worry	lips
mi yin	metal	west	white	fall	lungs	large int.	sadness	nose
ma yin	water	north	black	winter	kidneys	bladder	fear	ears

Practical use

This set of correspondences served predominantly to identify relationships. As described in the "Monthly Commandments" of the *Liji* (Book of Rites) and in the early Daoist compilation *Huainanzi* (Book of the Prince of Huainan), it was used to explain why certain actions should be undertaken in certain seasons. For example, it became a general rule that because Heaven and Earth make the myriad creatures blossom in spring, one should in that season sleep and rise early, loosen the hair, relax the body, and allow all beings to live, abstaining from killing. Spring was a time of giving and not of taking, of reward and not of punishment. By following these injunctions, humanity was believed to act in proper alignment with the *qi* of spring and to secure health and harmony for both body and society. Any actions against the dominant *qi*-flow, on the other hand, would cause harm to the liver, the organ associated with wood and spring, and would create chills in the summer. They might also arouse aggression and anger, the corresponding emotions, and make for social upheaval and unhappiness.

In other words, the correspondence system provided a relational and dynamic vision of the universe, seeing all social, physical, and psychological occurrences in terms of natural cycles and ongoing patterns. It placed human beings in a world that was not, as in modern science, governed by invariable laws but subject to a pattern of interaction that could be orderly or chaotic. It thereby both limited and empowered people. It limited them by placing them into a natural cycle which responded to their actions and demanded total adaptation for success and fulfillment. Yet it also empowered them because it gave them an active role in the interaction with all things, the power to either support or disturb the natural and political order.

The Chinese calendar

Another important aspect of Chinese cosmology is the traditional calendar. Like its Western counterpart, it distinguishes four seasons – sometimes adding Indian summer as a fifth in the middle – and marks them with the solstices and the equinoxes. Unlike the Western system, however, in China the solstices and equinoxes are not considered the seasons' beginnings. Instead, they are the high points of the seasons, which begin about six weeks prior to them. This creates eight major cadences in the year: two solstices, two equinoxes, and four seasons' beginnings. They are known as the Eight Nodes and roughly match the festivals of pagan or Wicca religion

In addition, the Chinese divide the year into twenty-four solar periods of about two weeks each, which are named after natural and weather patterns such as Insects Stirring, Great Heat, Slight Cold, Winter Beginning, and the like. Both the Eight Nodes and the twenty-four solar periods have played important roles in Daoist ritual and organization.

Beyond this solar calculation, the Chinese calendar is also lunar in that it measures the months according to the phases of the moon. The first of the month is always on the new moon, and the fifteenth on the full moon. Because the lunar year has only 354 days as opposed to the 365¼ days of the solar year, the New Year shifts backward every year. To correct for this and keep the beginning of the year in the spring, the Chinese add one month to their calendar, the so-called intercalary month, once every three years – a total of seven additional months in nineteen years. This keeps their time calculation on the correct level and maintains the continuity of always having the winter solstice in the eleventh lunar month, the spring equinox in the second, the summer solstice in the fifth, and the fall equinox in the eighth.

The sixty-year cycle

For a larger count of years, the Chinese depend on Jupiter, which revolves around the sun once in twelve years. They assign a specific zodiac animal (e.g. rat, ox, hare) to each year, as well as a so-called cyclical character or "heavenly branch" (e.g. *zi, chou, yin*). They also, under the Shang, used to have a ten-day week as the foundation of ancestral sacrifices, in which they numbered the days with another set of nominal characters, known as "earthly stems" (e.g. *jia, yi, bing*). Combining the stems and branches in all possible permutations, a set of sixty combinations evolved, which was then used to count the years – the so-called sixty-year or sexagenary cycle. It looks like this

year 1 = *jiazi* (1-rat)	year 10 = *guiyou* (10-rooster)
year 2 = *yichou* (2-ox)	year 11 = *jiaxu* (1-dog)
year 3 = *bingyin* (3-tiger)	year 12 = *yihai* (2-pig)
year 4 = *dingmao* (4-hare)	year 13 = *bingzi* (3-rat)
year 5 = *mouchen* (5-dragon)	year 14 = *dingchou* (4-ox)
year 6 = *yisi* (6-snake)	etc., until
year 7 = *gengwu* (7-horse)	year 59 = *renxu* (9-dog)
year 8 = *xinwei* (8-sheep)	year 60 = *guihai* (10-pig)
year 9 = *renshen* (9-monkey)	year 61 = *jiazi* (1-rat) = year 1

This cycle was formally established during the Han dynasty and the first *jiazi* (1-rat) year known is the year 4 C.E. Each new cycle, moreover, was seen as a new beginning, based on the idea that human life lasted for approximately sixty years and that, once it was over, a complete renewal occurred. The set of sixty was further applied to designate months, days, and hours, and is at the root of Chinese fate calculation even today – especially important in the planning of suitable marriages. Religious rituals of all traditions are scheduled according to the auspicious or inauspicious nature of the signs, and many of the most important Daoist rites occur once every sixty years to mark the renewal of the cosmos. In addition, Daoist and other millenarian movements have focused on certain years, such as the first year of the cycle (*jiazi*), as the starting point of a new age.

Deities, demons, and divine rulers

Beyond the natural patterns of yin-yang, the five phases, and the calendar, the Han universe – and in its wake the Daoist cosmos – was also heavily populated by divine figures, including nature gods, ancestors, and various other supernatural entities from a large variety of cultural and geographical regions. Striving to establish an integrated cosmic pattern while joining together numerous previously warring states into a solid empire, Han officials systematized and structured the multiplicity of divinities into an organized structure.

The Five Emperors

To begin, they took local gods from the regional states and arranged them in a system based on the five phases to create a five-fold central pantheon of deities, each associated with a specific cosmic direction, a color, and an essential power. Thus, a figure known as Zhuan Xu (Good Xu) became also known as Yandi (Fiery Emperor) and was associated with the direction of the south, the color red, and the power of rise and ascension. The central gods of the so-called Five Emperors were accordingly:

name	translation	direction	color	phase	quality
Zhurong	Blessed Melter	east	green	wood	straightness
Huangdi	Yellow Emperor	center	yellow	earth	planting
Shaohao	Lesser Brilliance	north	black	water	cohesion
Yandi	Fiery Emperor	south	red	fire	ascension
Di Ku	Emperor Ku	west	white	metal	sharpness

Not only spatially ruling the four quadrants of the world with the Yellow Emperor at the center, these five deities were also arranged chronologically – in this very order, which reflects the controlling cycle of the five phases – to represent the dynastic succession of Chinese prehistory. In this function they were placed between several other sets of sage rulers, beginning in high antiquity with the so-called Three Sovereigns (Sanhuang) and continuing through the Five Dynasties all the way into actual history. The Three Sovereigns were Fu Xi (Hidden Vapor) who first discerned the trigrams of the *Yijing* from patterns in the stars and arranged for Heaven and Earth to take their proper places; Nügua (Snake Woman) who fashioned the first human beings from mud and set up life on the planet; and Shennong (Divine Farmer), supported by Suiren (Fire Drill), who developed agriculture, social structure, and markets, and also brought fire to the people.

Dynastic succession

In the time of the Three Sovereigns, the world was in complete harmony, free from strife, war, hunger, and early death. Nature functioned smoothly and interacted beneficially toward all beings, so that there was enough food for everyone and people lived in a state of great peace, reaching extreme longevity of hundreds if not thousands of years.

The Five Emperors listed above, next, saw the further expansion and development of culture so that, for example, the first war in human history occurred under the

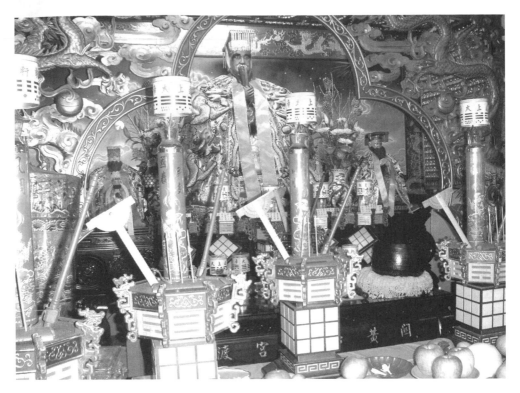

Figure 4.2 The Yellow Emperor, worshiped in Taiwan today

Yellow Emperor in his battle against an opponent for the throne known as Chiyu (Wormy Rebel). Their rule was still characterized by overall goodness, but the increased complexity of life caused various difficulties and people began to have shortened life expectancies.

Next came the Five Dynasties, led by the two paragons Yao and Shun, highly virtuous emperors who each ruled for a century or more. Great heroes in Confucian circles, these two are models of humility, personal sacrifice, and goodness among all Chinese emperors. The remaining three dynasties, often also listed as a separate entity, connect prehistory to the historical age. They are the Xia, Shang, and Zhou. They, too, were arranged according to the five phases, but unlike the Five Emperors, whose succession was governed by the controlling cycle, implying that one ruler had to overcome the other, the Five Dynasties were seen to have produced each other harmoniously. The story thus goes that Yao selected Shun and adopted him as his son and successor, while Shun appointed Yu, the first ruler of the Xia, because of his uncanny engineering abilities shown in controlling the great flood.

The new pattern therefore meant that after Di Ku, who ruled under the phase metal, Yao ruled under the sign of water, followed by Shun (wood), Xia (fire), Shang (earth), and Zhou (metal). The First Emperor of the Qin dynasty saw himself as an heir to the Zhou in this cycle and ruled under the sign of water, arranging all measures in multiples of six, garbing his officials in black, and in general manifesting water symbolism in various ways.

The Han dynasty, faced with a violent succession, dithered between using the productive or controlling cycles and had multiple legends that alternately associated the colors yellow (earth) or red (fire) with their rule. They eventually settled on the controlling cycle and saw themselves as ruling under the power of fire. Their end, moreover, was presaged by numerous prophesies that (according to the productive cycle) a ruler under the color yellow would arise – a ruler, moreover, who was inspired by a divine connection to Dao and also the leader of the first Daoist movement.

Center gods

Aside from the Five Emperors in charge of the main quadrants of the world, the Han pantheon also acknowledged various central powers located above and beyond them. Among them was first of all Heaven itself, the power of the Zhou pantheon that managed all life and stood in direct relation to the emperor, known as the "Son of Heaven" (*tianzi*). Making offerings to the deities of the directions all year round in accordance with the seasons in a special sanctuary known as the Hall of Light, the emperor would also report to Heaven on a regular basis and receive divine communications from this power.

A close next in potency to Heaven itself, but slightly more visible and accessible was the starry constellation of the Northern Dipper (Beidou), already described in the *Shiji* as being "placed in the center; . . . it governs all four cardinal points, separates yin and yang, and determines the four seasons. It balances the five phases and arranges the divisions [of time] and the levels [of space]. It fixates the various measures."

The Dipper, often also associated with the Pole Star (North Culmen, Beiji), was the central power of the universe and functioned in establishing its inherent order. Situated in the central palace of the sky, it was seen as the foundation of the world, the root of yin and yang, the pivot of all creative transformations, the bridge between sun and moon (day and night), and the ultimate source and arbiter of all living beings. The Dipper is the celestial match of the center on earth, a vertical nub where the middle of the earth is horizontal. What the Dipper is in the skies, Mount Kunlun is on earth: the vertical axis of the world, the polar center of the cosmos.

The Great One

Another central deity important in the Han pantheon was the Great One (Taiyi) an astral and abstract power both at the center of the cosmos and at the root of creation. The god personifies four things: the primordial state of the world before beings were created; the principle according to which creation takes place; the material energy of the world in its primordial form; and the basic characteristic of all there is, an abstract mark of existence. The One as the root power of undifferentiation is a close second to Dao itself. It is like the cosmic chaos Hundun, the primordial energy of all there is, the root power necessary to create and, by extension, to rule.

Matching the characteristics of the Northern Dipper, who represents a more actively governing aspect of primordial power, the Great One was similarly placed in the stars and venerated as an astral deity. Formally installed as the god of the center during Han times, he took over the place of the Yellow Emperor, relegating him and the other four emperors to a position of attendants. Losing his place in the center, moreover, the Yellow Emperor was established between the Red and the White Emperors. He soon became a key mediator between the celestial and human realms, representing the eternal learner and serving as the interlocutor in certain tales of the *Zhuangzi*, in the medical classics, and in sexual manuals.

The Ruler of Fates

Another important central figure in the Han pantheon was the Ruler of Fates (Siming). Not quite at the core of the entire universe, he was the chief of an underworld bureaucracy that kept close records on human deeds and attitudes and ordered people to die and be delivered to the underworld – not yet a hell but a rather shadowy place called Yellow Springs, where the dead resided and received ancestral offerings until such time when their spirits should return to the great flow of cosmic *qi*.

The powers of this deity are first documented in a manuscript excavated at Fangmatan, which describes the resurrection of a man named Dan in 297 B.C.E. Having killed another, he committed suicide and was buried after three days of public exposure, only to reappear, alive but not quite hale, after three years. His resurrection was effected through the workings of the underworld administration, to whom a surviving friend petitioned on the grounds that Dan had been taken before his allotted time had run out. Accordingly, "he made a declaration to the senior scribe of the Ruler of Fates, who then had a white dog dig up the pit to let Dan out." Reporting on his experiences in the otherworld, the wronged man explained: "The dead do not want many clothes. People sacrificing at tombs should not spit."

The celestial administration

The notion that the otherworld is hierarchically organized goes back to an ancient Chinese administrative ideal, formulated first in the *Liji*. According to this, the feudal ranking order consists of three dukes, nine ministers, twenty-seven high officials, and eighty-one secretaries, who are placed in concentric circles around one king residing in the center of his capital, which in turn is at the pivot of nine provinces, 120 prefectures, and 1,200 districts. Matching this complex Zhou bureaucracy, the supernatural realm was accordingly expanded from the original Shang pantheon to include multiple levels and intricate complexes.

Further formalized under the Han dynasty, the otherworldly administration was located to the inner depth of Mount Tai, the eastern of five sacred mountains who ruled the earth. Here the mountain god sits in judgment over the good and bad deeds of the dead and decrees appropriate punishments to be enacted through their descendants. Numerous bamboo slips found in tombs of the period accordingly contain petitions addressed to the Yellow Lord, the Lord of the Earth, or the Lord of the Underworld, including lists of grave goods and presents to be given to the responsible bureaucrats. In addition, there are funerary texts that function as a kind of passport or letter of introduction, by which a celestial envoy recommends the deceased to the netherworld authorities, thus assuring new arrival of a satisfactory integration into the subterranean territory.

Ghosts and demons

Should, however, the deceased not be received properly or miss the support of his descendants, he might well develop into a negative power and join the forces of demons, ghosts, specters, and hobgoblins that also populated the Han world. Hungry and desperate, these were a veritable horde of nasty creatures that lurked on the fringes of the visible world, ready to pounce on unsuspecting creatures. They could be unhappy or discontented dead, supernaturally empowered animals, or earth-based monsters. Some were people who had died violently, come back to wreak vengeance; others were ancestors neglected by their kin, hungry and in search of sustenance; yet others were mutant animals, creatures that somehow gained the power to change their shape and cause trouble.

To deal with these, people took basic precautions such as hanging demon-dispelling branches (preferably of peach wood) or talismans over their doors, muttering spells against ghosts whenever they entered an unknown area, or performing a divination before venturing out. Once a demon or ghost had made itself known, more active measures could be taken, such as throwing a slipper at it, holding up a mirror to reveal its true shape, or calling it by its name. Normally, these creatures could not stand these acts and would vanish forthwith. Sometimes, however, more extensive rites of exorcism were necessary, or perhaps a shamanic séance in which the demon was called out, identified, and properly vanquished.

However difficult the navigation of the supernatural realm, throughout all their interactions with the gods the Han people never lost sight of the ultimate state of perfect harmony that was at the foundation of all existence and could be recovered with proper personal and political action.

The ideal of Great Peace

Great Peace (Taiping) in ancient China meant a realm of total happiness and freedom, where justice prevailed and all cosmic and social energies circulated in a continuous, smooth rhythm. The term occurs first in a musical context, describing the total harmony and perfect accord of sounds. In its more political sense it appears in the historical records of the *Shiji*, denoting the establishment of perfect order. Great Peace was effected by good government that satisfied not only the common people but also the forces of Heaven and Earth, thus leading to a state of blissful harmony that would find the natural forces always beneficent and never destructive.

The state of Great Peace, Han people believed, had been fully realized in the time when the world was first created, under the rule of the Three Sovereigns. It had declined somewhat, but not too much, under the Five Emperors and been recovered again when the sage king Yao, came to power. According to some readings, notably those of a more Daoist persuasion known as the Huang-Lao school, it was most extensively realized under the government of the Yellow Emperor and could be recovered through veneration of this figure in coordination with following the guidance of Laozi.

Measures of Attainment

In either case, Han officials saw the way to recovery in paying close attention to cosmic patterns, closely observing the portents, reading the signs of Heaven and Earth, and performing the right rituals at the right times. It was also essential that ruler perfected his virtue and observed the proper rites in accordance with the five phases. Through these various measures, it was believed, human government could ensure the proper cooperation of yin and yang and thus establish a realm of Great Peace on earth – possibly after first passing through a period of chaos and destruction. Although attainable in the present, however, this state was not considered permanent nor was it seen as in total discontinuity with the present.

The emperor, moreover, who was to realize Great Peace and obtain the full blessings of Heaven, was believed to either be a sage himself (like Yao) or have the support of one (like the Yellow Emperor and his adviser Guangchengzi). Being part of the natural movement of Heaven, such a sage supposedly appeared at regular intervals, as part of a cyclical event that occurred every couple of hundred years or so.

Following this belief, Qin and Han emperors summoned magical practitioners to court in the hope that one of them might prove to be the key sage or that at least their insights into the workings of the cosmos would help them establish perfect government. Later, with a shift toward Confucianism, which became the foundation of the imperial examination system established in 136 B.C.E., Confucius rose to the status of main sage, his teachings venerated and interpreted with great devotion. At this stage, and unlike in later Daoist visions of Great Peace, none of these protagonists was considered a supernatural agent or divinely appointed. The ideal state of governance could still be obtained at the right cosmic moment with human means alone, provided the ruler proved himself worthy of the Mandate of Heaven.

The Mandate of Heaven

The Mandate of Heaven (*tianming*) appears first in the historical classic *Shujing* of the eighth century B.C.E. as a way in which Heaven (*tian*) directs the course of mundane events by ordering (*ming*) certain kings or feudal lords to take specific actions. Heaven, in these early days still closely linked with the high god of the Shang dynasty, referred to five different entities: a quasi-personified divine agent, the materially visible sky, the course of nature, the inherent pattern of events, and the representation of highest moral principle. Its order to govern, moreover, is closely linked with a moral dimension and a sense of temporality. "Nobody gets the mandate forever," the *Shujing* says. "As long as you have personal virtue, you can keep the throne. When you do not have the virtue anymore, the Nine Provinces will slip through your hands."

In the course of the Zhou dynasty and under the impact of five-phases cosmology, thinkers came to see Heaven increasingly as a natural force, the sum-total of cosmic organization that governs the inherent structures and cycles of life. Thus the Legalist Xunzi says: "Heaven has a constant regularity of activity. It did not exist for the sake of [the sage ruler] Yao nor cease to exist for the sake of [the cruel tyrant] Jie. Respond to it with good government, and success will result. Respond to it with misgovernment, and calamity will result." The Mandate of Heaven, already linked with the virtuous nature of a sincere and good ruler, was accordingly connected to specific omens or portents, such as the appearance of wondrous stones and charts or mythical animals (phoenixes, unicorns, and dragons). More explosively, however, it was also connected to the will of the common people whose contentment or distress become signs of a ruler's ability to govern. Good harvests and prosperity as well as peace and social harmony thus showed Heaven's acceptance and support of a certain ruler.

The inverse of this doctrine meant that if a ruler was about to lose the Mandate, Heaven would signal this fact through omens and portents, such as eclipses, falling stars, untimely weather, and natural disasters; the common people would be unsettled and even rise in rebellion. The notion, moreover, that "nobody gets the Mandate forever," that cosmic cycles as much as royal virtue change over time, was then connected with the doctrine of the five phases. Cyclical revolutions in government were seen as part of the natural course of events; dynasties actively began to govern under the auspices of certain phases.

Cosmic Cycles

As a result of this doctrine, whenever odd celestial phenomena were spied, floods or droughts occurred, or some form of social discontent arose, people looked to potential new rulers matching the next cosmic phase. They were expected to be associated with certain colors, symbolic numbers, and virtues. Ditties circulated, prophecies abounded, and omen-lore was rife. When the overall situation deteriorated more seriously, messianic figures arose and rebellions began. The stage, in other words, was set for the arising of the first organized Daoist movements with their own visions of ideal governance and a pervasive state of Great Peace.

Key points you need to know

- Traditional Chinese cosmology, which pervades the culture, works with a correspondence system based on the complementary forces yin and yang, terms originally referring to the shady and sunny sides of a hill.
- Their developmental stages are divided more subtly into a system of five phases, which is then matched with seasons, directions, colors, bodily organs, senses, and political patterns.
- They also manifest more subtly in the Chinese calendar with its twelve-year cycle (zodiac animals) and ten-day week, combined into a sixty-year pattern.
- Aside from cosmic forces, the Han universe was also populated by numerous deities: ancient sage rulers (Three Sovereigns, Five Emperors, Yao, Shun, Yu), gods of the center (Northern Dipper, Great One, Ruler of Fates), and other figures (celestial bureaucrats, ancestors, ghosts, and demons).
- This divergence could yet be pulled together in harmony through the attainment of a state of Great Peace, universal perfection on all levels of life. Key to this realization was the ruler, whose Mandate of Heaven was linked with natural phenomena and the happiness of the people.

Discussion questions

1. How can we apply yin-yang and the five phases in our lives? Is there merit in seeing life as continuously unfolding from one state into another?
2. How do the gods and celestial administrators create a sense of order in people's lives? Does it make sense to have a multiplicity of supernatural figures, both positive and negative?
3. What is the connection of religion and governance in other cultures? Is there still a tendency today to see government in cosmic terms?

Further reading

Csikszentmihalyi, Mark. 2000. "Han Cosmology and Mantic Practices." In *Daoism Handbook*, edited by Livia Kohn, 53–73. Leiden: E. Brill.

Graham, A. C. 1986. *Yin-Yang and the Nature of Correlative Thinking*. Singapore: The Institute for East Asian Philosophies.

Harper, Donald. 1985. "A Chinese Demonography of the Third Century B.C." *Harvard Journal of Asiatic Studies* 45: 459–98.

Karlgren, Bernhard. 1946. "Legends and Cults in Ancient China." *Bulletin of the Museum of Far Eastern Antiquities* 18: 199–365.

Lewis, Mark E. 1990. *Sanctioned Violence in Early China*. Albany, NY: State University of New York Press.

Major, John S. 1993. *Heaven and Earth in Early Han Thought: Chapters Three, Four, and Five of the Huainanzi*. Albany, NY: State University of New York Press.

Matsumoto, Kiiko, and Stephen Birch. 1985. *Five Elements and Ten Stems*. Brookline, MA: Paradigm Publications.

Shahar, Meir, and Robert P. Weller, eds. 1996. *Unruly Gods: Divinity and Society in China*. Honolulu, HI: University of Hawai'i Press.

Part II

Development

5 *Major schools of the middle ages*

In this chapter

Under the auspices of Han cosmology and pantheon, with a backdrop of *Daode jing* and *Zhuangzi*, the first organized Daoist communities emerged: millenarian groups inspired by visions of Great Peace, prophesies, and a variety of omens. They were the Way of Great Peace and the Celestial Masters. While the former rose in rebellion and were destroyed in civil war, the latter submitted to a local warlord and survived, then spread throughout China. Mingling with local cults as well as with alchemical cultivation groups, they gave rise to various new developments, most importantly the Highest Clarity revelations in the mid-fourth century, followed by the school of Numinous Treasure in the 390s.

While these schools flourished in the south, adopting large portions of Buddhist doctrine and practice, the Celestial Masters underwent a revival in the north, becoming the central force of the Daoist theocracy in the early fifth century and giving rise to the first monastic institution at Louguan. In the sixth century, moreover, the various Daoist schools began to integrate in a system known as the Three Caverns, which served as state religion under the Tang.

Main topics covered

- Celestial Masters
- Highest Clarity
- Numinous Treasure
- The theocracy
- The Three Caverns
- State religion

Celestial Masters

In response to a series of natural disasters and bad administration, various peasant revolts arose in the second century C.E. Among their leaders were also several figures inspired by direct contact with the divine who claimed to have the perfect solution to the world's problems and to lead the people into the new age of Great Peace – now seen as a major break with the present and lasting for a millennium. Two of these revolutionary leaders received their powers – including the ability to heal, make rain, and create social harmony – from a deity understood as the personification of the Dao and called, in the wake of Laozi and the Yellow Emperor, (Yellow) Lord Lao. They founded the first organized Daoist communities.

The Celestial Masters (Tianshi) – more formally known as the school of Orthodox Unity (Zhengyi) – started with Zhang Daoling, a magical practitioner and alchemist from central China who took up residence on Mount Heming in Sichuan. There, in 142, he had a vision of Lord Lao who told him that the end of the world was at hand. He was to instruct the people to repent and prepare themselves for the momentous changes by becoming morally pure so they could serve as the "seed people" of the new age of Great Peace. Closing the "Covenant of Orthodox Unity," the god appointed Zhang as his representative on earth with the title "celestial master" and gave him healing powers as a sign of his empowerment. Zhang followed the god's orders and, in an era characterized by continuous disasters, gathered thousands of people around him. As a token for his efforts, he took five pecks of rice from his followers, whom he organized into tight units and controlled with a strict moral code and ritual schedule, creating a semi-independent state on a religious and ritual basis.

Around the same time a similar organization sprang up in east China (Shandong). Founded by the visionary Gan Ji, it was known as the Way of Great Peace and in many ways followed the same pattern as the Celestial Masters. However, while the latter hoped to see the transformation of the world by natural means, the leaders of Great Peace decided to help it along and, in the next *jiazi* year (184,) rose in rebellion. They were called the Yellow Turbans after the yellow kerchiefs they wore to show their goal of replacing the Mandate of the Han with their government under the phase earth. After decades of bloody civil war, they were defeated and their organization ceased to exist. Their teachings remain in a fragmentary scripture, the *Taiping jing* (Scripture of Great Peace).

Later developments

Unlike the followers of the Way of Great Peace, the Celestial Masters saw themselves as advisers to a potent worldly ruler rather than his replacement. As a result, they survived and grew, under Zhang Daoling's grandson Zhang Lu even merging with another local cult run by a certain Zhang Xiu. The latter utilized a more stringent military-type organization and practiced formal ritual of confession and petition — both characteristics that were to become typical of the Celestial Masters in general. As a result of this merger Zhang Lu controlled a large territory in southwest China, which he divided into twenty-four districts matching the twenty-four solar periods of the year. He made amicable arrangements with the local governor and gave his organization a strong inner structure and ritual system.

After about thirty years of consolidation, battles ensued surrounding the end of the Han dynasty, and the warlord Cao Cao attacked the area. In 215, Zhang Lu submitted to Cao Cao, a move criticized by followers on both sides as an act of submission and weakness. In the event, Cao Cao became a powerful leader and decided not to tolerate a separate organization in his territory. He forcefully moved large numbers of Celestial Masters followers to different parts of the empire, where they spread their cult, transforming it gradually into a major organized religion.

As such they are still present today. The current Celestial Master, the sixty-fifth of his lineage, resides in Taiwan, and Celestial Masters priests control a wide network of Daoist temples and communities, specializing in purifications, exorcisms, and cosmic renewal rituals. Prohibited on the mainland for about fifty years under Communism, their practice is making new inroads there as well, notably in the southeastern provinces that are closest to Taiwan. In addition, an intact and functioning community of Celestial Masters Daoism is still found among the Yao in northern Thailand, who adopted the religion in the twelfth century.

Highest Clarity

When the Celestial Masters were forced to emigrate from their home base in Sichuan, they moved all over China, including also the southern region around the city of Nanjing. Here, in a small village near Mount Mao, they mingled with shamanic local cults that focused on communicating with spirits and the dead as well as with groups of alchemical seekers – heirs of the magical practitioners of the Han – who also went into ecstatic trances to receive potent recipes from a heaven known as Great Clarity (Taiqing). The result of this mixture, was a new set of revelations, received in the 360s and named Highest Clarity (Shangqing) after their heaven of origin. Being connected with the gods gave personal meaning and official validation to local southern aristocrats, who had been displaced in their official positions by the northern court elite after their flight south to escape from the onslaught of Central Asian hordes.

The revelations

The revelations began when two brothers of the aristocratic Xu family hired the medium Yang Xi (b. 330) to establish contact with the younger Xu's wife Tao

Kedou, who had died in 362. She appeared and told them about her status in the otherworld, explained the overall organization of the heavens, and introduced the medium to various other spirit figures. Among them were underworld rulers, divine officers of the dead, spirit masters of moral rules, denizens of the Huayang Grotto on nearby Mount Mao, as well as some leaders of the Celestial Masters, notably the former ritual master Lady Wei Huacun (251–334).

Together they provided the medium with a detailed description of the organization and population of the otherworld, and especially of the top heaven of Highest Clarity. They also revealed specific methods of shamanic travels or ecstatic excursions, visualizations, and alchemical concoctions. And they instructed the seekers on how to transmit the texts and their methods, while predicting a new golden age to come with the arising of Lord Goldtower, the Latter-Day Saint.

The Xu brothers wrote down everything Yang Xi transmitted from the otherworld, however disparate it may have seemed, and created a basic collection of sacred texts. They shared their new revelations with their immediate neighbors and relatives. The elder Xu became a full-time practitioner and vanished into the mountains in 348, never to be heard of again. His brother continued the family affairs and passed the texts on to his son Xu Hui (b. 341), who in 370 also vanished into the mountains, where he allegedly lived for another sixty years. His son Xu Huangmin (361–429) inherited the texts but did not take them quite as seriously, transmitting them far and wide and thus allowing them to be scattered in different parts of China. There they remained until they were collected again a century later by the Daoist master and alchemist Tao Hongjing.

Canonization

Tao Hongjing (456–536) was a descendant of Tao Kedou's native family and thus closely connected with the original revelation circle. A learned scholar and devout seeker, he gained favor with Emperor Wu of the Liang dynasty, who saw in him the potential provider of an immortality elixir. Tao established himself on Mount Mao and founded a center where practitioners could cultivate immortality, whether alone and celibate or communal and married. There he pursued alchemical and pharmacological studies, working on various elixirs and editing important manuals.

One day he came across an original Highest Clarity manuscript and was struck both by its powerful language and its high spiritual vision. He also noted the unusual quality of the calligraphy used, which he identified as the handwriting of the Xu brothers, and set out on an extensive quest to recover as many texts as possible. He eventually pieced together a close reconstruction of the original canon and compiled a record of the revelations, contained in his *Zhen'gao* (Declarations of the Perfected). Through his efforts the Highest Clarity scriptures became the center of a formal Daoist school, in due course honored as the highest form of Daoism practiced in medieval China.

Numinous Treasure

Toward the end of the fourth century, when Xu Huangmin began to distribute the Highest Clarity scriptures more widely and the original group started to lose its cohesion, yet another Daoist community began to grow. This was the Numinous Treasure (Lingbao) school, named after its key concept of precious talismans – characters in celestial script written on holy paper that symbolized the key powers of the universe and could both create social harmony and transfer people into the immortal realm. The new school began in the 390s with the inspiration of Ge Chaofu, a practicing member of Highest Clarity, who was particularly concerned with recovering the heritage of his own family, notably of the leading alchemist Ge Hong (283–343) and the magical practitioner Ge Xuan (164–244).

To do so, he proposed an alternative worldview, one which adopted the ideas of multiple segments of heaven, celestial administration, and an extensive host of divine beings from Highest Clarity, but which also returned to the cosmology of the five phases in combination with Han deities and practices and which placed a renewed emphasis on Celestial Masters ritual. He documented this view in various seminal works, which integrated manuals of the magical practitioners with Highest Clarity practices and new talismanic rituals.

Talisman power

In one text, the *Lingbao wufuxu* (Explanation of the Five Talismans of Numinous Treasure), he spells out how the five central talismans of Lingbao were not only powers of creation but stood at the root of all enlightened government over the millennia, and especially served the mythical ruler Yu in the control of the flood. Yu could not

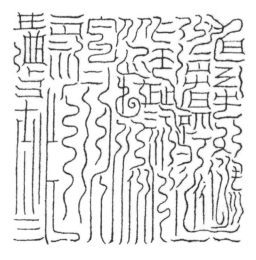

Figure 5.1 A talisman of Numinous Treasure

find a suitable heir for the talismans and instead hid them in a sacred mountain where they were found and illegitimately acquired by King Helü of Wu around the time of Confucius. The king was duly punished and the talismans vanished again until, so Ge Chaofu claims, they were offered in legitimate revelation to his ancestor Ge Xuan who duly made them accessible and equipped them with proper explanations, protective charms, and ritual prescriptions.

If treated correctly, the talismans would not only grant access to the otherworld and immortality for oneself and one's ancestors but also provide peace and harmony for family, village, county, and empire. The five central cosmic talismans, moreover, were only the tip of the iceberg – there were divine charts and diagrams for many geographical locations, such as the five sacred mountains and the ten great grotto heavens (underground immortal realms that connected sacred mountains), as well as for any number of personal and political designs. A separate set of talismans, moreover, linked with ancient magical practitioners and rediscovered in the fifth century, was claimed to have served the Three Sovereigns of high antiquity in their effort to create universal harmony. They formed the core of yet a separate school with a more active political agenda, known as the Three Sovereigns (Sanhuang).

As regards the Numinous Treasure school itself, over time it developed communal rituals for talisman activation that involved formal purifications and the sending of petitions to the otherworld. These rituals, known as purgations (*zhai*), in due course grew to be splendid, large-scale affairs with music, wine, and drama, led by professional masters and geared to move the cosmos in its roots. Not only were they extremely popular in the middle ages, making Numinous Treasure the dominant Daoist school in the fifth century, but they also formed the foundation of all Daoist ritual in later schools and are still practiced today.

The Buddhist impact

Another innovation of the Numinous Treasure school was its adaptation of Buddhism, which had arrived in China already in the first century c.e. but did not emerge as a strong religious force until the early fifth century, when the Central Asian scholar Kumārajīva (d. 413) from Kucha came to head a translation institute in the northern capital of Chang'an. Due to his efforts, Chinese Buddhists finally had texts that represented accurate presentations of doctrine and worldview, rules and rituals. Both metaphysical speculation and monastic discipline improved vastly, leading to a great upsurge in Buddhist activity in the country and inspiring Daoists to imitate the foreign religion.

Numinous Treasure masters integrated aspects of Buddhist cosmology, world-view, scriptures, and practices, and created a vast new collection of Daoist texts in close imitation of Buddhist sutras. They specifically adopted the notion of consecutive world ages or *kalpas*, the doctrine of karma and retribution, visions of hell and torture chambers for the dead, sets of systematic precepts and community rules, savior figures that would come and take people to the otherworld, as well as all sorts of new rituals and purification practices. Through their efforts Daoism in fifth-century south China transformed into a complex and sophisticated organized religion that has made a strong impact on Chinese culture ever since.

The theocracy

While all this was going on in south China, at the time divided into competing local states and governed by successive dynasties, the north was under the rule of a Central Asian people known as the Toba who had adopted the Chinese dynastic name of Wei. Alien to China, military in skill, and not well versed in the administration of vast empires, they had to rely on indigenous bureaucrats to administer their new realm. Unable to employ on Confucian officials who remained loyal to the Chinese emperor, they looked to local religious organizations to run the country for them. The result was the so-called Daoist theocracy, the first Daoist venture of major governmental involvement.

The leader of the theocracy was Kou Qianzhi (365–448). Born into a Celestial Masters family, he was an ecstatic visionary who practiced assiduously and received several revelations from Lord Lao between 415 and 423 that provided both personal and social guidelines. Receiving especially a set of thirty-six rules for priestly ethics and communal ritual called the "New Code," he went to court to propose his vision of a new Daoist empire to the prime minister Cui Hao who recommended him to the Toba rulers. They appointed Kou as the head of a state-sponsored Daoist administration which collected taxes, distributed welfare, held regular rituals, and in general maintained social harmony.

Kou presided over a central headquarters in the capital, which housed 120 senior Daoists in a monastery-like setting, and established Daoist institutions throughout the country. The high point of his career was reached in 440 when the emperor accepted Daoist initiation and changed his reign title to "Perfect Lord of Great Peace." The system fell into decline with Kou's death in 448 and ended in 451 with the execution of Cui Hao, who had become increasingly megalomaniac, gravely insulting both the rulers and rivaling Buddhist factions. The latter immediately took up the slack created by the Daoist failure and established an administrative system of so-called sangha-households through which they registered the people, collected taxes, and took care of welfare.

Louguan

Many of the Daoists displaced by the end of the theocracy, on the other hand, congregated in a new institution established by a local master called Yin Tong, who claimed to be a descendant of Yin Xi, the first recipient of the *Daode jing*. He asserted that his homestead in the foothills of the Zhongnan mountains (about 60 km southwest of the capital Chang'an, modern Xi'an) was the actual place where the famous transmission had occurred. He called it Louguan, the "Lookout Tower," in deference to Yin Xi's alleged astronomical observations and opened it to all practicing Daoists.

In the wake of the theocracy, Louguan grew significantly. It became the first major monastery of the Daoist religion and a great center for the collection and integration of the teachings. Its residents, known as the Northern Celestial Masters or the Louguan lineage, brought forth a number of important scriptures on precepts, rituals, ordination, and mystical attainments. They also formulated Daoist philosophy in a new mode, in a work called *Xisheng jing* (Scripture of Western Ascension) integrating the teachings of the *Daode jing* with the advanced myth of Lord Lao and the mystical stages they underwent in their practice. In the sixth century, they played an important role in court politics. In the civil war at the end of the Sui dynasty in the early seventh century, they actively supported the rising Tang rulers, who honored the institution with a new name and richly endowed it.

The Three Caverns

By the sixth century, then, the majority of leading Daoist schools were in place, supplemented by a variety of local traditions and lesser lineages that similarly emerged through the personal contact of individual seekers with divine figures. At the time the overall culture shifted strongly toward unification – the northern Toba-Wei empire being torn apart by internal conflicts and the various southern states getting tired of ever changing and increasingly corrupt dynasties. Part of the push for unification was the intellectual search for an integrating worldview, a doctrinal network that could hold the various factions and forces together. Various emperors accordingly staged major court debates among Buddhists, Daoists, and Confucians, hoping to either find one of them superior to the others or discover a way to harmonize all three.

As part of this integration effort, Daoists began to think of their religion as one and made various attempts at bringing the different schools into one system. Louguan masters hoped to develop a structure centered on Lord Lao; Highest Clarity followers proposed a central pantheon of thirty-nine deities. The system that eventually prevailed was known as the Three Caverns. Originally a bibliographic classification developed by Lu Xiujing (406–477), a member of both the Numinous Treasure and Celestial Master schools, the system followed the Buddhist Three Vehicles or paths to enlightenment: through listening, personal cultivation, and selfless service. In Lu's version, the Numinous Treasure school with its strong communal focus was placed at the top, Highest Clarity with its personal otherworld experiences ranked second, and the Three Sovereigns with their priestly emphasis on right government placed third. The Celestial Masters were placed at the very foundation of the entire pyramid. The same basic structure continued into the Tang, except that, in the sixth century, Daoists switched the placement of top schools, giving first rank to Highest Clarity.

Texts and gods

All Daoist texts were then arranged into three main categories, the works of each school associated with a special "Cavern" and a "Supplement" – the latter containing technical and hagiographic materials as well as materials from lesser schools. A fourth supplement was added to house the Celestial Masters at the foundation. The overall system, still used in the Daoist canon today, is as follows:

Cavern	School	Supplement
Perfection (Dongzhen)	Highest Clarity	Great Mystery (Taixuan)
Mystery (Dongxuan)	Numinous Treasure	Great Peace (Taiping)
Spirit (Dongshen)	Three Sovereigns	Great Clarity (Taiqing)
	Celestial Masters	OrthodoxUnity (Zhengyi)

The gods of the Three Caverns, moreover, were joined together into one group known as the Pure Ones or the Daoist trinity. Named after the three major heavens of the early medieval system, they had the Heavenly Worthy of Primordial Beginning (representing Highest Clarity) at the center, the Lord of the Dao (Numinous Treasure) to his left, and Lord Lao (adopted from both the Three Sovereigns and Celestial Masters schools) to his right.

The three deities further matched the Three Treasures of the religion, another concept adopted from Buddhism, i.e. *buddha* (enlightenment), *dharma* (teaching), and *sangha* (community of followers). In Daoism, they are the Dao, the scriptures, and the teachers. The gods represent the Three Treasures in the sense that the Heavenly Worthy is the creative power at the root of all existence, the Lord of the Dao is the revealer of scriptures and presenter of revelations, and Lord Lao is the practical teacher who provides instructions in various techniques and communicates most closely with humanity.

Figure 5.2 The Three Pure Ones (from *Myths and Legends of China*, by Edward T.C. Werner, (George G. Harrap & Co., 1922). Private Collection/The Bridgeman Art Library.)

TAKING REFUGE IN THE THREE TREASURES
With all my heart I surrender my body
to the Great Dao of the Highest Nonultimate.
With all my heart I surrender my spirit
to the Venerable Scriptures in Thirty-Six Sections.
With all my heart I surrender my life
to the Great Preceptors of the Mysterious Center.

Priestly ranks

The Three Caverns also provided the blueprint for the priestly hierarchy of integrated Daoism. It was a highly complex system, with major and minor ranks, that can be summarized according to seven main levels:

School	Rank
Zhengyi (Celestial Masters)	Register Disciple
Taixuan (Great Mystery)	Disciple of Good Faith
Dongyuan (Cavern Abyss)	Disciple of Cavern Abyss
Laozi (*Daode jing*)	Disciple of Eminent Mystery
Sanhuang (Three Sovereigns)	Disciple of Cavern Spirit
Lingbao (Numinous Treasure)	Preceptor of Highest Mystery
Shangqing (Highest Clarity)	Preceptor of Highest Perfection

The first three ranks were those of lay masters, while the last three were monastic, and the middle rank (Disciple of Eminent Mystery) signified a transitional stage that could be held either by a householder or a recluse.

Ordinations into these ranks began very early, with children being initiated first into the Celestial Masters level. After that, each level required extended periods of training, the guidance of an ordination master, and several sponsors from the community. In the Tang, when Daoism in this form – led by the patriarch of Highest Clarity – was the dominant religion of China, the most common ordination taken was Disciple of Good Faith. It involved receiving the *Daode jing* and several hagiographies of Laozi plus taking a set of ten precepts that included the five basic Buddhist prohibitions and five positive resolutions. The latter are:

6. I will maintain harmony with my ancestors and family and never disregard my kin.
7. When I see someone do good, I will support him with joy and delight.
8. When I see someone unfortunate, I will support him with dignity to recover good fortune.
9. When someone comes to do me harm, I will not harbor thoughts of revenge.
10. As long as all beings have not attained the Dao, I will not expect to do so myself.

The most elaborate actual ordination ceremony known from the Tang was the elevation of two imperial princesses to the rank of Preceptor of Highest Mystery in the year 711.

The multiplicity of medieval schools as well as their complex integration served as the mainstay of the Daoist religion through the middle ages and has left a major legacy to the present day. The schools represent the multifaceted nature of the religion, involving all sorts of religious communities, beliefs, and practices.

State religion

Integrated Daoism, with its complex canon, pantheon, and ordination hierarchy – and enhanced by new philosophical visions and encyclopedic presentations – came to serve as the state religion under the Tang. The ruling house, a family with the surname Li, declared Lord Lao to be their clan founder and elevated him to central deity of the dynasty. The god responded with a series of miracles.

Lord Lao's support

The first instance was his appearance in 617–618, when he showed himself to the commoner Ji Shanxing and ordered him to convey to the struggling Tang founder that he would indeed win the empire. In response to this, the emperor in 620 honored the god formally as "sage ancestor" of the dynasty and renamed the Louguan center Zongsheng guan. Next, a withered cypress at his birthplace in Bozhou began to blossom, which inspired Emperor Taizong in 633 to have the temple there restored. In 662, the deity arranged for the finding of a wondrous stone, and upon its being honored with due ceremony, appeared to express his approval in a vision shared by the entire court.

The most intense series of miraculous discoveries and appearances occurred under Emperor Xuanzong (r. 712–755), a serious follower of the religion who wrote several commentaries to the *Daode jing*, supported the collection of Daoist texts, and had frequent meetings with senior masters, ritual specialists, Daoist poets, and official patriarchs, such as Sima Chengzhen. His reign being particularly blessed, finds included a half-moon-shaped piece of jade that showed a picture of a musician immortal, a metal fish – three feet long and of purple and blue-green coloring – which made a spectacular sound when struck, and several "celestial treasures" – wondrous talismans buried in a stone container with a golden box and typically inscribed with red characters in an obscure ancient script.

Daoist institutions

Encouraged by these signs of divine approval, the emperor reorganized court liturgy, state administration, and the worship of the imperial ancestors along Daoist lines. Himself a learned Daoist who wrote several commentaries to the *Daode jing* and sponsored collections of Daoist thought, he supported the creation of Daoist rites, songs, and dances. For example, he supported a new liturgical choreography called the "Dance of the Purple Culmen" as part of official ceremony, thus changing the nature of court ritual toward a more Daoist mode. He also established a separate examination system based on philosophical Daoist classics – whose authors he divinized, honored with flowery titles (such as Sovereign Emperor of Chaos Prime for Laozi), and had worshiped in special temples.

In addition, the emperor established central state-sponsored monasteries in the two capitals that replaced existing ancestral shrines and centered around the worship of Lord Lao. They were extensive and grandiose in their layout and architecture and not only provided facilities for ancestor worship but also served as academies for training in Daoist classics and ritual. As part of this reorganization of imperial ancestor worship, the emperor further elevated all ordained Daoists to imperial family members, causing the renaming of Daoist monasteries from "temple" (*guan*) to "palace" (*gong*).

Spreading Daoist structures beyond the political center, he also set up state-sponsored institutions in each district, creating a tight network of political control through religious channels. Doing so, he continued a pattern first developed under Kou Qianzhi's theocracy, which too coopted and controlled religious organizations. In the wake of the latter, the Sui government sponsored religious temples as state-supporting institutions, establishing Buddhist temples on the five sacred mountains, in the capitals, and at important holy sites of the state. The Tang continued this practice, and in 666, Gaozong set up one Buddhist and one Daoist monastery in every prefecture. Emperor Xuanzong merely expanded it further, establishing Daoist institutions in all major districts. The role of these "temples," which held a statute of Lord Lao side by side with one of the emperors, was less to spread religion than to create a sanctified imperial network throughout the country.

In addition to these state-sponsored centers, there were 1,687 Daoist institutions (including 550 nunneries) registered in the empire in 739. Although they included some major teaching monasteries, for the most they were small hermitages. Located both in the cities and on mountains, they housed individual recluses or small groups of monks or nuns who went about their worship in a quiet, unassuming way.

Legal codes

However minor and unassuming, all clerics had to obey special legal codes that were put in place under the Tang. For one, the rulers took control of ordination and established a system of official registration, so that all ordained monks and nuns (Buddhist and Daoist) had to carry a certificate at all times. The rulers also set up new special legislation regarding priestly behavior. As documented in a special code for the clergy as well as in Tang legal codes, ordained clerics were not supposed to ride horses, possess military books, form cliques, solicit donors, or stay for more than three days with the same lay family. They must not participate in musical or other entertainments, or behave in any way rudely or abusively to elders or those of higher rank.

Punishments for transgressions were harsh, and offenders had to be handed over to the secular authorities for all serious crimes. For example, if recluses partook of improper foods or liquor they could be condemned to hard labor; if they wore clothes of silk or aristocratic colors, they could be defrocked and sent to hard labor. Similarly, if they stole or desecrated sacred objects, they could be punished by imprisonment, hard labor, or exile. If they engaged in fortune-telling and faith-healing they faced return to lay status and, if they still continued their charlatanry, were threatened by strangulation.

After a long and varied history of multiple revelations and social organizations, Daoism in the Tang had thus reached not only a pinnacle of internal organization but had come close to the center of power and was subject to stringent official policies and regulations. Closely allied to the Tang state, the integrated system of the religion did not survive its downfall and gave way to a major reorganization after the dynasty's collapse in 907. Nevertheless, it had created key doctrinal and ritual features, communal and organizational structures, as well as models for interaction with the state that set the stage for all other developments to come.

Key points you need to know

- Organized Daoism began in the second century C.E. with the two movements: Way of Great Peace and Celestial Masters. They were millenarian in nature and prepared people for the new age of Great Peace. The Way of Great Peace ended with the Yellow Turban rebellion in 184; the Celestial Masters transformed into an organized religion and are still active in Taiwan today.

- Highest Clarity goes back to a series of revelations in the 360s; carried by aristocrats, it was a small self-cultivation group to begin and only later, through the efforts of Tao Hongjing around the year 500, became a major Daoist school.

- Numinous Treasure began in the 390s. Based on Highest Clarity, it yet also incorporated Han cosmology and Celestial Masters ritual; in the fifth century, it became the main agent to adopt Buddhism into the Daoist system.

- The Daoist theocracy lasted for about thirty years in the early fifth century. It was centered in north China and created an administrative system for the foreign rulers. In its wake, the first Daoist monastery at Louguan came to flourish.

- In the sixth century, in the overall climate of unification, Daoists developed an integrated system to their teaching, known as the Three Caverns. They organize the textual materials, the pantheon, and the priestly hierarchy.

- Under the Tang, Daoism served as state religion. It was elevated to high prominence at court and in the capitals, and its institutions were present in every district of the empire. At the same time, it came under the close control of the state which took charge of ordinations, issued certificates, and established legal codes and punishments for improper behavior.

Discussion questions

1. How did other religions begin? What were the first Christian communities like? What about Islam? Do any of their beginnings bear a resemblance to Daoism?
2. What is syncretism? Can you think of other examples where religious systems adapt to other cultures and/or countries and integrate different beliefs and practices?
3. What exactly is a theocracy? How does it work? Are the other and/or modern examples? Is it a good form of government?

Further reading

Benn, Charles D. 1987. "Religious Aspects of Emperor Hsüan-tsung's Taoist Ideology." In *Buddhist and Taoist Practice in Medieval Chinese Society*, edited by David W. Chappell, 127–45. Honolulu, HI: University of Hawai'i Press.

Hendrischke, Barbara. 2000. "Early Daoist Movements." In *Daoism Handbook*, edited by Livia Kohn, 134–64. Leiden: E. Brill.

Kohn, Livia. 1991. *Taoist Mystical Philosophy: The Scripture of Western Ascension*. Albany, NY: State University of New York Press.

Kohn, Livia. 2000. "The Northern Celestial Masters." In *Daoism Handbook*, edited by Livia Kohn, 283–308. Leiden: E. Brill.

Mather, Richard. 1979. "K'ou Ch'ien-chih and the Taoist Theocracy at the Northern Wei Court 425–451." In *Facets of Taoism*, edited by Holmes Welch and Anna Seidel, 103–22. New Haven, CT: Yale University Press.

Ofuchi Ninji. 1979. "The Formation of the Taoist Canon." In *Facets of Taoism*, edited by Holmes Welch and Anna Seidel, 253–68. New Haven, CT: Yale University Press.

Pregadio, Fabrizio. 2006. *Great Clarity: Daoism and Alchemy in Early Medieval China*. Stanford, CA: Stanford University Press.

Robinet, Isabelle. 2000. "Shangqing – Highest Clarity." In *Daoism Handbook*, edited by Livia Kohn, 196–224. Leiden: E. Brill.

Strickmann, Michel. 1978. "The Mao-shan Revelations: Taoism and the Aristocracy." *T'oung Pao* 63: 1–63.

Yamada, Toshiaki. 2000. "The Lingbao School." In *Daoism Handbook*, edited by Livia Kohn, 225–55. Leiden: E. Brill.

Zürcher, Erik. 1980. "Buddhist Influence on Early Taoism." *T'oung Pao* 66: 84–147.

6 Ethics and community

In this chapter

Following this plethora of revelations, medieval Daoists lived in many kinds of communities, from fundamentally egalitarian millenarian and monastic groups through close-knit self-cultivation societies to state-sponsored organizations and lay-based religious associations. Within this multiplicity, they yet all subscribed to some core ideals, such as the close connection to Heaven, the importance of the family, and the observation of certain moral rules. Also common to all Daoist communities were the creation of a priestly establishment and ranking system, the formulation of social regulations, and the establishment of a ritual schedule that filled the year with various types of celebrations. Yet there were also unique aspects to each form of the Daoist life, a different ethical emphasis and different kinds of ritual practices.

Main topics covered

- The celestial connection
- Millenarian structures
- Self-cultivation groups
- Lay organizations
- The monastic life

The celestial connection

To live properly in the Dao, people have to realize that they and all beings form an integral part of nature and the greater universe, which functions in perfect harmony and is fundamentally good. Created in a series of transformations without a radical break from the pure, formless Dao, the universe manifests itself in a wondrous combination of manifold forces that ideally work together to constitute a cosmos of perfect goodness – a goodness that can be intuited by human beings as a sense of well-being and inner harmony but that also finds expression in moral and social rules. This goodness, moreover, once it is realized at any point in the world, radiates throughout the universe and contributes to a comprehensive harmony in Dao.

Daoist rules and community structures thus serve to create an attitude in the individual that realizes universal interconnectedness. They acknowledge that while the universe is essentially perfect, single entities can participate in this perfection to a greater or lesser degree. Ideal Daoists have realized their inner nature to the utmost and found perfection in who they were meant to be; they are able to spread the purity of Dao. People living in conflict and trouble, on the other hand, have not realized their true potential but have become removed from inherent harmony, developing patterns of disharmony and an inclination toward immoral and harmful actions. They are at odds with the universal forces and counteract the tendencies of Heaven and Earth.

Good and evil

Because all people in their essence are made up of the *qi* of Heaven and Earth, their actions and thoughts – including their hidden fantasies and secret intentions – have a direct impact on the functioning of the world. As outlined first in the fourth-century text *Chisongzi zhongjie jing* (The Essential Precepts of Master Redpine), people cause cosmic disharmony by disregarding Heaven and Earth, harming demons and spirits, cursing the wind and the rain, denigrating sages and scriptural teachings, or desecrating shrines and temples. Not only religious and cosmic violations, but all manner of social harm disturbs the cosmos: being unfilial toward their father and mother; digging up tombs to steal the valuables of the dead; cheating the blind, the deaf, and the dumb; throwing impure substances into food and drink; killing other beings; accusing and slandering others or spying on their affairs; obstructing roads and letting drains be blocked; stealing and cheating, destroying nature's riches, and in other ways harming society and the life around them. All these acts cause Heaven and Earth to be upset, leading to irregular weather patterns, eclipses, hurricanes, earthquakes, floods, droughts, and the like.

Warned by these signs from Heaven and Earth, Daoists realize that, being originally one with the root of the universe, they have the power to make the cosmos move in harmony by acting more and more in goodness – a moral goodness that abstains from harmful actions and supports all life. They replace negative and destructive attitudes with supportive and helpful ones. For example, as the *Chisongzi zhongjie jing* says, instead of "when burdened by debt, they wish that the moneylender should die and the debt expire," they now strive to pay back the money. When they see someone blessed with beautiful wives and concubines, instead of developing an intent toward adultery, they count their blessings and "realize that their own partner does not create quarrels or upheaval." They observe varying sets of precepts and prohibitions to gradually develop a greater awareness of Heaven and Earth; eventually they create good fortune for themselves, society, and the world at large.

The celestial administration

In addition to showing signs of disapproval through natural disasters, Heaven and Earth also unfold their effects on people's lives through the celestial administration which supervises human behavior and adjusts people's life expectancy in accordance with their deeds. Among the early Celestial Masters, this administration was described in terms of the Three Bureaus of Heaven, Earth, and Water, each with groups of officers who administered people's fates.

In the medieval schools, the system was expanded and the Daoist otherworld became an elaborate construction of manifold offices. The *Siji mingke* (Illustrious Regulations of the Four Ultimates), a fifth-century Highest Clarity text, describes the central offices in heaven:

1. The office to the left presides over transgressions of a yang nature, such as killing, theft of celestial treasures, unwarranted spread of sacred texts, cursing and swearing.
2. The office to the right presides over transgressions of a yin nature, including harboring schemes in one's heart, disobedience, planning harm to others, and never remembering the Dao.
3. The office in the center presides over more essential shortcomings, such as doubts and duplicity, lack of reverence and faith in heavenly perfection, desecration of heavenly treasures, and thoughts of removing the scriptures of the Dao or of defiling perfected writings.

Records and punishments

In each case, the celestial administrators keep a detailed record of every individual's deeds and intentions, for each sin subtracting an appropriate number of days from his or her life expectancy. They control a huge staff of divine guards, bailiffs, and local agents; they receive regular reports from the stove god installed in each family's hearth and from three divine agents that live within the person and are known as the Three Worms or Three Corpses. Half-animal, half-human in looks, they reside in the head, torso, and abdomen of each individual, where they monitor deeds and thoughts. Once in every sixty-day cycle, on the *gengshen* day (no. 57), they ascend to heaven to report to the celestial officers. If sins prevail, they receive orders to make the person sick, morally impure, or prone to misfortunes, leading eventually to disgrace, ailments, and death. To escape the clutches of the celestial bureaucrats and live a happy life, one must therefore act morally and with proper virtue, worship the gods, pay proper respects to Heaven and Earth, and practice regular meditations and rituals. One can also stay awake on the *gengshen* night, thus preventing the Three Worms from making their report, which will leave them disoriented and eventually cause their demise.

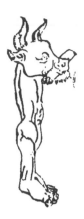

Figure 6.1 The Three Worms

If subjected to their noxious machinations, however, and engaged in any form of evil, retribution and punishment will not stop with the individual. Rather, the misfortune spreads to family and community, not only by affecting them immediately as the person gets sick, loses money, or is incarcerated, but also through something called "inherited evil." Spelled out first in the *Taiping jing*, this means that descendants and communities suffer the results of their elders' actions, leading to the crippling and early death of children and various kinds of troubles in neighborhoods and villages. With the spread of Buddhist karma and retribution, moreover, the sinner was also believed to undergo massive tortures in the underworld prisons and be reborn as various unpleasant creatures, such as a worm, a snake, a vulture, or the like.

Millenarian structures

While these concepts pervade Daoism in general, specific communities add their own unique patterns to the mix. Thus, for example, the earliest Daoist communities, the Dao of Great Peace and the Celestial Masters, were millenarian groups. As described by Victor Turner in his seminal work *The Ritual Process* (1969), millenarian groups are one form of *communitas*, i.e. a total or liminal institution, such as also found in monasteries, boot camps, asylums, and the like. Consisting of people who have placed themselves intentionally in a liminal or threshold situation, they are betwixt and between social positions or life stages – in the Daoist case no longer of the ordinary world and not yet of the realm of Great Peace. People in liminal phases are typically without status, property, insignia, rank, and position. Groups of this type tend to emphasize comradeship, simplicity, and obedience within their organizations while defining themselves radically against all outsiders through manifestly different garb, eating habits, sexual mores, and life style. The early Daoist communities match this description in many respects.

Ritual patterns

Religion dominated the administration of the organizations. Followers of the Celestial Masters were ranked hierarchically on the basis of ritual attainments, with the so-called libationers, leaders of the twenty-four parishes, at the top. Beneath them were the demon soldiers, meritorious leaders of households who represented smaller units in the organization. Members came from all walks of life and included many non-Chinese, and leadership positions could be filled by either men or women, Han Chinese, or ethnic minorities. At the bottom were the common followers, organized and counted according to households. Ranks were attained through ritual initiations, at which followers received lists of spirit generals for protection against demons. The earliest initiations were given to children at age seven, then continued at regular intervals, depending on the follower's devotion and community service. The list of spirit generals was called a register (*lu*) and was carried, together with protective talismans, in a piece of silk around the waist.

Each household paid the "five pecks of rice" tax or its equivalent in silk, paper, brushes, ceramics, or handicrafts. Its exact amount varied according to the number of productive members in each family. It was assigned and collected on the three major festival days of the year, the full moon day of the first, seventh, and tenth months. These days were called the Three Primes and celebrated in honor of the celestial administration which kept records of life and death, and consisted of the Three Bureaus of Heaven, Earth, and Water. Festivities involved large community assemblies and major banquets known as kitchen-feasts. Unlike on regular days when the consumption of meat and alcohol was prohibited, at these occasions wine would flow, animals were slaughtered, and everyone celebrated with enthusiasm, leading some critics of the movement to condemn their practices as "orgiastic." In addition, each smaller unit or village had a community or parish hall, where members would assemble to perform regular rituals, confess sins, and discuss local affairs.

Community rules

Everybody had to participate in these community events and perform community service, repairing roads and bridges and maintaining so-called lodges of righteousness where travelers could stay on their journeys. In addition, community life dominated the individual through sets of rules. The earliest such set is associated with the *Xiang'er* commentary to the *Daode Jing*. It guides followers to behave with obedience to the leaders and with reticence to their fellow members. They should not strive for positions beyond their status and abstain from sacrifices for popular gods. They must not to do evil, engage in warfare, accumulate riches, or praise themselves as great sages. On a more positive note, followers should develop a helpful and positive attitude within the community, controlling their senses and showing humility toward others. Advancing further, they should give active service to the Dao, preserve living things, and live in accordance with the patterns of the universe – never cutting down plants unnecessarily and especially not in spring time. The rewards are accordingly. Those who obey the highest rules become immortals, all others will extend their years and live happily ever after – surviving even the cataclysmic changes to come as the world ends.

Similarly, the fifth-century collection *Laojun shuo yibai bashi jie* (180 Precepts Spoken by Lord Lao) provides rules on practical living and emphasizes personal honesty and community life. The text prohibits fundamental infractions of cosmic order, such as killing, theft, adultery, abortion, intoxication, destruction of natural resources, and waste of food. It regulates the proper behavior toward community members and outsiders, forbidding specifically fraternization with brigands and soldiers, cruelty to slaves and animals, and familiarity when encountering outsiders and officials. Many details of daily life are regulated, and pettiness and rudeness are discouraged as much as the accumulation of personal wealth.

Sex and sickness

Beyond these community regulations, the Celestial Masters, as other total institutions, also took control over their members' bodies, notably in the arenas of sexuality and health. They exerted sexual control through an initiatory practice known as the "harmonization of *qi*." This involved formally choreographed intercourse between selected non-married couples in an elaborate ritual. Practitioners underwent this rite when they were promoted from one level of ritual standing to the next, enacting the matching of yin and yang in their bodies and thus contributing to greater cosmic harmony. In addition to the cosmic benefits, the rite also set followers far apart from mainstream Confucian society, thus enhancing cult cohesion and binding followers strongly to the leader.

Another aspect of physical control appears in the Celestial Masters' understanding of sickness and sin. Sickness was seen strictly in supernatural terms as the attack by a demon, who could only gain entry into a person's body if the latter was weakened by sin. As a result, all healing of the early Celestial Masters was undertaken through ritual and magic; acupuncture, herbs, and other medical treatments were expressly prohibited.

Concrete measures in the case of sickness, involved four steps. First the sick person was isolated in a so-called oratory to think of their sins and find a explanation for the illness. Once certain sins had been identified, a senior master would come to write them down – in triplicate and together with a formal petition for their eradication from the person's divine record. Next, the three copies would be transmitted ceremonially to Heaven (by burning), Earth (by burying), and Water (by casting into a river). The divine officials would then set the record straight, expel the demons, and restore the person's good health. Additional, supplementary measures of purification included the ingestion of "talisman water" (the ashes of a talisman dissolved in water), healing exercises, and meditations.

Self-cultivation groups

A completely different kind of Daoist community evolved through various self-cultivation groups, small (often aristocratic) assemblies of like-minded seekers who shared a common goal, such as the ecstatic encounter with deities (Highest Clarity), the creation of an alternative society (Ruan Ji, Liu Ling, etc.), or the concoction of an alchemical elixir (Ge Hong). Rather than an extensive community organization and manifold rules, they had sets of practice instructions and highly specific taboos which were not geared primarily toward cosmic purity or community cohesion but served to maintain and enhance internal energies, to create optimal conditions for successful practice.

For example the *Lingshu ziwen* (Numinous Book in Purple Characters) says: Highest Clarity Daoists followed a set of ten so-called Immortals' Taboos which prohibited violence, debauchery, stealing, intoxication, and laziness – all potentially damaging to the internal body gods – plus a series of dietary taboos. For example:

> Do not eat the flesh of animals associated with the day of your parents' birth. As and when you do so, your primordial body will lose its beginning, and your deepest root can no longer be accessed. Then the gods of the womb cry out in agony and the Scarlet Lord [of the heart] wails for affection. Your three spirit souls will be ruthlessly poisoned, while your material souls are tied firmly to the grave. As this meat enters your mouth, your destiny falls into the long night [of the underworld]. This is the fifth item that defeats the signs of immortality.

Similarly followers should not eat the flesh of animals associated with their own birthday, as well as those associated with certain days according to the sixty-day cycle (such as shellfish on "crab" day). They should also avoid urinating, spitting, and combing their hair while facing north, and on specific days should not dig the earth, look at blood, sell shoes, or take baths.

Beyond these general taboos, the behavioral guidelines of Highest Clarity were practice instructions, which involved exercises, incantations, and personal rituals, as well as methods of identifying the gods and ways of communicating with them.

Elixir concoction

Alchemical practitioners, too – whether magical practitioners, followers of Great Clarity, or members of Highest Clarity – followed a number of organizational guidelines and taboos. Thus any elixir concoction had to take place at exactly the right time and in exactly the right place. Ideally, it should begin at the height of yin –

at midnight of the winter solstice – and be done in a completely secluded spot with the right kinds of streams, hills, and trees for the proper flow of *qi*. Seekers began by setting up a furnace, typically a three-tiered brick oven, and completing various ritual purifications, including bathing, fasting, and avoidance of sex and blood. They put up protective talismans, offered a sacrifice to the gods, swore an oath of secrecy, and made a formal pledge to their master.

Next, the concoction proper began, a lengthy and complicated procedure that involved creating a chemical reaction on the basis of highly disparate and often poisonous substances, cooked according to cosmic instructions and surrounded by magical devices. The most commonly used drug was called cinnabar (*dan*), which is also the generic word for "elixir." It is a mercury-sulfite that dissolves into its parts when heated, then reconstitutes itself back into cinnabar (i.e. "reverted cinnabar"). Mercury, of course, is highly poisonous: taken in small amounts, it causes delusions and brain damage; in massive doses, it is fatal. Parallel to this concoction work, alchemists also hoped to create gold from base metals and to replicate the cosmic processes of creation for insights into, and power over, the innermost secrets of the universe. If and when the elixir had been created successfully, alchemists had to perform a thanksgiving sacrifice and give away large portions of the newly created gold. They could then take varying doses of the elixir, a gray-brown mud that was ingested either rolled into a pill or dissolved in liquid. Depending on the dose, they could attain magical powers, gain divine protection, find lightness and radiance in body and mind, and have the choice of either extending life on earth indefinitely or ascend to the immortals.

Lay organizations

Lay organizations differ from millenarian communities in that their followers join a specific school or association for devotional purposes while remaining the subjects of the worldly ruler and obeying the laws of the state. Their rank in civil society, their economic status, and their social connections are not predominantly defined through the religious organization. Their community does not control every aspect of their life, they do not pay taxes to religiously appointed officials, and there are no civil sanctions for failure to attend assemblies or ceremonies. Rather, members join voluntarily as their schedule permits, they give donations as they can, and they come back only if services prove efficacious and worthwhile.

Lay assemblies also differ from self-cultivation groups in that the overarching goal of their religious practice is not the complete transcendence of this world and the attainment of immortality or ascension. Rather, they follow their rules, perform their rituals, and observe their practices to enhance life on this earth, with the goal of creating greater health, happiness, and good fortune – a set of goals often expressed in Chinese popular religion in the deity triad Fu Lu Shou: a prosperous and extensive

Figure 6.2 The three gods Fu Lu Shou (Bibliothèque Nationale, Paris/Archives Charmet/The
     Bridgeman Art Library)

family, good social status and material well-being, as well as a long and healthy life
(posterity, prosperity, and longevity).

Communal worship

To this end, lay Daoists participated in regular communal services and took sets
of selected or temporary precepts in order to undergo minor ordinations, join an
elite group, or perform in a ritual. As formulated first under the theocracy and later
adopted into Numinous Treasure and the integrated form of Daoism, followers

observed daily, regular, and special rites, involving formal feasts and communal meetings. Feasts were divided according to major, medium, and lesser, lasting seven, five, or three days respectively. To prepare for a feast, members had to purify themselves by abstaining from meat and the five strong-smelling vegetables (garlic, ginger, onions, leeks, and scallions), as well as from sexual relations and contact with impure substances. A typical banquet, then, consisted of three courses – a vegetarian meal, wine, and rice – but those who could not afford all three could resort to only having wine. The ritual activity during feasts, daily services, and ancestral worship, moreover, all involved a series of bows and prostrations as well as the burning of incense and offering of a prayer or petition.

Special rites were also prescribed for funerals and sicknesses, the latter involving not only ritual prostrations and the sending of petitions but also the public confession of sins. In their ordinary lives, moreover, all members had to honor their elders and the civil officials, even more so if the latter were also priests of the religion. The priests in their turn, as officers among the celestials, had to behave with particular propriety and be a model to the community. In an adaptation of Buddhist rules, they were moreover bound by special behavioral regulations, such as moving about with a straight body and straight face, without turning to look either left or right. For example:

> When entering a parish hall to present a petition, in all cases be of upright posture and quickened gait, take your place on the right and left according to rank and exhibit seriousness and devotion. Do not allow men and women to intermingle or stand in the wrong place. Do not let them look around idly, chatter noisily, push and shove, or advance and retreat either too quickly or too slowly. (*New Code*)

Purgations

In addition, the Numinous Treasure school in the fifth century developed a new type of major public rite known as purgation. It involved participants chanting, praying, confessing their sins, presenting offerings and petitions to the gods, and generally coming to create a divine community on earth. One of their most spectacular festivals was the Mud and Soot Purgation, performed to alleviate the karma accumulated from the past and help the follower and his ancestors attain immortal status, envisioned as a bureaucratic transfer of registration files of the celestial administration. Participants would undergo symbolic punishments, such as being bound in fetters, hung upside-down, or ceremoniously beaten, while the audience would whip themselves into a frenzy, wail and weep, cover themselves in ashes, and roll around in the mud. A typical prayer is:

> For three days and three nights, through all the six [double-hour] periods,
> We carry out repentance for our pardon.

> May our millions of forebears and ancestors –
> all our fathers, mothers, uncles, brothers,
> Whether dead already or to die in future, down to ourselves, participating here –
> May we all be free from all the evil for *kalpas* still to come!
> For millions of generations, we have committed sins and accumulated burdens.
> Reverently we now trust in the rite of this Purgation.
> May our family be complete and ordered!
> May we be bathed and cleansed to purity!

It was also believed that large-scale ceremonies on behalf of the state and the community as, for example, the Yellow Register Purgation would create cosmic harmony in the larger universe and ease social and political tensions. Festivals of purgation were held at regular intervals, at the Three Primes, the Eight Nodes, and other major annual junctions, as well as on occasions important to religious or state institutions. The priests who conducted these festivals had to be formally ordained and were equipped with the most exquisite robes and implements. They exerted authority as celestial officials, reconfirming the inherent nature of Daoist ritual as a formal audience with the gods.

Daoist art

Another way in which communal Daoists offered prayers for the well-being of family, ancestors, and state was by sponsoring works of Daoist art, most importantly stone images. A typical the stele showed the image of a high Daoist god on the front and have inscriptions on the back and/or on the sides. After the artist had executed the image, the family would hire a priest and, in a formal consecration ritual, have the object placed on a mountainside to allow its easy communication with the otherworld.

About fifty such objects have so far been excavated, mainly from north China. Images are mostly of Lord Lao, but also of other high gods or of a group of deities that may also include a buddha or bodhisattva, showing that Daoist followers were not loathe to appeal to other, potentially efficacious gods. Inscriptions typically contain prayers for the dead, wishing that they may avoid the three bad forms of rebirth (as animal, ghost, or hell dweller) and instead come to life in the heavens; for the happiness and prosperity of currently living family members; for the imperial family and political peace; and for the liberation of all beings. In addition, there are occasional prayers for a prosperous human rebirth for the ancestors or for the coming of the true lord who will bring Great Peace.

> May the governors and rulers
> And all the officers who keep the earth in order
> Guide the people with bright virtue. . . .
> May the good teaching be spread widely,
> And the people follow it in happiness
> Looking up with hope. . . .
> May they have their wishes realized
> And their lives extended!

The monastic life

Monastic institutions represent the culmination of all the other kinds of religious community. They are liminal in the sense that their members have already left this world and are preparing for the next; they are centers for the practice of self-cultivation and have transcendence as their ultimate goal; yet they also form an important component of ordinary society where they play various roles: supporting the state, providing relief for the populace, training priests, and often serving in health care and education. Unlike Christian monasteries where the ultimate goal is the realization of selfless love and unlike Buddhist institutions which serve the attainment of enlightenment, Daoist monasteries hope to create a celestial space, a prototype of the ideal realm of the perfected on earth.

The first clearly known Daoist monastery is Louguan, which grew in the wake of the Daoist theocracy. Following its lead, many important institutions arose which soon not only trained Daoist priests and leaders but also became major centers of learning and economic and political power. Regulated by both state and religious statutes, monastics – both monks and nuns in equal measure and without gender-based discrimination – followed a schedule determined by ritual observances, transformed simple ordinary acts such as washing their face and hands and brushing their teeth into sacred activities, and elevated meals to major ceremonial occasions that blessed the heavens and all beings. They also tightly controlled all interactions both within the community and with members of the opposite sex, and submitted themselves to order and control in selfless obedience and abject humility.

The daily schedule

As the Celestial Masters scheduled their major annual festivals to coincide with administrative events in the heavens, so monastics arranged their cycles in accordance with nature and the gods and followed a daily schedule determined by ritual. Matching Buddhist convention, they divided the day into six periods of worship – midnight, cockcrow, dawn, noon, dusk, and early evening. First monastics observed a minor rite at cockcrow, consisting of prostrations and the chanting of incantations. The morning audience followed at dawn, a formal assembly of all members in honor of the deities, complete with hymns, prostrations, incense burning, and scripture reading. Breakfast was served afterward, and then there was unscheduled time until noon.

The noon meal was served around 11 a.m. It was a ceremony involving offerings, prayers, praises, and chants of repentance, whose timing coincided with the feeding of the heavenly sages in order to secure the greatest benefit for human practitioners. The afternoon was without formal services, followed by the evening audience at dusk and another, lesser rite in mid-evening. A sixth period of worship was scheduled around midnight. All around the clock, therefore, in addition to the high holidays throughout the year, Daoists followed the heavenly rhythm and arranged their lives in service of the divine. Just as their millenarian forebears, moreover, the consumption of food was a highlight in the ritual activities – although monks and nuns abstained from alcohol and meat throughout.

Monastic food

The noon meal was the central food event of the day. Monks and nuns (often living in so-called double-houses) lined up in full regalia and filed into the refectory in the proper order. They chanted a series of incantations, bowing repeatedly, then with precise movements unwrapped their set of five bowls and utensils. The meal itself began with the serving of grain (rice or millet), followed by a number of different dishes, usually vegetarian and made up of the five food groups as defined in a seventh-century text on monastic eating: *qi*, medicines, grain, fruit, and vegetables.

The food should be neither too hot nor too cold, too spicy or too bland, nor should it contain any harmful substances. Rather, it was to harmonize the blood and body fluids and create an overall sense of harmony in the body, supporting health and long life. Also, every taking of food came with a ritual of sharing it with all beings, from the gods above to the demons below, from the emperor and donors that made the meal possible to all people on earth.

Sex and alcohol

To transform their lives into that of immortals, Daoist monastics also had rules against intoxication and sexual contact. Both could seriously impede the flow of cosmic energies in the person and harm Heaven and Earth. More specifically, the rules warn against the development of uncontrolled behavior: sloth and torpor, violence and killing, eating meat, consuming the five strong vegetables, and disregarding taboos or the ritual schedule. These give offence to celestial officers, sicken the souls, bring nightmares and bad fortune, and cause bad karma and rebirth.

Alcohol specifically is blamed for ten kinds of problems, including unfilial, offensive, and belligerent behavior, sexual hankerings and rule violations, as well as riding accidents and getting lost on the road. Its consumption harms all forms of social interaction and leads to violence and aggression; also, its production is a perfect waste of thousands of pounds of good grain that could feed the people. It is, therefore, best to stay away from wine completely and instead create one's own inner liquor from refined saliva and *qi*.

Similarly, to prevent sensual attachments and sexual activity, men and women should remain separate and avoid all contact or discussions. If they do not even see an attractive person of the opposite sex, their minds will not get agitated. Daoists were, therefore, seriously segregated and had to remain distant whenever they found themselves in the presence of a person of the other sex. However, even for this rule there were exceptions. For example, Daoist monks were allowed to lecture lay women on the scriptures or help a woman in need. They were also – following the overarching Confucian codes of Chinese society – to support their mothers and sisters if other male members of their family could not do so, and in general behave honorably toward the other sex.

In all they did, moreover, they should keep in mind the greater harmony and benefit of the cosmos at large, avoiding all activities that would create disturbance among recluses, families, villages, country, and state. The goal of the religious Daoist life, however much centered on the individual or in whatever kind of community, never wavered from the universal vision of Great Peace. The harmony of Heaven and Earth was always at the core of all communal and religious Daoist activity – and still is to the present day.

Key points you need to know

- Daoist ethics focus on the creation of harmony within the community and the larger universe. All Daoist activities are closely connected to Heaven and Earth, who signal their disapproval through natural disasters, personal misfortunes, sickness, and harm.
- The earliest Daoist communities of the second century were millenarian in nature. They segregated themselves from ordinary society and lived a tightly regulated life full of community service, rituals, and restrictions.
- Self-cultivation groups at the same time had much less stringent regulations but dedicated themselves to the attainment of an otherworldly goal, such as ascension or immortality. Their communities were centered on the transcendent; their activities were governed by taboos and practice instructions.

- Lay organizations, such as the Numinous Treasure school and the theocracy, used religious ritual and community to enhance life on earth: personal good fortune, protection of ancestors, peace in the land. They engaged in large-scale rituals and also sponsored works of Daoist art.
- Monasteries, finally, became the central pillar of Daoism in the Tang dynasty, the training ground for priests and the core of holiness. They had strict schedules and tight rules and served to establish a replica of the immortal life on earth. Avoiding alcohol and sensual attachments, they also worked for the community, offering rituals for political stability and providing an economic network through the country.

Discussion questions

1. Why do people behave with goodness? What are some common motivations for people to do good? How do they compare to the Daoist vision of Heaven and Earth?
2. How are millenarian and monastic institutions similar and different? Can you think of other institutions that share some of the same characteristics? What are the potential benefits and dangers of such total institutions?
3. What are the main characteristic of an organized religion? If you were to found one, what would you need most essentially? What elements could be left out?

Further reading

Bokenkamp, Stephen R. 1997. *Early Daoist Scriptures*. With a contribution by Peter Nickerson. Berkeley, CA: University of California Press.

Campany, Robert. 2005. "Eating Better Than Gods and Ancestors." In *Of Tripod and Palate: Food, Politics and Religion in Traditional China*, edited by Roel Sterckx, 96–122. New York: Palgrave Macmillan.

Hendrischke, Barbara. 1991. "The Concept of Inherited Evil in the *Taiping Jing*." *East Asian History* 2: 1–30.

Hendrischke, Barbara, and Benjamin Penny. 1996. "*The 180 Precepts Spoken by Lord Lao*: A Translation and Textual Study." *Taoist Resources* 6.2: 17–29.

Kamitsuka, Yoshiko. 1998. "Lao-tzu in Six Dynasties Sculpture." In *Lao-tzu and the Tao-te-ching*, edited by Livia Kohn and Michael LaFargue, 63–85. Albany, NY: State University of New York Press.

Kleeman, Terry. 1998. *Great Perfection: Religion and Ethnicity in a Chinese Millenarian Kingdom*. Honolulu, HI: University of Hawai'i Press.

Kohn, Livia. 2003. *Monastic Life in Medieval Daoism: A Cross-Cultural Perspective*. Honolulu, HI: University of Hawai'i Press.

Kohn, Livia. 2004. *Cosmos and Community: The Ethical Dimension of Daoism.* Cambridge, MA: Three Pines Press.

Tsuchiya, Masaaki. 2002. "Confession of Sins and Awareness of Self in the *Taiping jing.*" In *Daoist Identity: History, Lineage, and Ritual,* edited by Livia Kohn and Harold D. Roth, 39–57. Honolulu, HI: University of Hawai'i Press.

7 Creation and the pantheon

In this chapter

While creation in ancient Daoism is mainly cosmogony, the natural evolution of the world from Dao, organized Daoists pose Lord Lao as conscious, active creator or, alternatively, see the celestial sounds and symbols of the primordial scriptures as the root cause and central power of creation. The latter, moreover, take the concrete shape of sacred spells and incantations as well as ritual talismans and cosmic charts. As such, they are activated in ritual practice to ensure adepts' direct access to the upper reaches of the universe. The universe, moreover, is now divided into thirty-six heavens, the lower twenty-eight of which remain in the realm of rebirth and are determined by the laws of karma and retribution. The upper heavens are for perfected human beings as well as immortals, who serve there in different administrative functions. In addition to these divine beings, Daoists also believe in the nature deities, specialized gods, ancestors, and ghosts adapted from popular religion.

Main topics covered

- Creation
- Spells, charts, and talismans
- Heavens and hells
- Gods, ancestors, and immortals

Creation

Early Daoist texts describe the creation in terms of cosmogony, that is, as an unfolding of natural processes from the underlying Dao. They have several models for this: the boring of seven sensory openings into the shapeless sack of cosmic chaos (Hundun), which creates the world and its culture but also kills formless primordiality (*Zhuangzi*); the productive unfolding of several stages from the Dao first to cosmic oneness, then to the twofold powers of yin-yang, and on to the three – yin and yang joined – from which the myriad beings arise that populate the world (*Daode jing*; *Huainanzi*); the division of the underlying oneness of the cosmos into the two forces yin and yang, followed by their further subdivision into different mixtures known as the four emblems (yang-yang, yin-yin, yang-yin, yin-yang) and from there into the eight trigrams and sixty-four hexagrams (*Yijing*); and the gradual transformation of the world through a series of initiatory stages such as Grand Simplicity, Grand Immaculate, and Grand Initiation that eventually give rise to High, Middle, and Low Antiquity, ruled by the various sage rulers and mythical heroes of old (*Yijing* commentaries; *Liezi*).

Lord Lao as Creator

Daoists of the middle ages change this fundamental outlook to develop several further models of world development. For one, they begin to see Lord Lao, the deified Laozi, not only as a personification of Dao but as an active, conscious creator who is set apart from the world and gives it shape. No longer a mere human philosopher or even a gifted immortal, he is now the root of the entire world, the representative of the order and creativity inherent in the cosmos. As Laozi comes to create the world, the beginning of his life extends back to the dawn of the universe, while his entire career is transformed into a celestial myth. Thus the *Laozi bianhua jing* (Scripture of Laozi's Transformations) of the late second century C.E. says:

> He rests in great beginning and wanders in the great origin,
> Floats through dark, numinous emptiness. . . .
> He joins serene darkness before its opening,
> Is present in original chaos before the beginnings of time.
> Beyond harmony of the pure and turbid,
> Moving along with Grand Initiation,
> He resides in the ancient realm of obscurity and vastness. . . .
> Alone and without relation,
> He has existed since before Heaven and Earth.
> Living deeply hidden, he always returns to be:
> Gone, the primordial; present, a man!

The Celestial Masters

Lord Lao as creator appears further in the *Santian neijie jing* (Inner Explanation of the Three Heavens), a fifth-century mythical outline of Celestial Masters' history. Here creation begins with Dao as the underlying creative power of the world, "dark and obscure, vast and open, and without prior cause." Revolving in emptiness and spontaneity, it "transforms and brings forth the Elder of Dao and Virtue," followed by the three highest heavens. Once they exist, the Dao as Great Nonbeing creates the three fundamental *qi* of the cosmos: mysterious, primordial, and beginning. They in turn intermingle in chaos and bring forth a primordial goddess called Jade Maiden of Mystery and Wonder, a name that combines the basic attributes of Dao with the formal title of a Daoist goddess. She next gives birth to the celestial version of Laozi through her left armpit. The god in this version is not Dao as such but its direct product, mediated through a series of transformations that bring forth heavens, spiritual powers, pure energies, and a mother figure. He is born supernaturally even in heaven. His emergence from the left armpit, moreover, borrows from the birth story of the Buddha, who leaves his mother through her right hip.

Next, Lord Lao creates the world. Under his guidance, mysterious energy rises up to form Heaven, beginning energy sinks down and becomes Earth, while primordial energy flows everywhere and turns into Water – thus forming the three basic agencies of the Celestial Masters' universe. In addition, the god creates three major continents with three countries each, where he places people and religions: Daoism in the center (China), Buddhism in the west (India), and the "Way of Clear Harmony" (a shamanic religion) in the south. Thus the world with its main continents and religions comes into existence.

Primordial symbols

A yet different take on the creation of the universe appears in the other medieval schools. In Highest Clarity, for example, the key to cosmic unfolding is the celestial existence of powerful cosmic charts and scriptures. Formed through a first coagulation of original *qi*, cosmic symbols existed from the beginning of the universe, in essence identical with the underlying force of all: uncreated, direct, primordial. Their recitation gave the gods, similarly primordial, the power to furnish being from emptiness. Not only cataclysms of creation, the scriptures are also key forces of survival. When the world, as it does periodically, comes to an end, the highest scriptures alone survive. The word for "scripture" (*jing*) is thus imbued with a new and more powerful meaning: the "going through" of the original graph becomes the "eternally surviving" of the religion.

Nothing but rays of pure light in the beginning, the primordial energies condensed to form heavenly signs and integrated scriptures. Made from jade, they are inscribed on tablets of gold in the highest heavens. Incredibly big and written in a form entirely unintelligible to human beings, they are stored on the Mountain of Jade Capital in Mystery Metropolis, the center of the Heaven of Grand Network. Only the highest and most refined of the heavenly host ever gain access to this subtle realm. However, these celestials on occasion transmit them to human beings – either in translation (as scriptural texts) or directly (as sacred signs in heavenly script).

Scriptural power

In either case, the galactic words have enormous power for their possessor and must be handled with great care. Recitation of the esoteric names of the heavens as much as of the scriptures themselves conveys immortal status on the believer. Holding original signs of Heaven is like having a passport to the higher spheres, a token of immortality, the possession of truth incarnate. In this sense, sacred scriptures in Daoism are more than containers of divine truth: they are powerful means of magic, seats of celestial potency, sounds of empowerment, signs of the ultimate.

The scriptures can subjugate demons, control natural phenomena, and enable seekers to journey to the otherworld. Copied carefully and handled only with proper ritual and through purification, scriptures must never be lost or used lightly. Never must one teach or even show a scripture to one not rightfully initiated.

Sacred sounds

The Numinous Treasure school agrees with this assessment of the primordial and creative power of scriptures and heavenly symbols, but it also adds the dimension of sacred sounds into the mix. According to their vision of the universe, there were originally five cosmic charts of the five directions, represented by the so-called Five Elders, adaptations of the Five Emperors of Han cosmology and the key deities of the world's beginning. Each god has his own special name, location, characteristics, and sacred spell. For example, the *Yuanshi wulao zhenwen* (Perfect Writings of the Five Ancient Lords of Primordial Beginning), the primary scripture of Numinous Treasure, says:

> In the east resides the First Ancient Lord of Green Power, with the Jewel of Peace, in the Forest of Blossoms. His spell is the pervading mysterious stanza of precious perfection that brings forth the spirit.
>
> In the south resides the Perfect Ancient Lord of Cinnabar Power, with the Jewel of Brahma, in the Realm of Flaming Yang. His spell is the precious numinous song that reaches to Heaven from the southern clouds. . . .
>
> The jade tablets of the Five Ancient Lords are all texts made from pervading emptiness and pure spontaneity. In their original form they rest hidden above the Nine Heavens on the Mysterious Terrace of the Seven Treasures in the Palace of Purple Tenuity in the Numinous Capital. There they are guarded by the five emperors and their spirit officers. In accordance with the ordinances of the mystery, they emerge only once in 40,000 eons.

Revelations of these sacred words, symbols, and sounds are thus rare occurrences that have to be treated with special care and must not be taken lightly. They come with the full force of primordiality and have tremendous powers that can be used both to advantage and to the creation of great danger.

Spells, charts, and talismans

As a result of this emphasis on sacred sounds and symbols, medieval Daoists paid close attention to their activation in religious practice. They worked heavily with spells, chants, and incantations to connect to the original sounds of Heaven; they made ample use of charts, signs, and talismans to adopt the celestial script into their lives.

For example, the Celestial Masters took control of the supernatural forces that pervaded their universe by fortifying their houses and bodies with talismans while learning to recognize the demons and call them by their proper names. They also visualized themselves as demon-conquering heroes and banished all malevolent forces through their powers, enhanced by the ritual formula: "Swiftly, swiftly, in accordance with the statutes and ordinances." Used in all ritual incantations and petitions of the Celestial Masters, this formula is still in use today and has, moreover, made its way into Japan where it is a key phrase among mountain hermits, the so-called Yamabushi.

A formal incantation against demons from a fourth-century text known as *Zhougui jing* (Scripture on Cursing Demons) runs as follows:

> The Celestial Master said:
> I am the scourge that kills all misfortunes under heaven,
> A changing body among men, I am a demon king.
> My body tall to sixteen feet, my face square and even,
> I have copper teeth, iron molars, and a tough, sharp beak.
> In my hands a grindstone and a boiling pot,
> I hurl the thunder, throw the lightning, and swing the lights of heaven.
> Stars and planets lose their course, the moon hides her shining,
> Whirlwinds arise, battering earth, the sun retains his brilliance.
> Grasses and ferns scorch and wither, trees lose their foliage.
> Mountains tumble, stones cleave asunder, I break all river bridges.
> My carriage holds an iron cage, shot with a silver lock,
> I beat it thrice in every month, sing six sacred songs.
> Thus I search out the many demons, valiant and strong,
> Succeed in killing off the numerous misfortunes.
> While I thus brandish divine spells, who would dare approach,
> Passing fast over a thousand miles, I free all from misery.
> Swiftly, swiftly, in accordance with the statutes and ordinances!

Incantations in Highest Clarity

Similarly, Highest Clarity practitioners as part of their visualization practice would chant incantations to the gods to come and empower them. Thus the *Tianguan sandu* (Three Ways to Go Beyond the Heavenly Pass) has:

> Oh, Yang Brightness of Mystery Pivot,
> Spirit Soul and Spirit of the Heavenly Pivot!
> Oh, Nine Lords of Highest Mystery –
> Merge and transform into one single spirit!
> Cut off my route to death at the Gate of Demons,
> Open my registers of life in the Southern Office!
> Let my spirit souls be free from the three bad rebirths,
> Let me come to life again as an immortal!

The religious practice that goes with an incantation like this is twofold: a visualization of the divine representatives of Dao and an ecstatic excursion to the heavenly abodes. Visualization typically begins with a period of purification (bathing, abstention, avoidance of sex, blood, and dirt) and takes place in an oratory. The adept begins by burning incense and bowing to the ten directions. He or she clicks the teeth to indicate his readiness for contact with the divine and loosens her clothing to settle on a meditation cushion before a small altar table. Then she visualizes either the seven gods of the stars of Dipper, the Heavenly Worthy, the Queen Mother, or Lord Lao surrounded by the four heraldic animals – tigers and dragons formed by starry constellations. The gods descend before him and offer him protection, join him in his own unique world to raise him to a celestial level of being. They may also communicate with him, describe for him the delights of the heavens, the ranks and orders of the immortals, or again take him up on a visit to the celestial realm.

Talismans and sacred charts

As concrete aids in this practice, Daoists use magical diagrams, charts of the universe, supernatural maps of sacred mountains, and potent talismans to activate the original powers of Dao. They all contain celestial signs and drawings that symbolize the essential power of a place, god, or heaven. They are used to empower the practitioner, granting him influence over the relevant entity and providing protection from all demonic and harmful influences.

More specifically, talismans (*fu*) go back to ancient identification devices used in military campaigns, where the general would break a token in half, then send one part off with his deputy and have the other half delivered to the connecting marshal at the other flank. When the two met, they would match their halves and find that, indeed, they carried the correct empowerment. In Daoism, talismans were

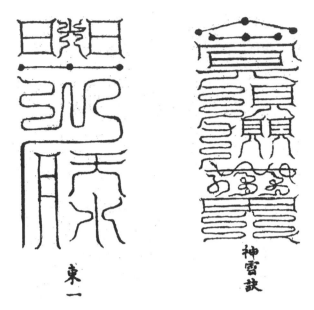

Figure 7.1 Classic talismans

used similarly, with the main difference that the matching half was the original in Heaven. Their earthly parts were rectangular pieces of wood, metal or, more recently, colored paper (usually yellow, red, or blue), inscribed in black or red ink with figurative signs and formal symbols, stylized characters and images, written. Depending on the situation, they serve as a manifestation of cosmic energies, a geomantic chart, the representation of a deity, an edict from the spirit world, or a god's immediate order.

Activating talismans

Talismans could only be handled and activated if the practitioner was in a high state of purity and mentally prepared to take on the powers they represented. All medieval Daoist schools made use of them for purification, exorcism, healing, and various rituals.

They were particularly dominant in the school of the Three Sovereigns, which strove to continue the activation of sacred talismans as used by the ancient sage rulers to govern the world in perfect harmony. Revealed to the hermit Bo He in the third century as writings in a cave, the talismans were later found on Mount Song, then passed down and linked with other cosmic charts. Followers of the Three Sovereigns school believed that the talismans guaranteed universal harmony. Safely stored in the higher heavens and accessible only to the gods, they were transmitted to earth by Lord Lao or the Yellow Emperor. Through them practitioners learned about the

Figure 7.2 The Diagram of the Great Ultimate

proper behavior, personal integrity, and correct procedures for the effective handling of the talismans.

As outlined in the *Badi jing* (Scripture of the Eight Emperors) of the Three Sovereigns school, to write a talisman, practitioners needed a special brush and ink. They began by purifying themselves with incense and by fasting in a secluded spot. They should act only at night and in a clean place, in perfect accordance with the phases of the moon. First they donned immortals' garb, then summoned the gods by writing the proper talisman. For the gods of Heaven, the characters should be written pointing upward; for those of Earth, downward. The deities would announce their presence after a few moments.

Sacred charts

Celestial symbols were further activated in diagrams or sacred charts (*tu*). Stylized cosmic maps of sacred areas, they came in three kinds. The first represents mythical geography or the true shape of a geographic feature; examples are the charts of the five sacred mountains, of mysterious grotto-heavens in their interior, of Numinous Treasure paradises, and of the underworld. The second type includes diagrams associated with the *Yijing*, which reveal the functioning of the universe and its cosmogonic principles; examples are the *Diagram of the Great Ultimate* and the *River Chart*, a sacred map of the universe brought to earth on the back of a dragon in the Yellow River. The third consists of representations of the body, syntheses of cosmogonic elements, depictions of body gods, the underworld, alchemical processes and talismanic elements; the best known is the *Neijing tu* (Diagram of Interior Passageways), a picturesque illustration of the world inside the body.

Heavens and hells

The world in Daoism, then, consists of multiple layers of realms both thisworldly and otherworldly. The majority of existence is subsumed in a comprehensive structure of thirty-six heavens, topped by the Heaven of Grand Network, also translated as the Heaven of Grand Veil, with its capital of Mystery Metropolis, also known as the (Mountain of) Jade Capital. Here the great celestial scriptures are stored, managed and guarded by the highest of deities, powerful representatives of Dao and elevated immortals.

The thirty-five heavens beneath this highest realm divide into five groups. There are first the Three Clarities – Highest Clarity, Jade Clarity, Great Clarity – the heavens that represent the three major schools of Daoism with their respective gods, scriptures, talismans, chants, and a host of divine administrators. Below them are the four "Brahma-Heavens," named after the central deity of the Hindu pantheon who represents the purity of the universe and the four ideal mental states (*brahmaviharas*): equanimity, love, compassion, and sympathetic joy. These four heavens are reserved for true believers, human beings who have attained a very high level of purity in their lives and minds and who are transposed into these divine realms of pure bliss. They can advance to become immortals in the Clarities or, like bodhisattvas, decide to return to the lower realms if they decide to assist humanity in its quest for peace and perfection.

The Three Worlds

The lowest twenty-eight levels of heaven are called the Three Worlds and are adapted from Buddhism. The lowest six form the World of Desire; the following eighteen are the World of Form; and the four heavens above them constitute the World of Formlessness. This is more or less the world people inhabit, their level determined by their dominant way of life. Are they mainly guided by desire and is their life governed by passion? Or do they follow fundamental principles, ethical rules, and inherent virtues that go beyond desire yet can still be expressed in form? Or are they spiritually advanced and have developed a strong intuition, a sense of rightness in themselves and in the universe, subject neither to desire nor to limiting rules? These highest of beings participate in the World of Formlessness and are poised for ascension into the Brahma Heavens or even the Three Clarities when all physicality is transcended

Figure 7.3 The Wheel of Life

The five paths of rebirth

The Three Worlds, unlike the higher heavens, are governed by the laws of karma and retribution. Here people transmigrate from birth to birth, passing repeatedly through five states of being, adapted from Buddhism. They are the realms of gods, humans, animals, hungry ghosts, and hell dwellers – leaving out the sixth Indian realm, that of titans (*asuras*).

These five states can be understood as both psychological states and cosmological planes. In the modern, psychological reading, each realm is associated with a particular attitude or emotion: gods are addicted to pleasure, human beings are fundamentally ignorant, animals run on instinct, hungry ghosts are driven by greed and desire, and hell dwellers are full of anger and hatred. We all pass through these states variously in our lives, but some people are dominantly more in one mode than another and can be described as living in that particular realm.

The Chinese traditionally have read these states more cosmologically and asserted that one can actually be reborn as an animal or a god and suffer or enjoy the kind of life that plane offers. Whether pleasant or unpleasant, though, as long as one is still in the Three Worlds and passes through the five paths of rebirth there is no permanent salvation or liberation and one has not reached the ideal state of immortality and divinity in the Dao.

Karmic punishments

Unfavorable planes of life in the Daoist system, then, are described as the "three bad rebirths," the "five realms of suffering," the "eight difficult conditions," and the "ten situations of intense suffering." As described in the fifth-century *Jieye benxing jing* (Scripture of Controlling Karma and Original Conduct), the three bad rebirths are in the hells, as hungry ghosts, or among animals, while the five realms of suffering include all areas of rebirth. The eight difficult conditions are life on the borders or among the barbarians; as a slave or servant; in poverty, as an orphan, or as a lowly person; as a sick person; as a mentally retarded, mad, or disabled person; in situations of trouble and distress; in a life without filial piety or compassion; and in a country that lacks Dao.

The ten situations of intense suffering, moreover, are specific punishments in the hells, envisioned as supernatural courts of inquisition and torture that were also adapted from Buddhism. The text lists them:

1. To have to step on the mountain of knives;
2. To have to climb the tree of swords;
3. To be thrown into the boiling cauldron;
4. To be tied to the hot iron pillar;
5. To have to lie on the bed of spikes;
6. To be tied to a fiery chariot and plunged into icy water;
7. To have one's head grasped and one's tongue twisted;
8. To have to swallow fire and to eat burning charcoal;
9. To be tied and locked up by the three officers, hit with metal cudgels, and beaten with iron staffs;
10. To come to life only to be tied in fetters, to be deeply in trouble and distress, and to be eventually killed.

Medieval Daoists adopted these tortures from Indian sources but they had clear reality also in that they reflected the actual means of extorting confessions from criminals in Chinese prisons. Later arranged in ten successive "courts of hell" and each associated with a particular kind of transgression, they are to the present day depicted in vivid detail on temple walls, providing massive deterrents for the faithful.

The workings of karma

The process by which one is affected by bad karma is gradual. As the sixth-century *Yinyuan jing* (Scripture of Karmic Retribution) describes it, people who live immorally and go against Dao will first encounter various forms of misfortune, such as disasters caused by water and fire, encounters with swords and weapons, capture and prison, evil winds and nasty demons. This will put great stress on their minds and cause increasing madness, while their bodies will suffer greatly from a variety of diseases and discomforts. Too sick to live yet not sick enough to die, they are caught in a living hell on earth.

Even after death, there is no respite. On the contrary, the real suffering starts in the various depths of hell for kalpas eternal. When they finally attain rebirth, they come back in the body of a domestic animal, as a pauper or despised person, crippled, dumb, or deaf, condemned to a life of suffering from hunger, cold, and chronic diseases. This situation, of course, gives rise to more inner tension and greed for food, wealth, and well-being, making it doubly difficult to create the good karmic conditions necessary for a better life. Moral behavior and formal precepts, therefore, form the first foothold in a new way of life away from evil and its bad consequences. Even the most elementary prohibitions against killing, stealing, and lying help to create a setting that allows relief and eventual growth in Dao.

Gods, ancestors, and immortals

Living in a positive relationship to Dao, moreover, means engaging in constant interaction not only with the community of the living but also with innumerable supernatural entities, most importantly forces of nature and the dead. They both, in traditional yin-yang pattern, come in a good and a bad form, so that there is a fourfold division of divine agents: gods and demons, ancestors and ghosts. The Chinese terms for these are the same: *shen* and *gui*, showing that, although they are different in position and power, there is no ultimately significant distinction between them.

Nature gods

Forces of nature include gods of soil and grain (worshiped in every village), the dragon gods who manage wind and rain, the Five Emperors of the five directions, the Sun God, the Moon Lady, the various powers of the planets and the Northern Dipper, as well as other marvelous deities. They each have highly specified and benevolent functions in the workings of the cosmos, representing pure powers of life and creation that help to steer the universe in its right course.

On the negative side, natural forces also manifest as demons that bring disasters and epidemics, cause earthquakes and locust plagues, and in general make life difficult. There are demons of fire that burn down people's houses, demons of thunder and clouds that create bad fortune, and demons of cold wind that cause sickness and infertility.

Ancestors

The divine and the demonic are also present within people and among the dead. In people, they are their material (*po*) and spirit (*hun*) souls. Characterized as yin and yang, respectively, they represent the earthly and Heavenly *qi* in the person and serve to ensure healthy instincts of self-preservation and survival as well as provide guidance toward intellectual or spiritual pursuits.

Having joined to form the person during gestation, after death they each return to their native realms: the *hun* or yang part to heaven, the *po* or yin part to Earth. Both continue to have both spiritual potency as well as some material nature, so that they need support and sustenance from the living. The *hun* soul thus becomes an ancestral spirit (*shen*), is represented in an ancestral tablet placed on the altar in the center of a traditional Chinese home, and there receives regular sacrifices from the living whom it protects in return. It is also envisioned to pass through the hells and descendants make every effort to ensure its smooth transit, having scriptures chanted and writs of pardon delivered to the underworld officers.

The *po* soul remains with the corpse and is buried in the earth under positive auspices and with full regard to directional fengshui; it receives grave gifts – real objects in antiquity, clay and straw replicas but real food in the middle ages, and paper images today – and is the object of an extensive family visit at Qingming, the Pure and Bright Festival in the fourth month. It, too, protects the living but can become a haunting influence if not satisfied properly.

In some cases, the ancestor is considered so meritorious, having been a person of high exemplary standing and great virtue, that his powers are too good to be used by just one family. In this case, he or she is elevated to a deity in a public process not unlike beatification in the Catholic church. Once appointed, the god can be associated with tasks specific to his expertise – as for example, Guandi, the God of Wealth – or can become an official in the celestial hierarchy, such as a village or city god.

Ghosts

Ghosts (*gui*) are the lost dead, people who have died violently or far from their kin, otherworldly manifestations of unfortunate animals, or otherwise harmed creatures who cannot find rest. They are exceedingly numerous and typically hungry, with a limited degree of consciousness that guides them to possible sources of nourishment – incense and food offerings. They gobble up sacrifices originally meant for ancestors, seek sexual congress with beautiful girls or boys, possess harmless people to get them to do their wishes, and in general wreak havoc wherever they appear.

A typical countermeasure is to throw a shoe as soon as one spots them, calling out their names if one can identify them, or using peach wood to make a sacred bow and arrow for one's defense. Talismans and exorcisms complete the armory of unsuspecting citizens constantly surrounded by otherworldly malevolence.

An alternative remedy is to provide regular offerings for the ghosts – as done in grand scale at the annual Ghost Festival in the seventh lunar month – and thus appease them or even assure their cooperation. In some cases, one or the other ghost may turn benevolent and emerge as an efficient protector of the community or healer of the sick. In this case, his or her worship increases dramatically: the ghost becomes a god. Many such deities are local, and their cult fades again as their efficacy declines. In some cases the actual corpse is enshrined and the deity looks black – later images, too, replicating this feature.

All these supernatural agents, gods and demons, ancestral spirits and ghosts depend on their close interaction with the living. The living and the otherworldly help or harm each other and exist in a mutual relationship, having no real independence in the universal scheme. They are deeply embedded in the complementary nature of yin and yang.

Immortals

Above and beyond all these figures, however, there is a group of deities that reside above the Three Worlds and do not participate in the mutuality system. These are the immortals and perfected beings of Daoism, who are also of two kinds: either uncreated or created, born form pure celestial energies or transformed from a human base.

Celestial perfected include the pure gods of the Dao, who are not forces of nature but stand beyond nature at the root of existence and represent the core heavens and scriptures of the religion. Transformed immortals, on the other hand, are human beings who, either through an elixir or a variety of practices have found direct access to Dao and succeeded in transforming themselves completely.

In either case, immortals are part of the pure level of Dao at the root of creation, beyond the yin-yang division of the mainstream cosmos. They stand alone and interact with other beings entirely on their own terms. No feeding or forcing is possible. Like bodhisattvas or Western gods, one can pray to them but their response, if it ever comes, is entirely an act of grace and not based on a mutual relationship of any kind.

Transcendence

Immortals are physical beings, as everything in the Chinese universe is physical in a more or less subtle form. But while the gods of the mainstream pantheon consist of high yang energy and the dead of high yin, immortals are beyond either, having bodies of ultimate yang that makes up the base of all other forms of *qi*. To transcend to this level, human beings – who consist of a lucky mix of yin and yang – have to undergo long periods of physical and meditation practices to transform to increasingly purer levels of yang and eventually go beyond all. After having created a new, transcendent type of body, they pass through death, always the gateway to the otherworld, as the mere falling-away of their human form, shedding the body "like the skin of a cicada" to allow the free flight of the immortal entity within.

The successfully transformed immortal is duly rewarded with a position in the celestial administration, usually beginning as a lowly manager in the realm of the dead, the Six Palaces of Fengdu, then gradually working his way up to the higher realms in centuries of dedicated service. Higher administrators, in communications from the otherworld, are often also identified as meritorious ancestors of devout Daoists and popular gods from the mainstream pantheon. Created by the personified Dao or pure celestial scriptures, arranged in a complex system of multiple heavens, and populated by familiar figures, the Daoist otherworld thus actively continues mainstream Chinese beliefs while yet transforming them in a new vision.

Key points you need to know

- The Daoist universe is created from the Dao either by evolution or through the agency of Lord Lao or the sacred sounds and signs of the scriptures. Daoists gain access to the otherworld by using the primordial sounds and signs in the form of incantations and spells or talismans and cosmic charts.

- They strive to attain the higher of altogether thirty-six heavens, overcoming the tribulations of karma and retribution which rule the lower twenty-eight, also known as the Three Worlds, a concept adapted from Buddhism. The World of Desire, moreover, also includes several undesirable realms of rebirth, such as that of animals, hungry ghosts, and hells.

- The various heavens and deities are also present in the human body, which is a replica of the universe and houses a variety of gods, palaces, and passageways. In the higher reaches of heaven, immortals serve as celestial administrators along with nature gods and divinized human beings. At the same time, Daoists also subscribe to the beliefs of popular religion, including worship of nature deities, ancestors, and divinized humans.

Discussion questions

1. How do the Daoist visions of creation compare to other creation stories? Are they more or less plausible? In what ways are they similar or different?
2. Is there anything in the Daoist vision of heaven and hell that reminds you of Western or other comparative concepts? What are some common themes in such visions?
3. What are some uses of sacred signs and sounds used in rituals or group organization?

Further reading

Bokenkamp, Stephen R. 2007. *Ancestors and Anxiety: Daoism and the Birth of Rebirth in China*. Berkeley, CA: University of California Press.

Eberhard, Wolfram. 1967. *Guilt and Sin in Traditional China*. Berkeley, CA: University of California Press.

Despeux, Catherine. 2000. "Talismans and Sacred Diagrams." In *Daoism Handbook*, edited by Livia Kohn, 498–540. Leiden: E. Brill.

Girardot, Norman. 1983. *Myth and Meaning in Early Taoism*. Berkeley, CA: University of California Press.

Jordan, David K. 1972. *Gods, Ghosts and Ancestors*. Berkeley, CA: University of California Press.

Major, John S. 1993. *Heaven and Earth in Early Han Thought: Chapters Three, Four, and Five of the Huainanzi*. Albany, NY: State University of New York Press.

Seidel, Anna. 1969. *La divinisation de Lao-tseu dans le taoïsme des Han*. Paris: Ecole Française d'Extrême-Orient. Reprinted 1992.

Teiser, Stephen F. 1994. *The Scripture of the Ten Kings: And the Making of Purgatory in Medieval Chinese Buddhism*. Honolulu, HI: University of Hawai'i Press.

8 Religious practices

In this chapter

Daoist religious practices can be personal or communal, focus on meditation or ritual. They all require initial purification through abstention from impurity and fundamental health built through longevity practice. The latter involves a moderate lifestyle together with efforts at *qi*-regulation, notably through diet, exercise, breathing, and sexual control. Also common to both ritual and meditation is the importance of mental concentration, learned through exercises of focused one-pointedness, and of visualization, the internal seeing of energies, deities, and ecstatic journeys to the stars.

Beyond that, Daoist meditation involves specific practices to attain quietude and concentration, a variety of methods called "observation" that allow practitioners to identify fully with Dao, and visualization methods that enhance the *qi* in the inner organs and cosmicize the body. Ritual, moreover, in the Daoist tradition is a combination of ancient Chinese sacrifices and traditional court ritual. The core of the rite is an audience with Dao as celestial deities. It involves extensive preparations, detailed orchestration of all aspects, the formal invitation of numerous deities, and a series of incantations of repentance followed by prayers for harmony and good fortune. It concludes with a large communal banquet.

Main topics covered

- Longevity techniques
- Breath and sex
- Meditation
- Visualization
- Body transformation
- Ritual activation

Longevity techniques

The Daoist path has both an individual and communal dimension. On the communal level, advanced Daoists serve as priests and advisers, ritual specialists and intermediaries between this world and the divine, aiding people in their ascent to Heaven and granting them release from the tortures of hell. While communal practice involves extensive ritual training, it also means a thorough transformation of self in terms of cosmicizing the body, activating different levels of *qi*, and acknowledging the nature and importance of supernatural agencies. By the same token, individual practice is never far removed from the community of believers and always also involves ritual awareness and a close connection to the gods. In other words, all different kinds of Daoists, whatever their specialization and main orientation, in some form or another undertake the full variety of religious practices.

Daoist practice involves a large variety of specific techniques that originated in different segments of Chinese culture and society. The longevity methods, for example, go back to medical sources and originally formed part of preventative medicine. Many meditation and certain ritual techniques similarly are of Buddhist origin and were integrated after the foreign religion had food a strong foothold in the country. In the Tang dynasty (618–907), two leading Daoist masters, the physician and alchemist Sun Simiao (582–683) and the Highest Clarity Patriarch Sima Chengzhen (647–735), created a formal systematization of practices, from the elementary moderation of lifestyle through various forms of physical refinement to stages of meditation and ascent to immortality.

The following presentation follows their outline, but it should be understood that in actual reality Daoists did not follow a set structure. Rather, they adapted the plethora of practices to their specific needs, placing great emphasis on some and leaving out others. They could also, as again documented in Tang sources, specialize so that there were alchemical masters, exercise specialists, herbal pharmacists, sexual practitioners, and various kinds of meditation leaders.

Moderation

Most outlines of Daoist practice begin by emphasizing the need to establish harmony on the personal level. This means that one should live as healthily as possible in close adaptation to the natural cycles of day and night and the changes of the seasons. The fourth-century *Yangsheng yaoji* (Long Life Compendium), for example, cites the ancient immortal Pengzu as saying:

> The method of nourishing life consists mainly in not doing harm to oneself. Keep warm in winter and cool in summer, and never lose your harmony with the four

seasons – that is how you can align yourself with the body. Do not allow sensuous beauty, provocative postures, easy leisure, and enticing entertainments to incite yearnings and desires – that is how you come to pervade the spirit.

The most important advice is to remain moderate in everything, since any excess will harm the lungs and kidneys: to eat and drink with control, to stay away from various luxuries that lead to a weakness of *qi*, and to keep speech and laughter within limits.

Continuing, the text cites Pengzu again and points out that heavy clothing and thick comforters, spicy foods and heavy meats, sexual attraction and beautiful women, melodious voices and enticing sounds, wild hunting and exciting outings, as well as all strive for success and ambition inevitably lead to a weakening of the body and thus a reduction in life expectancy. In the same vein, various mental activities harm key psychological forces and bring about a diminishing of *qi*, which takes one further away from Dao and reduces life. In other words, harmony with Dao manifests itself in mental stability and physical wellness, and any form of agitation or sickness indicates a decline in one's alignment with the forces of nature.

Diet

On the basis of a healthy and well-adjusted lifestyle, practitioners then conform to a Daoist diet, which essentially means eating moderately (never to complete satiation) and in natural balance by partaking of all the food groups associated with the five phases and matching foods to the seasons.

As described by Sun Simiao in his *Sheyang lun* (On Preserving and Nourishing [Life]), one should eat warming foods in winter and cooling foods in summer; prepare foods in accordance with the celestial constellations; observe the various food taboos associated with one's astrological signs; use locally grown and organic ingredients as much as possible; and systematically and in accordance with one's personal constitution supplement regular foodstuffs with herbal and mineral substances.

As practitioners become more proficient at controlling their diets, they can gradually wean themselves from ordinary foodstuffs, replacing grains and heavy foods with raw vegetables, fruits, and nuts. They can then increase herbal supplements, liquid nourishment, and concentrated internal guiding of *qi* to the point where they do not need any food to sustain themselves but can live entirely on *qi*. This process of removing ordinary food in favor of breath is called "abstention from grain" (*bigu*). As all dietary cultivation, the idea here is to create a well-adjusted body where the *qi* flows smoothly and in a regular rhythm, to lighten the body's structure in favor of subtler energies and a finer cosmic awareness.

Healing exercises

Another way of opening and lightening the body is through the practice of healing exercises (*daoyin*), first outlined in the medical manuscripts of the Han. Beginning with the school of Highest Clarity, Daoists expanded and systematized these practices. Placing a greater emphasis on internal awareness without completely giving up on physical movements, they developed integrated sequences and associated them with famous immortals of old, such as Master Redpine and the long-lived Pengzu, or linked with specific animals, often hardy specimens such as dragons and turtles.

The Turtle Way

For example, the fifth-century *Daoyin jing* (Exercise Classic) describes a series of practices called the "Turtle Way of Guiding the Qi." It involves several medical exercises, such as the following:

> Kneel upright and interlace your hands behind your back. This is called the sash tie. It relieves constipation and benefits the belly.
>
> Kneel on the floor and interlace your hands underneath your shins. This relieves excessive yin.

Doing so, practitioners tighten the abdominal muscles and lengthen the back, thus massaging the inner organs and releasing tension. They thereby open the pathways of *qi*, balance yin and yang energies, and engage with a subtler dimension of their physical being.

Next, the Turtle Way suggests inversions to let the *qi* move in various directions. It says:

> With both hands holding on to a rope, pull yourself up, then hang upside down, so that the legs are above the torso. This relieves dizziness in the head and craziness due to wind.
>
> Pull up with both hands and reverse yourself, so you hang from the rope with your back at the top. This relieves lack of concentrated essence and failure to digest properly.

These exercises involve placing the head below the heart, thus reversing blood flow to the brain which causes a relief of dizziness and mental confusion. They also alleviate heaviness in the legs and lower body, aiding digestion and the overall balance of circulation.

Another set of Turtle Way practices pays conscious attention to breath. One method involves covering the mouth and nose with a garment and holding the breath for the count of nine, then gently releasing it through the nose. Alternatively one can raise the head like a turtle and hold the breath for a count of five, then rub the tongue around the mouth and swallow the saliva.

Medieval and later texts record a large number of similar practices, in all cases asserting that, as Master Redpine says in to the *Daoyin jing*, "if done regularly, the practice will make your hearing keen, your vision bright, and your years extended to great longevity, with none of the hundred diseases arising."

Breath and sex

Daoists also engaged in breathing techniques without body movements, with the goal to sublimate the body's energies further. Best known is a practice of exhaling with specific lip positions and throat movements that created breaths with certain sounds while stabilizing their related organs. Already mentioned in the *Zhuangzi* and Han manuscripts, these were later systematized into a set called the Six Breaths (today the Six Healing Sounds). They are:

1. *Si*, a gentle, relaxed exhalation that lets the breath escape between slightly opened lips; it is associated with the lungs.
2. *He*, a strong breath with open mouth accompanied by a guttural rasping through tightening of the throat at the base of the tongue; it expels heat and aids the heart.
3. *Hu*, the standard term for "exhale," is a blowing out of breath with rounded lips; it supports the spleen.
4. *Xu*, a gentle expulsion of breath with open mouth; it balances the liver.
5. *Chui*, a sharp expulsion of air with almost closed lips; it, expels cold and aids the kidneys.
6. *Xi*, traditionally the sound of sighing, is a soft exhalation with the mouth slightly open; it supports the Triple Heater, a uniquely Chinese organ which absorbs *qi* from food and breath and directs it to the vital organs.

In addition, Daoists practice guiding the *qi* as outlined in the ancient inscription discussed earlier. They breathe in deeply, mix the breath with saliva in the mouth, then swallow it and consciously direct it to different parts of the body, nourishing the organs and moving freely through the energy channels.

Sexual control

Yet another way of accessing and sublimating *qi* in the body is through sexual energy or essence (*jing*). Emerging from the body's primordial *qi*, it is present in people from birth in limited amounts and centers in the Ocean of *Qi* (abdomen, lower elixir field) in men and in the Cavern of *Qi* (chest, middle elixir field) in women. Essence governs the kidneys and reproductive organs as well as the bones, marrow, teeth, brain, and

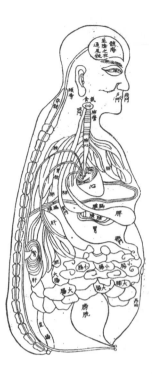

Figure 8.1 The energy channels in the body

overall energy system of the body; it easily diminishes through sexual engagements.
As a result, both Chinese medical and Daoist practitioners focus on conserving the
stock people have originally and on replenishing what is lost.

People conserve essence by limiting the frequency of its loss through ejaculation
and menstruation as well as by using massage techniques that keep the *qi* flowing.
They replenish it by working on its "return" or "reversion" into primordial *qi* with
the help of both partner and solo practices. The latter involve developing a state of
excitement and then, instead of allowing the *jing* to flow out of the body, mentally
and with the help of self-massages make it move up along the spine and into the head,
guiding it along the microcosmic orbit and thus enhancing the body's vitality.

Levels of practice

Sexual practices are undertaken on three levels, reflecting different intentions or
mind-sets:

(1) among ordinary people they are part of marital intercourse and focus largely
on healing and conservation;
(2) among longevity seekers they are known as "reverting sexual energy to nourish
the brain;" they can be undertaken individually through meditative refinement or

involve active intercourse, sometimes with multiple partners who are brought to orgasm while the practitioner retains *qi*;

(3) in organized Daoism sexual practices are known as "harmonization of *qi*" among the early Celestial Masters and as "dual cultivation" in the eternal alchemy of late imperial China. Ritually transformed ways of intercourse, these techniques are employed to enhance oneness with Dao and often lead on to solo practice, where yin and yang are isolated within the practitioner's body and refined into subtler forms of energy, ultimately leading to the internal creation of a spirit being that will survive this body and ascend to the higher heavens as an immortal.

Meditation

A different and somewhat subtler way of attaining *qi*-balance, sublimating the body-mind, and connecting to Dao is the practice of meditation. Meditation is the inward focus of attention in a state of mind where ego-related concerns and critical evaluations are suspended in favor of perceiving a deeper, subtler, and possibly divine flow of consciousness. Daoists engaged in several major forms of meditation, notably concentration, observation, and visualization.

Concentration

Concentration is one-pointedness of mind. It involves complete control of attention and the absorption in a single object – a sound, a visual diagram, a concrete entity, or the breath – with the goal of calming the mind and quieting internal chatter.

The earliest form of Daoist meditation described in the texts is a form of concentration: the quietist simplicity encouraged in the *Daode jing*, which comes with a general withdrawal of the senses and a reduction of mental input. Practitioners focus on breathing or the inner flow of *qi* and strive to gain a balance and one-pointedness of mind, gathering their attention in stillness so that they can be receptive to the purity of Dao. A similar set of practices is also outlined in the *Neiye*, which guides adepts to a deep, nonacting quietude and a profound alignment with the natural transformations.

Guarding the One

A more complex form of concentration appears in a method known as "guarding the One." Here practitioners sit in a restful pose and focus their attention on one single object, defined as "the One." This can be an abstract principle, a sense of power at the root of creation, a point inside the body, a central constellation in the stars, or Lord Lao as present in the body.

In the latter form, the One resides in the scarlet palace of the heart or in the purple chamber in the head, the center of vital energy in the middle or upper parts of the body. Also called the Perfect Great One of the Yellow Center, he looks like a baby and appears clad in purple robes while sitting on a golden throne. In his left hand, he holds the handle of the Northern Dipper; in his right hand he has the Pole Star, signifying his power at the central command of all. Guarding the One in this version combines the various other modifications of the practice; still mainly aimed at the establishment of one-pointed concentration and inner tranquility. It is already a form of visualization which dominates medieval Daoist practice.

Observation

Observation – also called insight, mindfulness, or awareness meditation – is a form of practice that encourages openness to all sorts of stimuli and leads to a sense of free-flowing awareness. It often begins with the recognition of physical sensations and subtle events in the body but may also involve paying attention to outside occurrences. Early Daoist examples of this practice appear in the *Zhuangzi*, which describes the fasting of the mind as a replacing of ordinary sensory patterns with pure *qi*-mentation and sketches the practice of sitting in oblivion with its complete forgetfulness of self and others.

Sitting in oblivion

In Tang Daoism, aided by the integration of Buddhist insight practice, sitting in oblivion became a major Daoist technique. Sima Chengzhen, in his *Zuowang lun* (On Sitting in Oblivion), presents a detailed outline, describing it in seven stages. From a basis of "respect and faith," practitioners leave the world (at least temporarily) to "intercept karma," then practice concentration to "tame the mind" and gain one-pointed focus. The fourth step, "detachment from affairs" is a first reevaluation of one's being in the world, the development of a sense of inner flow and connection to Dao.

After this, adepts move on to "true observation" to overcome their attachment to any personal identity, be it defined through the body or the mind. The body is just flesh and bones that are bound to rot sooner or later; the mind is just a succession of thoughts and ideas that have no constancy and no permanent center. It is just as well to give up all attachment to these fleeting phenomena and see the end of life as merely a change of residence of the spirit. "Thus," the text says, "relinquish all desires and abide in nonexistence. Be placid, pure, and well-rooted, and turn to observation. Whatever you loved before will not only cause weariness and disdain."

The last two steps are an enstatic immersion in a deep trance called "intense concentration," which allows practitioners to find a root in the depth of Dao; and an ecstatic freewheeling out of all body-centered reality into the spheres above where alone "realizing the Dao" is possible. The ultimate goal is complete disconnection from all worldly affairs and the attainment of immortality in the heavens above.

Inner observation

Closely connected to this practice and also formulated in Tang sources is an inner observation (*neiguan*), which consists of careful introspection of body and mind under the auspices of Chinese medicine and Daoist body gods. Practitioners find the body a microcosmic replica of the starry heavens above, full of palaces and chambers, gods and deities. This cosmic body, moreover, is governed by the force of spirit – primordial, formless, and ever-changing – which works through the human mind and governs life perfectly. Instead of trying to follow sensory impressions, make judgments, and develop critical evaluations, people learn to be at rest in their original cosmic nature and let the intuition of the spirit guide them through life.

Visualization

Visualization means the mental focus on a specific scene or sequence of events, such as energy flows, deities, cosmic patterns, saints' lives, or potential future events. The scenes are either seen with complete detachment or involve the participation of the practitioner. In either case, visualization opens the consciousness to more subtle levels, allowing the powers of the unconscious to manifest themselves and bringing new dimensions to the practitioner's life.

Also called creative imagination, visualization is an important method used today in a variety of contexts, from sports training to business presentations. In the Daoist world, it was called "actualization and imagination" (*cunxiang*) and applied both internally and externally, that is, it served as a form of intensified concentration to enhance the health and empowerment of the body and was also a means to ecstatically travel to the otherworld and engage with the deities, not unlike the cosmic journey of the Great Man.

Organ vision

The earliest visualization practice described in Daoist texts involved seeing lights of different colors in the body, matching the energies of the five phases with their directions and related inner organs. As the *Taiping jing shengjun bizhi* (Secret Instructions of the Holy Lord on the Scripture of Great Peace) describes it, one should begin by sitting quietly with eyes closed until a brilliant light arises in the mind.

This light will initially be red, with prolonged practice it will turn white. After another long stretch, it will be green. As you penetrate these lights, they will come nearer and nearer and eventually merge into one brilliance. Nothing is not illuminated within; the hundred diseases are driven out.

Each light, moreover, is connected to its matching inner organ so that, for example, the green light is directed to the liver, the red light to the heart, and so on. The lights vitalize and strengthen the inner organs, creating health and long life as well as a sense of cosmic connection.

The Five Sprouts

An expanded version of this practice as undertaken in Highest Clarity is known as absorbing the Five Sprouts, the subtle, germinal energies of the five directions. As outlined in Sima Chengzhen's *Fuqi jingyi lun* (On the Essential Meaning of the Absorption of *Qi*), at dawn when everything awakens to life and is full of potential, adepts begin by swallowing the saliva while holding sacred talismans and chanting purifying invocations.

They face the direction in question, usually beginning with the east, and in their minds visualize its *qi* in its appropriate color. A general mist in the beginning, it gradually forms into a ball, sort of like the rising sun, then through further concentration shrinks in size and comes closer to the adept. Eventually the size of a pill, the sprout can be swallowed and guided mentally to the organ of its correspondence. A suitable incantation places it firmly in its new receptacle, and gradually the adept's body becomes infused with cosmic energy and partakes more actively in the cosmos as a whole. The incantations are short and to the point. For example:

> Green Sprout of the East:
> Be absorbed to feed my [internal] green sprout [liver].
> I drink you through the Morning Flower [root of upper teeth]. (3a)
> Vermilion Cinnabar of the South:
> Be absorbed to feed my [internal] vermilion cinnabar [heart].
> I drink you through the Cinnabar Lake [root of lower teeth].

By ingesting the sprouts, Daoists partake of the inherent power of the celestial bodies and feed on the pure creative energy of the universe its most subtle form. Increasingly joining the germinal energy of the universe, they become lighter and freer, learn to appear and disappear at will, overcome the limitations of this world, and attain immortality in the heavenly realm.

Body transformation

Another way of creating a sense of cosmic reality in the body is through internally traveling through its various parts, uncovering the larger universe as represented in microcosmic form within. Already Han cosmology and Chinese medicine saw the body as a network of *qi*-storage areas and energy channels, a replica of nature and the cosmos.

Medieval Daoists advanced this vision to see the body as a veritable storehouse of divine agencies, palaces, and figures, patterned in many ways on the constellations in the stars. As outlined in the *Huangting jing* (Yellow Court Scripture), a fourth-century meditation manual, and depicted in later charts, such as the *Neijing tu* (Chart of Internal Passageways), they would develop concentration and with slow and conscious breathing move mentally into their heads, entering through the Deep Valley of the nose and passing between the sun and the moon (left and right eyes) to visit the paradise mountain of Mount Kunlun or Laozi's palace of the Yellow Court in the head.

To attain entry, they sounded the gong or musical stone placed in the Dark Towers of the ears through an exercise called "beating the heavenly drum." With both palms covering the ears, the index and middle fingers are snapped to sound against the back of the skull. They thus produced reverberations that created a sound not unlike distant drumming.

Figure 8.2 Beating the heavenly drum

Internal travel

Practitioners thus entered to the divine realm of the head, made up of Nine Palaces that were each the residence of divine beings who also lived – simultaneously and correspondingly – in the stars. Most important among them were the Hall of Light, located in the center of the eyebrows about one inch into the head; the Grotto Chamber, one inch further in; and the Niwan Palace beyond it, the upper elixir field and residence of the three highest lords of the universe.

Moving lower from there, they would come to the Flowery Pond, i.e. the mouth, made up Jade Fluid or Sweet Spring, i.e. saliva. Crossing the pond over its central bridge, i.e. the tongue, adepts reach the deeper regions of the body. First there is the Twelve-Storied Tower, i.e. the throat, followed by the Scarlet Palace (heart), the Imperial Granary (stomach), the Purple Chamber (gall), the Great Wall (large intestine), and many others more. Going ever deeper, another cosmic region is reached. Here there is Yellow Court (spleen) with another set of Dark Towers, the kidneys.

Seeing the body as a replica of the universe and traveling through its depths, Daoists would develop a cosmic sense of self, an identity made up of flowing passageways and divine palaces rather than the bones and blood of ordinary physical existence. The very foundation of being, the root of personal identity, would be sublimated and cosmicized to create a sense of oneness with the universe.

Ecstatic excursions

The most advanced and complex form of visualization is the practice of ecstatic excursions, and adaptation of shamanic soul travel to the far reaches of the universe, into the starry constellations above, and eventually to the highest heavens gods and immortals. The practice typically begins with a period of purification and ritual preparation, after which ecstatic visits to the otherworld usually start with a tour around the far reaches of the earth. They then move on to an imitation of the planets' movements, especially of the sun and the moon, in an effort to make the body into a replica of the universe and gain control over its rhythm.

Once perfectly aligned, adepts reach out to visit the higher spheres of the planets and superior heavens to eventually approach the central axis of the world at the Dipper. Here they establish themselves in the quiet center of Dao, around which everything else revolves, thus becoming one with the root of creation. On their way, moreover, they encounter numerous gods and immortals, from whom they learn cosmic secrets and receive instructions for further attainment. By ecstatically traveling through the far cosmic reaches, adepts turn themselves increasingly into denizens of the otherworld, often finding their heavenly life more rewarding and more real than their existence on earth.

Figure 8.3 Visualizing the arrival of celestial deities (Source: Tianguan sandu)

Divine relations

Another form of bodily transformation is through energetic exchange with a divine agent. As described in the *Xuanzhen jingjue* (Scripture of the Mysterious Perfected), a technical manual of Highest Clarity, adepts visualize the pure energy of the sun or the moon, then imagine a goddess in its midst, called Jade Maiden of Highest Mystery. On her head she wears a purple cap, her cloak and skirt are made of vermilion brocade.

With prolonged practice, the Jade Maiden grows stronger and more vivid until she is felt present in the flesh. Adepts then imagine her to emit a red energy from her mouth, which fills the space between the light rays of the sun or the moon. They allow the rays to merge and combine with the morning light of the Jade Maiden, then open their own mouth to absorb the celestial power, guiding it through their body.

In a more advanced form of the practice, adepts imagine that the Jade Maiden presses her mouth tightly upon their own and allow her energy fluids to enter deeply into them. At this time, they are to chant the following:

Oh, Purple Perfected of Great Empyrean,
Hidden Goddess of the Hall of Light!
Oh, come out of the sun and enter the moon,
You celestial light of enchanting fragrance!
May your mouth emit red energy –
Oh, let it drip into my Three Primes!

If adepts manage to continue this practice regularly for five years, "the Jade Maiden will descend and lie down to share your mat. She might even divide her shape for you into a host of like jade maidens who will serve your every whim." A sublimated form of sexual harmonization as practiced in Celestial Masters ritual, this visualization makes the adept an accepted partner of the divine and full denizen of the otherworld, transported from his mundane individuality to the realm of utmost perfection.

Ritual activation

Just as every meditation exercise is preceded and accompanied by certain ritual actions – purifications, prostrations, burning of incense – Daoist rituals are deeply imbued with meditative practice and in fact any ritual can only be as efficacious as the meditative powers and efforts of its officiating priest.

Daoist ritual follows traditional Chinese forms which divides into sacrifice (*si*), purification (*zhai*), and thanksgiving or offering (*jiao*). In ancient China, and still in Confucian and popular rites today, the central part of the ceremony is the sacrifice, the presentation of ritual objects such as wine, tea, rice, sweets, and animal carcasses to the gods and ancestors. Following this there is a communal feast, when the food offerings are shared by the congregation. Purification, moreover, is a set of preparatory measures undertaken before conducting or joining the sacrifice, also commonly undertaken before extended meditation practice. The third and concluding part of the ceremony, offering, is a kind of merit-assuring rite after the successful sacrifice, with the goal of inducing the gods to give their blessings to humanity. All these rituals are, moreover, accompanied by specific spells, prayers, and incantations.

Kinds of rites

In addition to its roots in ancient sacrifice, Daoist ritual adapted traditional Chinese court formalities and came to place less emphasis on the sacrifice of objects than on facing the gods in formal audience. Before long, Daoists replaced the blood sacrifices of old with the presentation of written documents, such as petitions, memorials, announcements, and mandates. They still underwent purification as a preparatory measure, but their central focus shifted to the offering and they eschewed all killing of animals or blood sacrifices.

The Numinous Treasure school of the fifth century added a further dimension under Buddhist influence, expanding the purification into a formal fast or retreat, during which participants observed moral rules in addition to the five precepts, joined monastic meditation practice, listened to monks' lectures, and had the opportunity to confess their sins. Beyond that, medieval Daoists developed the purgation, a spectacular public and major communal ritual. It involved several days of communal chanting and praying, the confession of sins, and presentation of offerings. In the Song dynasty, this emphasis on offering led to a renaming of the central Daoist rite as "offering" (*jiao*) which is today known as the "festival of cosmic renewal."

The ritual setting

All purgations and offerings are undertaken for a specific purpose and under the sponsorship of clearly defined agents or donors. For example, the state could decide to arrange for a ritual to enhance peace and protection against enemies. Monasteries or major temples would hold rites as part of seasonal and clerical festivals, such as at the Three Primes. Communities might sponsor a festival to enhance cohesion, give thanks to the gods, and create renewal. And, last but not least, private individuals on occasion donated to a Daoist rite to expiate sins, encourage healing, or pray for success in business. In all cases, the scope and length of the rite depended on the amount of support made available to the officiants.

Once basic arrangements are made and an auspicious date and place are found, the rite begins with the establishment of a sacred space, usually a three-tiered altar to represent the key levels of the universe. It may be set up inside an established temple structure or arranged as a temporary facility in a specially cordoned-off area. Its essential feature being the audience with the celestials, it is essential that the area be completely secure, protected with exorcistic formulas and surrounded by benevolent spirits.

Key protagonists

Before any ritual commences, all active participants have to undergo a series of purifications and preparations which may take up to a month. Traditionally a group of five central officers was appointed: a Ritual Master of Lofty Virtue, a Cantor, a Purgation Overseer, an Incense Attendant, and a Lamp Attendant.

The Ritual Master was the key protagonist and formed the central focus of the purgation; he visualized the gods and commanded the divine presence, and tended to remain in isolated purity to focus on his inner powers. The Cantor was the main organizer: he orchestrated the movements of the Ritual Master, made sure the intention of the donor (to create peace, heal a disease, pray for renewal, or offer repentance) was clearly expressed in the memorials, scheduled all activities, and gave cues to the sound, light, and incense crews. He also led the congregation in chanting and responses, thus his appellation "cantor."

The Purgation Overseer, next, was the on-site manager of the event. He interacted most closely with the donor, making sure he and his associates (officials of state, community leaders, or family members) were well aware of all the rules. They had to begin purification three days before the scheduled event, needed proper housing set up for visiting Daoists, could only use ritually acceptable food for the offerings, and must never turn any visitor away or impose a fee for anyone participating. They also had to wear the right clothes, ornate and formal but not imitating priestly vestments, and give a donation in accordance with their wealth to show their devotion.

The Incense and Lamp Attendants, finally, were in charge of the concrete set-up, making sure that the burners were well stoked so that the incense could rise continuously throughout the celebrations and that the lamps were plentiful and distributed widely, lit in good time to create a festive and brilliant atmosphere. Supporting these central ritual officers, there were many others, especially groups of musicians to strike the bells and chimes, sound the gongs, drums, and bamboo clappers, and play the reed pipes and stringed instruments. There would also be staff members to direct people and answer questions. The entire atmosphere and organization must have been similar to the staging of a major theatrical production, and indeed there was a close relationship between ritual and theater in traditional China.

Ritual procedures

Once the actual rite begins, the Ritual Master – garbed in splendid vestments and adorned with an elaborate headdress – with the help of incantations, sacred hand gestures, and visualizations invites the deities to descend and participate. He often starts by visualizing a colored cloud of *qi* that transforms into the image of a god dressed in appropriate garb and equipped with the right attributes. Gradually he populates the sacred space with all various gods, ancestors, and people.

The priest visualizes each group of participants and asks them to take their seats. Daoist gods sit to the north so they can face south as did the emperor of old. Popular deities are established to the south, facing the superior Daoist gods. Heavenly bureaucrats of yang quality, administering the living, earth, and dragon spirits, are in the east; those of yin quality, ruling the dead, water, and tiger spirits, are in the west. People occupy the southeast, and the various other types of spirits are in the remaining corners.

Next the Ritual Master orchestrates a series of formal acts to inform the celestials that a major audience is being prepared. This includes raising sacred banners, beating drums, lighting lamps, and burning incense. Using another practice common in meditation, the priest clicks his teeth a number of times to let the gods know that something of importance is going to happen.

Over several days, then, various kinds of rites are being performed, combining formal acts and chanting of repentance with the submission of memorials and petitions to fulfill the specific purpose of the rite. As the activity draws to a close, the Ritual Master thanks the gods for their attendance and politely sends them off again to their various celestial homes. The ritual concludes with a large banquet, joined by everyone – friends and foes alike – to celebrate the successful cosmic invigoration of the community.

Key points you need to know

- Daoist religious practice divides into meditation and ritual. They both have in common that they require a period of purification, a strong self-control, a healthy body, good mental focus, and extended visualization practice.
- To gain a strong body and long life, Daoists practice moderation and control their *qi* through a harmonious diet, healing exercises, breathing, and sexual control. Beyond longevity practice, meditation involves various methods of concentration, such as quietist simplicity, inward training, and guarding the One; certain types of observation or insight, such as fasting of the mind, sitting in oblivion, and inner observation; and various forms of visualization, such as nourishing the inner organs, absorbing the five sprouts, actualizing the gods, ecstatically traveling to the otherworld, and engaging in relations with divine beings.
- Daoist major rituals used to be called purgations but are now known as offerings. They last many days and may be sponsored by the state, a temple, a community, or a family, in each case serving a specific purpose. After extensive preparations of ritual space and personal purification, the Ritual Master, assisted by various helpers, invites the gods to participate through visualization and, with chants of repentance and petitions for good fortune, creates a new level of harmony in the world.

Discussion questions

1. Do Daoist longevity methods work? How do they compare to Western recommendations for health and long life?
2. What is meditation? What are some commonly known examples in today? How do they compare to what Daoists are doing?
3. What is ritual? How does it function in our lives? Are there daily rituals in addition to religious ones? How important is a priest in the performance of ritual?

Further reading

Benn, Charles D. 1991. *The Cavern Mystery Transmission: A Taoist Ordination Rite of A.D. 711*. Honolulu, HI: University of Hawai'i Press.

Benn, Charles. 2000. "Daoist Ordination and *Zhai* Rituals." In *Daoism Handbook*, edited by Livia Kohn, 309–38. Leiden: E. Brill.

Johnson, David, ed. 1989. *Ritual Opera – Operatic Ritual: "Mu-lian Rescues His Mother" in Chinese Popular Culture*. Berkeley, CA: University of California, IEAS Publications.

Kohn, Livia. 1987. *Seven Steps to the Tao: Sima Chengzhen's Zuowanglun*. St. Augustin/Nettetal: Monumenta Serica Monograph XX.

Kohn, Livia, ed. 1989. *Taoist Meditation and Longevity Techniques*. Ann Arbor, MI: University of Michigan, Center for Chinese Studies Publications.

Kohn, Livia, ed. 2006. *Daoist Body Cultivation: Traditional Models and Contemporary Practices*. Magdalena, NM: Three Pines Press.

Robinet, Isabelle. 1993. *Taoist Meditation*. Translated by Norman Girardot and Julian Pas. Albany, NY: State University of New York Press.

Schafer, Edward H. 1978. "The Jade Woman of Greatest Mystery." *History of Religions* 17: 387–98.

Wile, Douglas. 1992. *Art of the Bedchamber: The Chinese Sexology Classics Including Women's Solo Meditation Texts*. Albany, NY: State University of New York Press.

Part III

Modernity

9 *Modern Daoism*

In this chapter

With the end of the Tang dynasty in 907 the integrated, state-supported system of Daoism collapsed and the religion began to reorganize into new structures, matching the social conditions of the Song dynasty. New masters emerged who catered to the needs of the merchant and literati classes and some of whom founded new schools. Largely lay-based, exorcistic, and devoted to martial deities, these schools linked themselves to the Celestial Masters. A major exception was the school of Complete Perfection, which was monastic and ascetic and established an independent system. These two schools became the only government-recognized venues of Daoism in late imperial China, providing an administrative umbrella for numerous sub sects and lineages. The government, moreover, enhanced its policy of strict control and established both administrative offices and stringent regulations. Certain emperors went beyond this, however, and developed a strong devotion to the religion, even identified themselves as Daoist gods. While the official face of Daoism thus became more controlled – centralized and standardized – local cults continued to flourish and bring forth deities and rituals of their own. Some of these deities rose to national prominence, adding a new dimension to the Daoist religion.

Main topics covered

- New texts and gods
- Ritual masters
- Complete perfection
- Imperial adaptations
- An expanded pantheon

New texts and gods

The integrated system of the Three Caverns, with the patriarch of Highest Clarity at the top and the systematic ordination hierarchy below, depended to a large extent on the imperial support of the Tang. The dynasty, badly shaken by the rebellion of An Lushan in 755, went into decline and increasingly suffered from incursions by local warlords until it collapsed completely in 907.

Daoism suffered from these circumstances but also adapted, developing strongholds in local centers – most famously the Black Sheep Temple (Qingyang gong) in Chengdu, Sichuan, as well as on various sacred mountains – and creating ritual and worship forms that involved protection from and enhancement of martial powers. A leading master at the time was Du Guangting (850–933), a master at the Tang court who later served a local Sichuan ruler. Seeing cataclysmic changes on the horizon, he made a strong effort to maintain and record traditional forms, leading extensive ceremonies and writing numerous works on Daoist worship, ritual, cosmology, geography, and hagiography.

Figure 9.1 A martial Daoist deity

New texts

In a more forward-looking development, Daoists of the late Tang also received revelations on Daoist rites for their changing social and political environment. A typical example is a set of six texts that contain sacred spells and talismans associated with the Dippers of the five directions. Linked explicitly with Lord Lao, they purport to record a second major revelation to Zhang Daoling in 155, after he received the Covenant of Orthodox Unity in 142. In content, these texts outline devotional measures of protection involving scriptural recitation and formal rites for the Dippers, preferably undertaken on one's birthday, the new moon, or other auspicious days. For example:

> The True Lords of the Six Stars, the Divine Lads of the Six Stars, the Generals of Fire Bell – whenever you recite this text with utmost sincerity and pray to them with a pure heart, they will respond immediately. As long as you are diligent in worship and in the petition's presentation, the perfected sages will descend to protect you from all harm and extend your years. You will live as long as the Dao.

Typical for the newly emerging Daoism, the texts focus on protection, exorcism, and healing; they invoke large numbers of potent, often martial deities; they work with sets of specific spells and written talismans; and they promise immediate support, speedy rescue, and efficient delivery from all evil.

New gods

These new methods were therapeutic, exorcistic, and mortuary rather than liturgical, meditational, or ascetic in nature. They served a rapidly rising merchant class who benefited greatly from an improved infrastructure, the invention of printing (paper money), and an overall increase in literacy. They were also very attractive to the literati who had to prove themselves in imperial examinations instead of being carried by aristocratic lineages.

Given almost two centuries of civil war as the Tang declined and the continued threat from Central Asian federations under the Song, their pantheons, moreover, were dominated by martial, humanized, and historicized deities rather than by cosmic powers, immortals, or emanations of Dao. Major figures accordingly include the Black Killer (Heisha) and the Dark Warrior (Xuanwu), both famous for their demon-slaying powers and threatening appearance – known from visions. The latter was a constellation in the northern sky, who appeared first in the Han dynasty as the mythical animal of the north, depicted as an intertwined turtle and snake. By the Song, he had acquired human shape and appeared with:

> his face stern and striking, his hair unbound, . . . he was wearing a breastplate of gold and a belt set with jewels. His hand brandished a sword, his feet were bare,

and round his head there shone a halo of light, while the ends of his sash floated in the breeze.

Ritual masters

The religious specialists who received such revelations and carried the methods of the new gods among the people, moreover, were only rarely Daoist priests (*daoshi*), i.e. formally ordained masters who underwent a process of examination and certification, clearly affiliated with a temple and an established school. Much more frequently they were ritual masters (*fashi*), lay practitioners beyond formal organizations whose lineages were vocational rather than hereditary. They lived in the communities or among the families they served or traveled through the villages and towns of the

Figure 9.2 Holy gestures in Daoist ritual

country, performing exorcisms, establishing protection, and effecting cures among the populace.

Ritual masters could be members of the literati elite and serve the official class; they could also be illiterate and part of the common folk. Some followed entire sets of texts and methods as formalized in newly arising schools; others became proficient in merely one technique or connected to one specific deity. They might work on their own or in conjunction with a spirit-boy who would go into trance under the guidance of the master. Though trance the master would become a celestial officer or the deity himself. From this position of power, he then commanded any disturbing forces to cease and desist while inviting benevolent protectors to come and serve. In all these activities, ritual masters were, moreover, in close competition with itinerant monks and tantric masters who performed similar services under Buddhist auspices, as well as with shamanic spirit-mediums who traditionally controlled the exorcism and protection market in the countryside.

Modern Daoists

The ritual masters, more colorful and less organized that earlier Daoists, set the tone of Daoist practice for the late imperial and modern periods. Unlike medieval practitioners, who belonged to formally established schools that existed as corporate entities with the right to train, approve, and certify, modern Daoists are independent and work predominantly through lineages. Although both imperial and modern governments require formal adhesion to one of the two main orders, in actual reality it is a matter of personal choice to study a particular text or practice and allegiance is mainly to one's personal teacher.

Some Daoists stay with one teacher and one system; some study with several different masters and become holders of multiple lineages; others move on to become fully ordained by undergoing government-sponsored training at major centers. There is, thus, a two-tiered system of organization and practice of Daoists today that goes back to the Song-dynasty emergence of ritual masters in addition (and sometimes opposition) to formally ordained Daoist priest.

Song schools

Some ritual masters in the Song, then, received new revelations with the help of spirit-mediums or rediscovered spells and talismans in obscure mountain grottos. In some cases, they assembled disciples and formed schools of their own – although they usually took care to somehow link them with the Celestial Masters who had been appointed chief Daoist administrators by the court.

Most pervasive among all new schools were the so-called Thunder Rites (*leifa*), a popular form of exorcism and protection that invoked the deities of the celestial

Department of Thunder, which had a direct and efficacious impact on human events. An early school that made use of them is called Heavenly Heart (Tianxin). It can be traced back to the ritual master Tan Zixiao (fl. 935) who received a revelation regarding a new dimension of Heaven: the Bureau for Exorcising Deviant Forces, ruled by the Northern Emperor and administered by the Black Killer, Dark Warrior, and Heavenly Protector. When his successor Rao Dongtian found a collection of sacred talismanic texts in a cavern on Mount Huagai in 994, the school developed a full set of practices which included rites of the Celestial Masters, ecstatic excursions of Highest Clarity, and various local traditions of healing and exorcism. It continued to flourish locally and was formally codified in 1116.

Another Song school is called Youthful Incipience (Tongchu). It goes back to Yang Xizhen (1101–1124), the son of a rice merchant who entered the Huayang Grotto on Mount Mao (Jiangsu) and came back with a new ritual system that, too, included Thunder Rites and various forms of exorcism; it was also linked with Zhang Daoling and the Celestial Masters. The same pattern holds also true for various Numinous Treasure methods. One set of diagrams and rituals was rediscovered on Mount Longhu (Jiangxi), the headquarters of the Celestial Masters, by the ritual master and rainmaker Liu Yongguang (1134–1206). Another set was developed by Ning Benli (1101–1181), a southern seeker who traveled to various sacred mountains before settling on Mount Tiantai (Zhejiang). He codified various surviving rites while joining them with new exorcistic practices. His work *Shangqing Lingbao dafa* (Great Rites of Highest Clarity and Numinous Treasure) in sixty-six chapters is a major compendium of the time.

Complete Perfection

In contrast to these dominantly exorcistic and therapeutic schools which arose for the most part in the south, a Daoist movement in north China – that would in due course become the other officially recognized Daoist order – focused on individual transformation and was characterized by monasticism, ascetic practices, and mystical experience. This was the school of Complete Perfection (Quanzhen), founded by Wang Chongyang (1112–1170), a member of the local gentry in northwest China (Shaanxi) who served as an official in the military administration of the Central Asian dynasty under the Jurchen-Jin (who had conquered north China in 1125).

In 1159, aged forty-eight, Wang retired from office and withdrew to the Zhongnan mountains near modern Xi'an, where he built a thatched hut and began to lead the life of an eccentric hermit. There he had a revelatory experience, spiritually meeting the two immortals Lü Dongbin and Zhongli Quan from whom he received various secret methods. Thus inspired, Wang intensified his dedication and asceticism, losing his sanity to the point where he dug himself a grave called "the tomb of the living dead." In 1167, he burned his hut to the ground while dancing around it. Then he moved to Shandong in eastern China, where he preached his visions and began to win followers. He founded five religious communities and spread his teaching until his death in 1170.

The Seven Perfected

Wang's work was continued by seven disciples, six men and one woman, known collectively as the Seven Perfected. After observing the standard three-year mourning period for their master, they went separate ways to spread his teaching in different parts of north China, each founding various communities that developed into separate lineages (*pai*). The most important among them was Qiu Chuji (1148–1227), better known as Master Changchun, the founder of the Longmen (Dragon Gate) lineage.

As patriarch of the school, he was summoned to see Chinggis Khan in his Central Asian headquarters in 1219. Since the Mongols by this time were well on their way to conquering China (and to ruling as the Yuan dynasty) and were likely to endanger the lives of many people, Qiu could not refuse the summons. Despite his advanced age of seventy-two years, he undertook the strenuous, three-year journey in the company of eighteen leading disciples. This was documented in the *Xiyou ji* (Journey to the West), translated into English by Arthur Waley as *The Travels of an Alchemist*.

Qiu seems to have established good communication with the Khan, although he could not give him the secret of immortality. As he was leaving, the Khan appointed him the leader of all religions of China and exempted his followers from taxes and labor. This, in one stroke, made Complete Perfection the most powerful and popular religious group in north China and thus contributed greatly to its lasting prominence.

Sun Buer

The only female member of the Seven Perfected was Sun Buer (1119–1182), born as Sun Yuanzhen in a small town in the Ninghai district of Shandong. The daughter of a powerful local family, she received a classical education, then married the landowner Ma Danyang (1123–1183) and raised a family.

In 1167, Wang Chongyang arrived in Shandong and set himself up in the southern gardens of Ninghai on a piece of Ma's property. He built himself a hermitage and entered a 100-day retreat, which lasted from the first of the tenth month to the beginning of the new year. When he finally emerged, he began his career as a teacher and religious leader, naming his new movement Complete Perfection. Ma Danyang became his eager follower, but his wife was not pleased at all – seeing his teachings as a major force come to disrupt her family life, social standing, and local comfort.

Some accounts even suggest that rather than entering his retreat voluntarily, Wang Chongyang was incarcerated in his hermitage by an irate Sun who wanted him out of her life so badly that she tried to starve him to death. When he was still alive after 100 days, not only had he perfected his personal sainthood but had also made a reluctant convert of Sun, whom he renamed Buer (Nondual) for her single-minded dedication to whatever cause she chose. The story of the retreat, embellished variously, became a model for later monastic practice. It is also a classical statement on the conflict women undergo between their social role and their religious calling.

After more dissension with the religious leader, Sun eventually became a model student and ordained as a nun of Complete Perfection. Residing at the local Shandong center, called the Golden Lotus Hall, she received the Daoist title "Serene One of Clarity and Stillness," which provided the name of her future lineage (Qingjing pai). Trained in internal cultivation and meditative absorption, she was also made privy to several sets of sacred writs, received in trance through spirit-writing, and learned to perform advanced rituals, exorcisms, and magical feats. After Wang's death, she moved to Luoyang, where she set herself up in a dilapidated temple called Grotto of the Immortal Lady Feng. Choosing this residence, she symbolically inherited not only a female lineage but also a claim to exorcism and eccentricity. She attracted quite a following and eventually ascended to heaven in broad daylight.

Later developments

Through the work of Qiu, Ma, Sun and other first-generation disciples and supported politically by the Mongol rulers, Complete Perfection spread through north China and made numerous converts. Many communities entrusted local temples to their clerics for management, and people often formed lay congregations of adepts eager to learn self-cultivation techniques.

Under the Ming, which established stringent controls of all religious organizations and favored the Celestial Masters as Daoist administrators, Complete Perfection temples were absorbed by local religious communities, the patriarchy disappeared, and the unified order loosened. It was only under the Qing, when the Manchu rulers supported a monastic organization with strong Confucian overtones, that the school reemerged and organized itself along modern lines.

At this time Wang Changyue (d. 1680), abbot of the White Cloud Temple (Baiyun guan) in Beijing – the old headquarters of Qiu Chuji and thus seat of the Longmen lineage – established a monastic hierarchy divided into beginners, intermediate practitioners, and celestial immortals. He compiled sets of precepts for each, making sure that the Confucian virtues of filial piety and loyalty were prominently in evidence, and codified appropriate training requirements and ordination rites. Doing so, he ensured that Complete Perfection became the favored order of the new rulers.

As a result, within a few decades the Longmen lineage came to dominate the religion, gaining control of most major Daoist monasteries and supporting the foundation of new communities. It grew into an extensive geographical and administrative network that has remained in place to the present day.

Imperial adaptations

As is already evident from the previous discussion the imperial court loomed large in the development of modern Daoism. In general, it exerted influence in three different ways: through administrative control systems; by choosing certain deities, masters, and practices for imperial protection; and in the personal devotion and sponsorship of individual rulers.

Administrative control

The Song dynasty continued control measures initiated by the Tang, requiring ordained priests to carry a certificate at all times and to obey a set of legal codes specifically designed for recluses. They also appointed the Celestial Master – a descendant of Zhang Daoling – as leading Daoist administrator of the country. However, faced with the rise of the ritual masters who operated on the fringes of the established system, they did not enforce these measures too strongly.

Under the Mongols, administrative control passed to the new school of Complete Perfection who managed their own enclaves, supervised the Celestial Master in south China, and also had power over Buddhist and other temples. They abused this privilege, were harshly criticized, and even persecuted. In 1281, Daoist books with the exception of the *Daode jing* were proscribed and burned; temples were confiscated or handed over to Buddhists; many recluses had to return to the laity, and the power of Complete Perfection was significantly reduced.

The Ming dynasty

Modern forms of administrative control were put in place under the Ming dynasty. Their first ruler, Emperor Taizu (r. 1368–1399), suspicious of all independent organizations – like those that had brought him, a poor peasant, to power in the first place – decreed a new set of measures that remained in place until the founding of the Republic of China in 1911. First, he made all religious affairs subject to approval by the Ministry of Rites, which now housed a Bureau of Daoist Registration with branch offices in each province, prefecture, and district. These offices controlled ordinations and issued certificates. They decreed which monasteries could hold ordinations, when, and for how many initiates, making sure the number of recluses was restricted to serve the government's needs.

Next he limited access to ordination. Men could only join an order between the ages of fourteen and twenty; women could not become nuns while still of child-bearing age. Soldiers and artisans were excluded categorically. Those who made it into the ordination system not only had to carry their certificate at all times but also had their movements and whereabouts monitored through the so-called All-Knowing Register. Third, he severely curtailed the number of private temples and required them to have an official stamp of approval. These measures reduced enthusiasm for the religious path among the populace, effected a high level of standardization among institutions and practitioners, and encouraged local and popular groups beyond the scope of imperial oversight.

Later measures

The Manchu rulers of the Qing dynasty continued the same overall pattern, supporting organizational standardization through the Longmen lineage of Complete Perfection while providing the Celestial Master with a priestly staff of twenty-seven officials in the Ministry of Rites. They relied on the former to survey Daoist priests and institutions and on the latter to help with rain-making, flood control, and exorcism. In the eighteenth century, they lost interest in Daoism, demoted the Celestial Master in rank and influence and paid less attention to Complete Perfection. Still, the networks of both organizations remained, one lay and village-centered, still focusing on purification, exorcism, and communal protection; the other monastic and temple-based, with a main concern for cultivation and moral uprightness.

State-protectors

Just as the Tang found a state supporting deity in Lord Lao, the ancestor of the ruling house, so the Song elected a powerful god as their official protector. In the Dark Warrior, the martial force of the north, they found a power behind the moving energy of the universe worthy of their devotion. Already under Emperor Taizu (r. 960–76), his cult was raised to national status, inspired by a manifestation of the Black Killer, who claimed to be an assistant of the Dark Warrior and appeared specifically to protect the dynasty.

The imperial standing of the Dark Warrior was greatly enhanced under Emperor Zhenzong (r. 998–1022), when a series of "heavenly texts" were discovered, a turtle and snake (the emblem of the god) made a miraculous appearance in the capital Kaifeng (Henan), and a healing spring bubbled up nearby. He saw further elevation under Emperor Renzong (r. 1023–1063), who, in 1055, had a series of 104 frescoes painted that showed the god's protection of the state in five distinct areas: political administration, military success, climate control, healing of diseases, and prevention of disasters. The emperor also ordered a first collection of Dark Warrior mirabilia and supported the compilation of a holy biography of the god.

Emperor Huizong (r. 1100–1125) had a vision of him as mighty warrior with stern face and loose hair. Both the Yuan and Ming dynasties associated him with political power and venerated him in officially sponsored sanctuaries. Under the early Ming, the Yongle Emperor (r. 1403–1425) greatly expanded the god's center on Mount Wudang (Hubei). He also supported the religion by sponsoring the collection and printing of the Daoist canon, still the main repository of Daoist materials today (see Appendix). The Dark Warrior was duly supported by both leading Daoist schools and grew vastly in popularity. As hero of the vernacular novel *Beiyou ji* (Journey to the North), he has sanctuaries today all over mainland China, in Taiwan, Hong Kong, Singapore, Thailand, and in overseas Chinese communities.

Emperors as immortals

While the court in general sought to control religious organizations and coopted the benefits of Daoist worship for their dynasties, certain emperors went much further and became serious devotees of the religion. Most prominent among them are Huizong of the Song (1082–1135, r. 1100–1125) and the Jiajing Emperor of the late Ming, Zhu Houcong (1507–1567, r. 1522–1566). Both came to power as younger sons and were seriously dedicated to the arts – calligraphy, painting, ceramics, poetry, and philosophy – which they sponsored, collected, and practiced themselves. They supported the collection of Daoist texts, sponsored temple construction, and actively designed extensive gardens that replicated immortals' paradises. They also engaged in Daoist practices – notably alchemy and internal cultivation – and surrounded themselves with Daoist masters as personal advisors.

Emperor Huizong

Huizong in particular had the house of his birth converted into a Daoist shrine, and built two new palaces richly adorned with Daoist art. He also worked on a major garden project, the Genie Park, in the northeastern quadrant of Kaifeng, a large area with an artificial lake and mountain, a network of streams, grottoes, and waterfalls, and an extensive rock collection from many regions of China.

In 1107, he engaged the services of Liu Hunkang (1035–1108), the twenty-fifth patriarch of Highest Clarity, to learn about healing and exorcism. Following his guidance, he sponsored the collection of liturgies for the Golden Register Purgation, a service specially designed to ensure the welfare of the imperial house. After Liu's death, he summoned an ascetic Daoist to serve as a medium in communications with a deceased consort. He was succeeded by a clairvoyant who provided healing talismans and aided the emperor in his prayers for rain.

The most influential Daoist adviser under Huizong, however, was Lin Lingsu (1076–1120), who claimed to have received a revelation from a Heaven known as Divine

Empyrean (Shenxiao) that identified the emperor as the elder son of the Jade Emperor, the Great Emperor of Long Life (Chengzhen dadi). This god, using sacred materials from this newly discovered heaven, would be the harbinger of a new age and establish peace on Earth. The Divine Empyrean system, which developed into yet another new Daoist school, integrated the pantheon of Highest Clarity and followed the cosmology of Numinous Treasure. It employed talismans, diagrams, lamps, seals, and pennants in elaborate rituals. Unfortunately, despite – or as some critics say, because of – Huizong's preoccupation with celestial matters, the capital was conquered by the Jurchen in 1125, the court had to flee, and the emperor's reign ended in disgrace.

The Jiajing Emperor

None of this stopped the Jiajing Emperor of the Ming dynasty to engage in very similar pursuits. He, too, had various Daoist advisers, supported and practiced Daoist arts, engaged in numerous Daoist prayers and rituals – especially for his weak health and the conception of an heir (born in 1533) – identified himself as a the incarnation of a Daoist deity, the Thunder God, and created an extensive spiritual realm in the Western Park (Xiyuan), located to the northwest of the Forbidden City in Beijing. Unlike Huizong, however, the Jiajing Emperor completely withdrew from the halls of government and for the last twelve years of his reign lived in Western Park, fully dedicating himself to Daoist practice and the recovery of his original immortal nature. He exerted a huge impact on the Daoist dimension of Chinese architecture, arts, and literature.

Other emperors, too, without going quite as far, were supportive of the religion, opening new venues for Daoists, such as employment in the Office of Divine Music, and sponsoring Daoist-inspired and ritual works. New schools of Daoist painting developed; Daoist themes appeared widely in paintings, murals, and on ceramics; Daoist sanctuaries and training facilities were expanded; and Daoist collections were supported and published. There was thus a new expansion of the religion, reaching from the court through ordained Daoists, ritual masters, and community assemblies to remote corners of the empire.

An expanded pantheon

As the religion expanded through new schools and under imperial sponsorship, so the pantheon took on a new form. Daoists began to integrate popular deities, making them part of their traditional hierarchy and thereby adapting to two major changes: the greater importance of local cults and regional centers, and the increased importance of deities that were personal protectors and related directly to the populace – as opposed to the pure energies of the Dao, who were essentially bureaucrats and could only be accessed through the mediation of a Daoist priest.

A well-studied example is the Three Immortals of Mount Huagai who rose to prominence around the year 1100 and were first venerated by the local elite. Responding to an imperial edict of 1085 to present local deities for general worship to the court, which was followed by Huizong's call for Daoist scriptures and sacred materials, local leaders enhanced their cult and presented them to the court. First coexisiting with the Daoist school of the Heavenly Heart, which had a major center at Mount Huagai, the Three Immortals were eventually integrated into the Daoist pantheon – advancing from local wonderworkers to active manifestations of the Three Pure Ones. In a very similar fashion, Daoists adopted various popular gods and made sure they were given official rank and title through senior divinities.

The City God

A clear example of this is the City God, a divine officer in the popular pantheon, usually identified as the ancestral spirit of a local benefactor who serves both as the divine protector for the area and the people's mediator to the celestial administration. Daoists adopted this figure by creating a celestial archetype, a single central City God who resides in the heavens of the Dao and receives his powers from Lord Lao. The fourteenth-century *Chenghuang jing* (Scripture of the City God) describes him:

> Representing the sagely Dao, he is lofty and illustrious.
> He shows no favor, no one-sidedness,
> But is public and loyal, upright and straight. . . .
> He has the authority of heaven and orders all on earth,
> Cuts off all evil and dispels all killing.
> He protects the state and guards the country,
> With great merit aids the gods of soil and grain . . .
> He commands eighteen perfected marshals,
> And has a million divine generals at his call.

It then points out that the power of the god is entirely due to his position and role in the overall Daoist pantheon and that he is in every way an inferior officer in the hierarchy of the Dao.

Mazu

A similar case holds also true for the Celestial Consort (Tianfei or Mazu), the protectress of fishermen in Fujian as well as of traveling merchants elsewhere who grew from a Song dynasty local saint into one of the most popular Chinese deities. She, too, was empowered by Lord Lao, who gave her a Daoist title and is said to be at the root of her powers to slay demons, dispel disasters, and rescue humans from difficulty. Her specific portfolio is defined clearly in the *Tianfei jing* (Scripture of the Celestial Consort) from the early Ming dynasty. According to this, she took the following vow:

> From this day forward, whether a traveling merchant or resident shopkeeper seeking assets in doing business, whether farmers in their sowing or artisans in their professions, whether troops in transit engaged in battle arrays, whether there be difficulty in childbirth that is not resolved, whether there be disturbances from public wrongs, whether there be any abusive language that results in grief and injury, or whether there be any malady or affliction to which one is inextricably bound and from which there is no respite –
>
> Should anyone [so mentioned] reveal reverence and respect and call my name, then I will offer immediate and trustworthy response and cause them to attain whatever they wish.

The popular and immediate nature of the deity thus remains intact. She gives support and reassurance to ordinary people, exerting celestial powers on their behalf, rescuing them from difficulties, and granting their wishes. But she is now also a Daoist goddess in that she has a bureaucratic rank and receives her powers ultimately from the Dao.

Figure 9.3 A popular Daoist god

Other deities

Other popular deities adopted into the Daoist pantheon at this time include the Goddess of the Morning Clouds (Bixia yuanjun), the daughter of the Lord of Mount Tai, who was first revered locally then became a national figure. Her special powers deal with women, whom she helps to conceive, keeps safe during pregnancy and delivery, and helps in many other ways.

Then there is the Mother of the Dipper (Doumu), originally a Hindu goddess named Marîcî, daughter of Brahma and personification of light, who rose to great veneration in Tibet. Governing the stars of the Dipper, who are in charge of all natural and personal events, she rules human destiny and saves people from peril.

In addition, there is also the God of Literature (Wenchang), originally a Sichuan hero who became known for his efficacious support of struggling scholars. He, too, was officially appointed by Lord Lao and rose to occupy a position in the expanded Daoist pantheon.

The Eight Immortals

A still different set of new Daoists appear in the Eight Immortals, a group of seven men and one woman who, since attaining immortality, have continued to serve humanity by manifesting in séances and providing inspiration. As a group, they were first stylized in theater plays of the thirteenth century, portrayed as an eccentric and happy lot who respond to pleas in emergencies and grant favors and protection. They remain highly popular today, as symbols of long life and happiness, appearing on cards for happy occasions and in restaurants for good luck and enjoyment. They play an active part in Chinese folk culture and have been featured time and again in comic books and popular movies.

Lü Dongbin

Most important among them is Lü Dongbin, identified not only as the revealing deity of Complete Perfection but a frequent guest of spirit-writing sessions and instructor of techniques. Depicted as a Confucian gentleman with aristocratic features and a sword, Lü is best known for the story of the "Yellow Millet Dream," in which he lives mentally through an entire official career while the millet is not even cooked. Waking from his dream, he realizes the futility of worldly endeavors and dedicates himself to Dao. Following another of the Eight Immorals, Zhongli Quan, for his training, he undergoes ten tests of his selfless nature and sincere dedication to the Dao, emerges victorious and becomes a highly respected and very popular immortal.

He is the only one among the group who merits separate temple complexes, such as the Palace of Pointing South (Zhinan gong) on the outskirts of Taipei and the

Figure 9.4 Lü Dongbin

Palace of Eternal Joy (Yongle gong) in Ruichong (Shanxi), which shows him and the celestial host in splendid murals.

Ironcrutch Li

Another popular figure in the group is Li Tieguai or Ironcrutch Li, who also has power over life and death. The story is that he was an expert in ecstatic excursions and once decided to go up into the heavens, leaving his corpse-like body behind for an entire week. To make sure nothing happened to it, he ordered a disciple to keep watch, but the boy got called away. Assuming that his master would not return anyway, he cremated the body.

When Li returned, he found his body gone and entered that of a recently dead man who happened to be an old, crippled beggar. To help himself get around, he used an iron crutch, thus his name, yet despite his transformation he lost none of his vigor or magical powers. Like Lü and the Dark Warrior, he is a fighter at heart and many stories, novels, comic books, and even movies show his martial exploits, combining in a fashion typical for this new form of Daoism, physical vigor with deep compassion and magical powers with a tremendous sense of humor.

Key points you need to know

- Modern Daoism begins with the Song dynasty in the tenth century, after the collapse of the integrated system of the Three Caverns at the end of the Tang. Its main representatives are the ritual masters, unorganized lay practitioners who perform various rituals and services for the populace.
- As Chinese society is dominated more by the merchant class and the educated elite, so religious concerns shift toward exorcism and healing, often with the help of trance practices. Many new schools arise that focus on this aspect of practice. They tend to link themselves with the Celestial Masters.
- One school is notably different: Complete Perfection, founded by Wang Chongyang in 1170, is monastic, ascetic, and focused on personal self-cultivation. Supported by the northern rulers and the Mongol emperors, it becomes the second leading school of modern Daoism.
- The fate and shape of the religion is closely connected to the imperial court. The government establishes stringent regulations for all practitioners; it coopts Daoist gods and ritual for state protection; and some emperors – especially those who believe themselves to be incarnations of Daoist deities – greatly support the religion.
- Balancing this centralized control, modern Daoism also flourishes in the countryside and comes to adapt to various local cults and popular gods into its pantheon. Important deities include the Eight Immortals, the City God, the goddess Mazu, as well as a number of Buddhist and other deities.

Discussion questions

1. How do the two aspects of religion – communal and personal – interrelate? Is one preferable over the other? Are they compatible? Should religion be focused more on personal salvation or on community coherence?
2. Reflect on the relation of religion and state. How has the state exerted control over religious organizations in the past? How have churches influenced politics? What is the contemporary situation?
3. Is there anything comparable to the multiple gods and immortals of the Daoist pantheon in other religions? Do other countries and cultures have local cults and popular deities? How do they work with religious multiplicity?

Further reading

Boltz, Judith M. 1987. *A Survey of Taoist Literature: Tenth to Seventeenth Centuries*, China Research Monograph 32. Berkeley, CA: University of California.

Davis, Edward L. 2001. *Society and the Supernatural in Sung China*. Honolulu, HI: University of Hawai'i Press.

DeBruyn, Pierre-Henry. 2000. "Daoism in the Ming (1368–1644)." In *Daoism Handbook*, edited by Livia Kohn, 594–622. Leiden: E. Brill.

Ebrey, Patricia. 2000. "Taoism and Art at the Court of Song Huizong." In *Daoism and the Arts of China*, edited by Stephen Little and Shawn Eichman, 95–111. Berkeley, CA: University of California Press.

Esposito, Monica. 2000. "Daoism in the Qing (1644–1911)." In *Daoism Handbook*, edited by Livia Kohn, 623–58. Leiden: E. Brill.

Goossaert, Vincent. 2007. *The Taoists of Peking 1800–1944*. Cambridge, MA: Harvard University Press.

Hymes, Robert. 2002. *Way and Byway: Taoism, Local Religion, and Models of Divinity in Sung and Modern China*. Berkeley, CA: University of California Press.

Kleeman, Terry F. 1994. *A God's Own Tale: The Book of Transformations of Wenchang, the Divine Lord of Zitong*. Albany, NY: State University of New York Press.

Komjathy, Louis. 2007. *Cultivating Perfection: Mysticism and Self-Transformation in Quanzhen Daoism*. Leiden: E. Brill.

Skar, Lowell. "Ritual Movements, Deity Cults, and the Transformation of Daoism in Song and Yuan Times." In *Daoism Handbook*, edited by Livia Kohn, 413–63. Leiden: E. Brill.

Yao, Ted. 2000. "Quanzhen – Complete Perfection." In *Daoism Handbook*, edited by Livia Kohn, 567–93. Leiden: E. Brill.

10 Reaching for the Dao

In this chapter

Modern Daoists in many ways continue the practices of the medieval system, working communal rituals to multiple deities and engaging in personal self-cultivation. The central focus is still to connect to the Dao through a variety of practices, however, the methods take on new forms. Thus immersion into trance plays a much greater role, both for exorcistic purposes and to gain information from the otherworld. Similarly, self-cultivation develops into a new system called internal alchemy which makes use of traditional body practices and meditations but places them into the context of alchemical transformation.

Another new dimension is the emphasis placed on martial arts as an extension of healing exercises and physical cultivation. Most prominent in this context is the emergence of taijiquan, which begins in a military and Confucian environment, then develops into a form of Daoist discipline. On another plane, Daoist thought plays a role in the philosophy of late imperial China which is dominated by Neo-Confucianism but also places great importance on unifying the various theoretical systems in an intellectual trend known as "harmonizing the three teachings." Last, but not least, Daoist themes are made prominent in a variety of vernacular novels that feature the quest for immortality, the adventures of the Eight Immortals and Lord Lao as a martial hero.

Main topics covered

- Trance practices
- Internal alchemy
- Healing and martial arts
- Philosophical speculation
- Vernacular novels

Trance practices

Entering a deep trance to connect to the gods is part of shamanistic practice and has played an important role in Daoism from the beginning. Most medieval revelations of sacred texts and divine instructions occurred in altered states of consciousness, with the seeker in deep meditative absorption or a spirit-media in ecstatic trance. Practitioners of Highest Clarity cultivated their trance ability to engage in soul travel to the stars and interact with the gods, whom they often met in vivid encounters. Daoist masters, whether in ritual or meditative settings, were otherworld officials and had the means of direct communication with the divine.

In the Song dynasty, this emphasis on trance states gains a new level of importance. It is activated in two main modes: by a ritual master, often with the help of a spirit-boy, for the purpose of exorcising demonic and unwanted forces; and by community leaders, through a professional spirit-medium, to gain information and instructions from benevolent deities.

Exorcism

The exorcistic use of trance states is most clearly documented in a Song rite known as Summoning for Investigation (*kaozhao fa*), employed as a cure for demonic possession and various other unexplained and hard-to-cure symptoms, such as erratic behavior, imaginary conversations, hallucinations, fixations, incomprehensible speech, and the like. The family notices the symptoms, finds no ordinary way of helping the person, and invites a Daoist priest or ritual master to perform the rite.

To begin, the master transforms himself into a spiritual entity – a deity or spirit-general with whom he has a close connection. While performing ritual steps, sacred hand gestures, and incantations, he visualizes the deity within his body and mentally creates a cosmic scenario for his transformation, then spiritually becomes a god. Once he is a divine official, he can command all sorts of spirit forces and wield all kinds of wondrous weapons that will allow him to perform the task at hand.

In a second step, the afflicting entity is identified and coaxed to present itself. The master – with the help of talismans, incantations, and gestures – mentally orders a troupe of lesser divinities to bring it into concrete presence: into a mirror, a basin of water, or another reflecting object. At the same time, the patient is asked to blow on this object, thus making sure that the captured entity is indeed the one causing the trouble. Positive identification is made as the patient opens his eyes and describes the entity he sees in the object, giving him the chance to condense and externalize the root cause of his affliction.

A trance-induced cure

In a third step, the master reintroduces the demonic entity into the patient. This is done quite forcefully. Visualizing a group of divine bailiffs binding and pushing the demon, the master inhales cosmic *qi* and mixes it with a mouthful of water. As the bailiffs force the entity into the patient, the master spits the *qi*-water over him, putting him into trance and causing a shaking or trembling. The patient who has externalized his affliction as a demonic entity is forced to accept on a subconscious level that his affliction is in fact none other than himself.

While in this trance state, the patient-cum-demon is subjected to an interrogation by the master, stating his reasons for creating the affliction and the means necessary to end it. Should the patient be too weak or too young to speak, the trance state is induced in a surrogate, a family member or professional medium to be possessed in his stead. In all cases, the root cause of the problem is identified and potent measures can be taken. In some situations, the master may negotiate a deal with the afflicting powers; in others, he may guide the negative aspects to remove themselves; in yet others, he may install a plan for remedial action to be taken in the patient's waking life.

The rite concludes with the master thanking the entity for its cooperation and waking the patient to normal consciousness while dismissing the supernatural helpers and extricating himself from his divine persona.

Spirit-writing

Another major use of trance techniques in modern Daoism is for the purpose of gaining information and instruction. Undertaken by literati as much as by commoners, but most often by Daoist community groups, this usually involves a technique called spirit-writing or the planchette.

A form of automatic writing, the practice took place in a sacred setting, such as a temple, an association hall, or a special room inside a devotee's residence. The hall typically contained a square table, on which was the planchette: a wooden tray covered with sand or incense ashes and surmounted by a T-shaped frame made of peach or willow. Its top featured a three-pronged sharp stick, about two feet long, ideally cut on a particularly good day from the southeastern side of a tree exposed to the rising sun. Held by two spirit-mediums, who went into trance, this stick would trace characters into the sand of the tray, thus conveying the divinities' message.

Ceremonial procedures

The spirit-writing ceremony was usually held on an auspicious day and in front of a congregation of devout seekers. Before inviting the spirit to descend into the stick, devotees offered food or flowers, burned incense, drew talismans, recited incantations, and underwent ceremonies of purification. As the spirit entered the stick it began to move automatically, tracing characters on the sand planchette. In addition to the two medium in trance, officials in charge of the ceremony include a reader who identified and recited the characters and a scribe who wrote them down. After the deity had left again, the community would offer thanks and proceed to put the instructions into action.

Certain groups or individuals would communicate with particular deities – very commonly the immortal Lü Dongbin – in each case presenting specific questions for their consideration. In some cases, deities also initiated communication, by appearing in a dream and commanding a session. They usually responded to the needs of the community, but it also happened that they revealed entirely unexpected and unheard-of information. Daoist gods and immortals have been known to channel complete autobiographies, lengthy practice instructions – such as taijiquan sequences – and extensive poetry collections. Spirit-writing is still widely practiced in Daoist circles today, and there are some groups who will not make any decision without first consulting their leading deity.

Internal alchemy

While trance techniques play an important role in Daoist communities, many practitioners – including all monastics and ritual leaders – also engage in personal self-cultivation. The dominant system for this is internal alchemy (*neidan*), which combines concepts of operative alchemy with visualization of body gods, the transformation of sexual essence and other forms of *qi*, medieval forms of meditation, and cosmological speculation associated with yin and yang, the five phases, lunar and solar cycles, and the *Yijing*.

Adopted by all Daoist schools since the Song dynasty, internal alchemy appears in a multitude of forms and teachings. Different schools and lineages place varied emphasis on physical, meditative, ritual, or ecstatic practices and envision the process in somewhat different cosmological and psychological terms. As centuries passed, further schools created still different forms of practice, including entire systems specifically for women (*nüdan*). They also integrated more traditional Confucian thought in the overall climate of "harmonizing the three teachings." Yet within this great variety, inner alchemy – then and now – typically begins with a preparatory phase of moral and physical readiness, which involves practicing longevity techniques, setting one's mind fully on the Great Work, and learning to control the mind with breath observation and concentration exercises.

Beginning the great work

Once ready, practitioners typically pass through a series of three transformations: from essence (*jing*) to energy (*qi*), from energy to spirit (*shen*), and from spirit to Dao, consciously and actively reversing human gestation and cosmic creation.

They begin by focusing on essence, the tangible form of *qi* that sinks down periodically from its original center in the Ocean of *Qi* (abdomen) in men and in the Cavern of *Qi* (chest) in women, manifesting as semen and menstrual blood respectively. To revert essence back to *qi*, men allow a feeling of arousal to occur, then guide the flowing energy back up along spine and into the head, thus "subduing the white tiger." Women, when they feel menstrual blood sink down from the Cavern of *Qi*, massage their breasts and visualize it rising upward and transforming into *qi*. Over several months, this will cause menstruation to cease, the "beheading of the red dragon."

Both then circulate the newly purified *qi* in the microcosmic orbit, guiding it along the central channels of the torso and opening a series of passes along the way. Not only strengthening the body and enhancing health, this *qi*-circulation eventually leads to the manifestation of a concentrated pearl of primordial *qi* – newly formed in men, latently present from birth in women. The first stage concludes when the pearl coalesces.

The immortal embryo

The second stage is the same for men and women. It focuses on the transformation of purified *qi* into spirit. The pearl of dew is developed into the golden flower with the help of transmuted *qi*. For this, yin and yang are identified as different energies in the body, each described with different metaphors depending on the level of purity attained. Typically there are the following:

yang = heart = fire = trigram *li* ☲ = pure lead = dragon = red bird;
yin = kidneys = water = trigram *kan* ☵ = pure mercury = tiger =white tiger.

At each stage of the transmutation process, the energies are given different names and different metaphors are employed. Eventually adepts learn not only to mix them in the abdomen but to revolve them through an internal-body cycle that includes not only the spine and breastbone but leads all the way to the feet and is known as the macrocosmic orbit. Gradually one's energies are refined to a point where they become as pure as the celestials themselves. Spirit emerges as an independent entity; the pearl opens up to give rise to the golden flower, the core of the immortal embryo in the lower cinnabar field.

Once the embryo starts to grow, adepts switch their practice to nourish it for ten months with embryo respiration. Not only nurturing the embryo, this practice also makes the adept increasingly independent of outer nourishment and air. While the first phase was easier for men, this stage is easier for women because they are naturally endowed with the faculty to grow an embryo. After ten months, the embryo is complete.

Realization

Adepts then proceed to the third stage. The as yet semi-material body of the embryo is transformed into the pure spirit body of the immortals, a body of primordial *qi*. After it is nourished to completion, it takes birth by moving up along the spine and exiting through the top of the head. This signifies the adept's celestial rebirth and is accompanied by the perception of a deep inner rumbling, like a clap of thunder. After passing into the celestial spheres, the spirit communicates with the gods, thus transcending the limitations of the body.

Once the embryo has been born, it grows through a further meditative exercise known as "nursing for three years." Gradually getting used to its new powers, it moves faster and travels further away until it can go far and wide without any limitation. As the spirit enters into its cosmic ventures, the adept exhibits enhanced faculties

Figure 10.1 The immortal embryo exits the body

and gains powers of direct interaction with the gods. These powers are also essential for the successful performance of Daoist ritual, so that all superior masters require thorough training in the procedures of internal alchemy.

Healing and martial arts

Beyond ritual and spiritual attainments, Daoists also engage in physical cultivation, for the purpose of healing and/or to prepare for more advanced undertakings. Practices developed in the middle ages continue and are standardized, such as the Six Healing Sounds and various exercise sequences associated with animals and famous immortals. Most popular among the latter is a set of practices called the Five Animal Frolics, which still plays an important role in qigong today. In addition, matching the demon-dispelling and martial nature of Daoist gods since the Song, martial practices become more prominent and develop into new forms. Best known among them is taijiquan or "Great Ultimate Boxing."

The Five Animal Frolics

The Five Animals Frolics is an exercise sequence that mixes standing and moving practices associated with the crane, bear, monkey, deer, and tiger. While animal-patterned exercises are documented as far back as the *Zhuangzi*, this system appears in historical sources for the first time in the official biography of the physician Hua Tuo of the second century C.E. It notes that he developed it on the basis of earlier movements to keep the body smooth and flexible.

> The practice aids the elimination of diseases and increases the functioning of the limbs and joints. Whenever a disorder is felt in the body one of the Animals should be practiced until one perspires freely. When perspiration is strong, one should cover the affected parts of the body with powder. In due course the body becomes lighter and more comfortable and a healthy appetite will return. (*Record of the Three Kingdoms*)

The first description of the actual practice appears in the early Tang in a work associated with Sun Simiao; it outlines a series of rather vigorous movements, geared to induce sweat and cleanse the inner organs. A later form, documented in the Ming collection *Chifeng sui* (Marrow of the Red Phoenix), has more gentle moves and places more emphasis on the breath.

This same version also occurs with illustrations showing female practitioners in the *Wuqin wu gongfa tushuo* (Illustrated Explanation of Five Animal Dance Practice). The preface explains that a woman living in the seclusion of the family home who wishes to cultivate herself should begin by setting up a quiet spot for her practice, then create some heat (with unspecified method) to accumulate *qi*. Next,

Figure 10.2 A woman practices the Five Animal Frolics

she should take the *qi* and circulate it through the arteries and meridians of her body until she feels it full and overflowing. Then she can practice the Five Animal Frolics to eliminate all diseases and allow the emergence of subtler energetic levels. After this, she should pursue more meditative practices that lead eventually to the elixir refinement of internal alchemy.

Five Animals today

Today the Frolics play an active part in qigong, using a basic form that is much longer and more complex than any traditional methods recorded. Each Animal now has between five and ten different exercises so that, for example, the Bear has eight standing practices, such as Bear Pushes Paws, Bear Pushes Back, Bear Extends Paws, and Bear Double Push, followed by four variations of the Bear Amble that range from a basic form through Bear Ambles with Fists to Pointing to the Sun and Holding the Moon.

This new version was developed in the early 1980s by Jiao Guorui and Liang Shifeng. It has since grown into over twenty variations which the Chinese government hopes to standardize into one officially recognized version. In addition to making the movements more sophisticalted, each Animal is now also linked with a cosmological entity, an inner organ, a section of the body, specific qualities, and with certain healing effects:

animal	cosmos	organ	body area	effect	quality
crane	heaven	heart	muscles	breathing	lightness
bear	earth	kidneys	lower back	inner focus	rootedness
monkey	humanity	spleen	joints, wrists	openness	agility
deer	spirit	liver	calm mind	subtlety	patience
tiger	body	lungs	whole body	awareness	strength

As a result, the Five Animal Frolics has become a comprehensive system of healing and long life, aiding ordinary people as well as religious seekers. The development, moreover, is typical for other healing exercises and Daoist techniques of body cultivation.

Martial arts

Martial arts are a form of physical practice geared toward fitness and self-defense in combination with ethical principles. They inherit two traditional value systems: ancient Confucian chivalry, which encouraged the practice of archery and charioteering as tools for aristocratic self-cultivation and emphasized honor, respect, good manners, precise timing, balance, and composure in all actions; and traditional Daoist concepts of bending and softness, expressed most clearly in Sunzi's *Art of War*, which stressed flexibility, yielding, humility, nonviolence, inner focus, and wisdom.

Martial practice is divided into hard and soft or outer and inner forms. That is to say, forms that focus on muscle and strength building, teach fighting techniques, and work toward the defeat of the opponent tend to be hard or outer; those that encourage a strong internal awareness and also have healing and even spiritual benefits are classified as soft or inner. Especially the latter were not alien to the religious institutions of medieval China, and historical records suggest that fighters from the Buddhist Shaolin monastery and the Daoist Louguan temple helped the Tang rulers win the empire. However, the practice remained esoteric and only emerged as part of popular culture in the Ming and Qing dynasties – another aspect of the transformation that created modern Daoism with its ritual masters, local cults, and widespread social appeal.

Unarmed combat

Martial practice started to spread significantly in the sixteenth century, when the Ming dynasty was in decline and looting bandits and marauding armies made self-defense a priority. At this time, groups of monks became famous for their fighting skills, especially with the staff. Unarmed combat (*quan*, lit. "fist"), on the other hand, became dominant only in the seventeenth century, when the incoming Qing rulers prohibited all use of weapons among non-military fighters. Both monastic and civil militias accordingly developed new techniques, combining defensive moves with the age-old practices of controlled breathing and healing exercises.

Among monastics, this occurred most prominently at the Buddhists' Shaolin Temple (Henan) and the Daoist Mount Wudang (Hubei), the sacred site associated with the Dark Warrior and a major center of Ming imperial worship. Within civil militias, it was most prominent in the southern part of the country, where it led to the development of taijiquan and other strengthening routines. Both kinds of martial practices, moreover, came to influence the modern tradition of healing exercises, and their patterns still form an active part of qigong.

Taiqiquan

Legend has it that taijiquan began when the Daoist immortal Zhang Sanfeng, a hermit on Mount Wudang, looked out the window of his hermitage and saw a crane fight with a snake. The two animals turned and twisted in such a complex pattern, neither gaining the advantage of the other, that the immortal saw in them the workings of pure Dao, the cosmic interaction of yin and yang. He promptly started to imitate their movements and created the first sequence of the practice – which he later, together with other patterns, a collection of poetry, and his complete autobiography, channeled to the Sichuan Daoist Li Xiyue (1806–1856). Zhang in due course became the patron saint of the practice; he is also the main link to Daoism which – however much it may have favored martial practices – originally had no part in its development.

Historically the beginnings of taijiquan can be traced to the military officer Chen Wangting who, after fighting the Manchu conquest in the 1630s, retired to his hometown and began to teach martial exercises consisting of five routines and a sequence of 108 moves. Transmitted through the family, his methods were organized into a slightly less martial system by his descendant Chen Zhangxing

Figure 10.3 The Taiji symbol

(1771–1853), leading to what is today known as the Chen-style, a series of rather simple moves in the four directions. The Yang-style, on the other hand, goes back to Yang Luchan (1799–1872), who originally studied Shaolin boxing, then became a student of Chen Zhangxing. His practice is softer and rounder, with wide arm movements, circular patterns, and intricate flexing in the wrists and arms. Spread by his sons and developed further into various sub-lineages, it is the most popular form of taijiquan today.

Joining the cosmos

In the original creation of this self-defense form, Master Chen used healing exercises in combination with military training. He also followed the dominant thought of the time, which combined Daoist and Neo-Confucian thinking, and picked the popular Taiji (Great Ultimate) diagram, which was first published in 1613, to symbolize his practice. This diagram, representing the state of the universe at the time of creation, appears in medieval Daoist charts adopted by internal alchemists and Neo-Confucians.

Taijiquan is executed exclusively from a standing position and involves continuous movements that are choreographed into lengthy and complex sequences. It eschews the development of large muscles and powerful strength in favor of internal suppleness (*jin*), a springiness in tendons, sinews, and ligaments. Rather than using the mind to systematically guide *qi*, practitioners keep it open and relaxed, allowing the *qi* to flow smoothly in all directions and the spirit to be receptive to all stimuli. The practice thus combines an open and relaxed meditative awareness with soft, slow, and focused body movements; its overall goal is to flow along with the Dao at creation in a smooth, supple, and relaxed way.

Philosophical speculation

Another area of Daoist development since the Song dynasty is philosophical speculation. Throughout the centuries, Daoists continued the tradition of intellectual awareness, cosmological speculation, and ethical consideration first documented in the ancient philosophers. Every generation saw new commentaries to the *Daode jing*, and Daoists continued to apply the terms and ideas of the *Zhuangzi* in their presentation of immortality. They also interacted variously with other schools of thought, and under the Tang widely integrated Buddhist concepts and systems of thought into their own modes of theoretical speculation, opening their own tradition of Daoist scholasticism.

In the Song dynasty, Confucianism rose to a new level of prominence. Its thinkers integrated concepts and systems from other schools and developed a fondness for the "harmonization of the three teachings" (*sanjiao heyi*), in their Neo-Confucian mode claiming that there was only one Dao and one *qi* and that people could attain essential harmony by following various paths and modes of thought. Confucian thinkers accordingly adopted Daoist cosmic charts and longevity methods as well as Buddhist principles and meditations. While Confucian intellectuals thus actively engaged in inner alchemy and used its vocabulary to explain their vision of the progress toward universal virtue and oneness with Heaven and Earth, Daoists opened new forms of thought that integrated ideas of Confucianism and Buddhism. Especially practitioners of taijiquan developed a philosophy to go with their practice that actively merged the three teachings.

Harmonizing the three teachings

A typical way of joining the three teachings was to see Confucianism as maintaining society through its emphasis on moral values, Chan Buddhism as concentrating on the cultivation of inner nature through meditation, and Daoism as encouraging bodily transformation through the enhancement of inner nature and destiny.

In Ming Confucianism, moreover, several Daoist concepts became prominent. They include the vision of Dao as the pure underlying essence of the universe as expressed in the *Daode jing*, the refinement of the inner elixir and its proper timing, the original power of *qi* and its cultivation by inner circulation, the regulation of breath as a means to concentration and good health, embryo breathing as a form of gaining inner subtlety, and the use of the trigrams and hexagrams of the *Yijing* to mark progress.

Confucian thinkers

Confucian thinkers such as Wang Dao (1487–1547), Zhan Ruoshui (1466–1560), Wang Yangming (1517–1579), and Lin Zhaoen (1517–1598) would use these concepts, often in conjunction with Chan Buddhist meditation practice and Daoist ways of breath control. With their help these thinkers explained the inner development of subtler states of mind, which led them to the realization of "innate knowledge" – seen as a function of *qi* – and the true self. This in turn was found essential for the unfolding of bright virtue that connected everyone to the cosmos, the goal of Neo-Confucian realization.

According to this view, everyone is inherently part of the larger universe and connected with it through principle (*li*) and *qi*-energy. These abstract/mental and concrete/physical aspects of existence were further related to Buddha-nature and karmic retribution, as well as to Daoist ideas of inner nature and destiny. Both aspects have to be cultivated equally for the ideal state to arise, a state that in the three teachings is called, respectively, oneness with Heaven and Earth, nirvana, and immortality.

Vernacular novels

The various aspects of Daoism at the time were, moreover, made popular in various novels that couched traditional themes in enjoyable language and tales of the miraculous. One that integrates the three teachings is the *Roupu tuan* (*Carnal Prayer Mat*; trl. by Patrick Hana), ascribed to Li Yu (1611–1680). The book's hero works his way to Buddhist enlightenment in a moralistic Confucian society with the help of Daoist sexual techniques. Moving from one partner to the next, engaging in extensive, highly creative sexual relations that are described in great, even pornographic detail, the hero eventually comes to realize that the universe is one at its core and that there is no need for major techniques of one sort or the other.

Another story full of Daoist motives that has remained widely popular to the present day is Wu Chengen's (d. 1582) *Xiyou ji* (Journey to the West), also translated as *Monkey* (by Arthur Waley). It tells the adventures of the monkey king Sun Wukong who steals the peaches of immortality from Kunlun and is reformed – since he cannot be killed – by having to accompany the pilgrim Xuanzang (596–664) who actually traveled to India to obtain Buddhist scriptures. On they way they encounter all sorts of monsters and magical situations, which the monkey successfully overcomes with the help of Daoist techniques.

Tales of Daoists

There are also various novels that involve Daoist specifically, similarly full of magical feats and wondrous adventures. One of them is the *Qizhen shizhuan* (Seven Daoist Masters; trl. by Eva Wong), written by an anonymous author around the year 1500. The book retells the story of Wang Chongyang and the Seven Perfected of Complete Perfection, including their various feats, complete with magical powers and supernatural connections.

Another is the *Dongyou ji* (Journey to the East; no trl.), written by Wu Yuantai (fl. 1566), using a title adapted from the popular *Xiyou ji*. This is a story about the Eight Immortals and their adventures as they travel east across the sea toward realization of the Dao. It describes each immortal's cultivation of perfection as well as their joint travels. It also recounts the hagiography of Lord Lao, outlining his birth under the Shang, his exploits on earth, the transmission of the *Daode jing*, and his various appearances in Chinese history.

Very similar exploits are also ascribed to the Dark Warrior, the official state protector since the Song. They are recounted in the *Beiyou ji* (Journey to the North; trl. by Gary Seaman) by Yu Xiangtou (fl. 1588–1609). The book outlines the multiple lives and extensive trials of the Dark Warrior, showing his progress from human crown prince to divine emperor and detailing his appearances on earth and the miracles he worked on behalf of humanity.

A different kind of fictional work is the *Zhang Sanfeng quanji* (Complete Collection of Zhang Sanfeng, trl. by Shiu-Hon Wong), channeled by Li Xiyue in the nineteenth century. It outlines the life and manifestations of Zhang Sanfeng together with a history of his Daoist lineage and a number of biographical notes on hidden scholars, hermits and wise men. It also presents Zhang's inner alchemical techniques and Daoist doctrines as well as a collection of his poems and philosophical notes. The latter detail the immortal's take on the harmonization of the three teachings, understanding of human life, and key ethical precepts.

Creation of the gods

A yet different from of Daoist tales, which caters to the increasing popularity of the martial arts, emerges in the novel *Fengshen yanyi* (Creation of the Gods; trl. by Zhizhong Gu), attributed to either Xu Zhonglin (d. 1566) or Lu Xixing (*c.* 1520–1601). The book describes in mythological fashion the fight of the rising Zhou dynasty against the last tyrant of the Shang in the second millennium B.C.E.

In each case, developments on earth are paralleled by activities in the heavens, and Lord Lao appears repeatedly to support the fight of the righteous Daoist group, the Promulgating Sect (Shanjiao), against the opposing Intercepting Sect (Jiejiao), led by the Grand Master of Heaven. This latter group lays various traps for the advancing Zhou army, and time and again Lord Lao is asked to give advice and support, provide weapons and help, mastermind battle plans, or seek truces and adjudication.

A Daoist Battle

For example, called upon to help spring a particularly nasty trap, the Daoist god joins the battle, becoming manifest as a saint on a blue fairy ox and taking an active hand in the fighting. Supported by another god, the Heavenly Worthy of Primordial Beginning, he begins by trying to parley with the enemy; then, still on his faithful ox, he enters the trap to engage his divine opponent in one-on-one combat. Auspicious lights flash forth, white mists rise up, magical charts turn into bridges, walking sticks become wondrous weapons, and swords glitter with numinous brilliance. Then, in the middle of the battle

> Laozi suddenly pulled in his rein and jumped out of the combat circle. He pushed his fishtail coronet to one side, and three columns of gas released from his head transformed into three immortals, called the "clarities."

These three immortals identify themselves as representatives of the Three Clarity heavens and together with Lord Lao proceed to attack his opponent from all sides. Not being real, they cannot harm him, but they distract him sufficiently so that the god can hit him with his divine stick. Eventually the two fighters break up and retire to reassemble their forces.

Next, Lord Lao and the Heavenly Worthy decide they need two extra immortals to break the trap and invite two buddhas from the western Pure Land to join them. Protected by auspicious clouds, flowers, jade necklaces, and precious pearls, they proceed to attack with Buddhist relics and lotus blossoms, and successfully enter the trap. Lord Lao promptly sends a crash of lightning across the field and makes a yellow fog spring up. Thus protected, the heroes force the nasty rebel to his knees and make him flee for his life, scattering his followers in all directions. This supernatural defeat at the same time opens the road for the Zhou army to advance.

Tales such as these as well as the various other novels, therefore, spread Daoist ideas and mythical themes among the populace, creating the image of the religion that is still dominant today and remains alive in kungfu movies: a strong emphasis on Lord Lao and the Dark Warrior, a deep veneration for the Eight Immortals and Seven Perfected, a unique way of being in the world, and a sense of the miraculous and martial.

Figure 10.4 A Daoist practicing the sword (By kind permission of www.wudangquan.net)

Key points you need to know

- Modern Daoism since the Song dynasty appears in various modes and social contexts. Institutional religion tends to focus on exorcism and fortune-telling, often with the help of trance practices, activated through mediums or spirit-writing.
- Individual cultivation centers on the practice of internal alchemy, which integrates medieval forms of longevity practice and meditation with *Yijing* speculation and the concoction of alchemical elixirs. It outlines the progress toward immortality in three stages, transforming essence, energy, and spirit into the purity of Dao.
- Among the wider populace, Daoism continues to be known for its healing exercises, as prominently exemplified in the Five Animal Frolics. New in the field is the increasingly popular emphasis on martial arts, notably the unarmed combat of taijiquan, which integrates ancient philosophical principles and notions of chivalry with physical practice.
- Thinkers at the same time strive to integrate the three teachings – Daoism, Buddhism, and Confucianism – into one system, asserting that there is only one ultimate reality and that all religions have a valid form of access to it.
- Beyond all this, Daoist motives and figures features prominently in vernacular novels, a new aspect of Chinese culture in the Ming dynasty. Daoist hagiographies are reformulated and embellished with magical tales, and many heroes exhibit Daoist powers and martial prowess.

Discussion questions

1. How do religions relate to trance techniques? Do many religions make use of them? Are they honored or despised? What role can trance states play in religious practice?
2. What kind of Daoist motives do we find in kungfu movies? Think of movies like *Crouching Tiger, Hidden Dragon*, *Kungfu Hustle*, and the like and examine them from a Daoist perspective.
3. What role does religion play in art, philosophy, and literature? It is essential or marginal? How does this change over historical periods? Do you personally prefer religious themes?

Further reading

Ching, Julia. 1976. *To Accumulate Wisdom: The Way of Wang Yang-ming*. New York: Columbia University Press.

Davis, Barbara. 2004. *The Taijiquan Classics: An Annotated Translation*. Berkeley, CA: North Atlantic Books.

Davis, Edward L. 2001. *Society and the Supernatural in Sung China*. Honolulu, HI: University of Hawai'i Press.

Despeux, Catherine, and Livia Kohn. 2003. *Women in Daoism*. Cambridge, MA: Three Pines Press.

Jordan, David K., and Daniel Overmyer. 1986. *The Flying Phoenix*. Princeton, NJ: Princeton University Press.

Kohn, Livia. 1998. "Taoist Scholasticism: A Preliminary Inquiry." In *Scholasticism: Cross-Cultural and Comparative Perspectives*, edited by José Ignacio Cabezon, 115–40. Albany, NY: State University of New York Press.

Shahar, Meir. 2007. *The Shaolin Monastery: History, Religion, and the Martial Arts*. Honolulu, HI: University of Hawai'i Press.

Skar, Lowell, and Fabrizio Pregadio. 2000. "Inner Alchemy (*Neidan*)." In *Daoism Handbook*, edited by Livia Kohn, 464–97. Leiden: E. Brill.

Wang, Shumin, and Penelope Barrett. 2006. "Profile of a *Daoyin* Tradition: The 'Five Animal Mimes'." *Asian Medicine – Tradition and Modernity* 2.2: 225–53.

11 *Daoism in China today*

In this chapter

The fate of Daoism in China today is closely linked with politics. Suppressed from the founding of the People's Republic in 1949 until the Four Modernizations in 1978, it has made a gradual come-back but remains under tight control. All Daoist institutions are state-owned, monastics are paid by the government, several bureaus compete for revenues and administrative power, and training centers require courses in Marxism as preparation for full ordination. Still, temple compounds are growing on the five sacred mountains, on Daoist mountains, and in all major cities. People choose the Daoist life for a variety of reasons: to take refuge from civilian life, do community service, rise in the official hierarchy, become a hermit, or establish a Daoist-based business.

As the religion has grown, so have its ritual activities, the most notable being the Grand Offering to All Heavens, which is now being performed every five or so years. The latest event of this kind was in Hong Kong in 2007, with hundreds of Daoists in attendance. Its cultivation practices, too, are taking off in unprecedented ways, Daoists increasingly adopting qigong while developing traditional martial arts, such as taiji quan.

Main topics covered

- Recent developments
- Structure and administration
- Daoist lives
- Ritual activities
- The Qigong connection

Recent developments

Daoism, together with all other religions of China, was the victim of the political transformation of the twentieth century. After World War II ended with the capitulation of Japan in 1945, the Chinese engaged in civil war, the Communists (CCP) under the leadership of Mao Zedong (1893–1976) battling the Republicans (Kuomintang), led by Chiang Kaishek (1888–1975). It ended in 1949 with the flight of the Republicans to Taiwan and the establishment of the People's Republic of China on the mainland.

Throughout the period leading up to this, religion had a difficult time. Monastic life was attacked as a form of escape from a country that badly needed workers and soldiers, while popular practices were condemned as superstitious and wasteful. Traditional myths and stories were debunked while gods toppled and organizations declined. On the other hand, trance activities, health techniques, and martial practices continued to flourish, if on a smaller level and often in secrecy. Communism exacerbated the situation. Its official doctrine followed Karl Marx in seeing religion as an opiate for the people, necessary only while their living conditions were horrendous. Religion would naturally evaporate once the true realm of freedom under the dictatorship of the proletariat was realized.

Communist policies

With no patience to wait for the natural demise of religion, the Communists suppressed it radically. In 1952, private holdings of land were outlawed and all was collectivized into communes. Religious organizations were dissolved, monks and nuns returned to the laity, and temples made into schools, assembly halls, garrisons, or storage facilities. In 1958, during the Great Leap Forward, every commune was encouraged to have its own steel mill, and all metal was confiscated to be used for industrial progress; many statues and religious artifacts found their way into the furnaces.

During the Cultural Revolution (1966–1976), young people (Red Guards) were encouraged to do away with all remnants of culture. All sorts of artifacts and what remained of temple buildings were destroyed, desecrated, and defaced. This only ended with the death of Mao Zedong in 1976 and the new leadership of Deng Xiaoping (1905–1997), who in 1978 began the Four Modernizations. As a result, since 1980 religious organizations and practices, as well as the academic study of religion, have undergone a revival.

New religions

Exploiting this freedom, in the 1990s various groups under the umbrella of the sanctioned health practice of qigong (lit. "working with *qi*") grew into large-scale

Figure 11.1 A community temple

organizations and recouped traditional religious patterns. In addition to healing exercises, they taught devotion to deities, chanting of sacred scriptures, taking of precepts, and obedience to group leaders. Typical groups included Zangmigong (Tantric Qigong), essentially a new religion based on Tibetan Buddhism, and Zhonggong (Central Qigong), an organization that led practitioners to Buddhist-style liberation.

There was also the notorious Falungong (Dharma Wheel Practice), founded in 1992, which proposed exercises and meditations in combination with ethical principles for the attainment of supernatural powers and transcendence into heaven. Refusing to bow to government regulations, they were outlawed in 1996. Since 1999, this group – and with it various other qigong and religious organizations – have been actively suppressed, creating once again a repressive atmosphere for personal religious cultivation.

Structure and administration

After 1949, all religions had to organize themselves under state law. Daoists, dominantly of the Complete Perfection school with headquarters at the White Cloud Temple in Beijing, accordingly formed the Chinese Daoist Association

(CDA). It began in 1956 with Yue Chongdai as president, who was succeeded by Chen Yingning (1880–1969) in 1962. The association held a national conference of Daoist representatives, which also included the Celestial Masters based on Mount Longhu, and created a basic forum for interaction with the state. Nothing much happened during the Cultural Revolution, when it had to lie low.

Since 1980, the CDA has held national meetings every five years, founded local associations in all major cities and provinces, sponsored Grand Offerings in 1993 and 2001, arranged for formal ordinations, established several training centers for monastics, and developed official contacts with Daoists all over the world.

Training and ordination

While the Celestial Masters on Mount Longhu routinely train priests and have held regular ordinations since 1995, the main training center for monastics (now only monks) is at the White Cloud Temple in Beijing. A second center has recently opened on Mount Qingcheng in Sichuan. A school especially for nuns was established on Nanyue (Hunan), the sacred mountain of the south, in 2005. Training usually lasts for two years, with classes of 50–100 students that are selected upon examination from local temples, where they were apprenticed to an established Daoist.

The system works on two levels: a would-be Daoist finds a master and, after some basic training and with family approval, is officially adopted into his or her lineage. This involves an initiation ceremony with the transmission of sacred texts, a vow to continue the tradition, and the bestowal of a religious name. Both Complete Perfection and Celestial Masters follow this system; there is no requirement to be a monk or nun. Also, masters typically specialize in certain kinds of texts, rituals, or practices, and disciples may decide to study other methods as well. In that case, they move on to other teachers and become holders of multiple lineages. Most Daoists in China remain on this level; so-called "ordained" foreigners, too, participate here.

The second level involves training at a large, state-sponsored center for the full two-year program, studying Chinese culture, foreign languages, temple administration, Marxism-Leninism, as well as Daoist history, ritual, music, literature, thought, cultivation, and so on. Graduates undergo full ordination to Daoist monk or nun, live in temples full-time, and become organizational leaders. Many begin by being religious enthusiasts but come out despising Daoist doctrines and practices, their highest loyalty being to the state. Full, large-scale ordinations were interrupted by war and Communism, and none was held between 1927 and 1989. Since then, three major ceremonies have been organized, each ordaining several hundred Daoists.

Multiple bureaus

Temples and monasteries have a semi-democratic management; they work largely through committees and elect their leaders. Their first supervising agency is the local Daoist association, whose administrators include ordained Daoists as well as supportive lay followers.

Above and beyond this, temples and practitioners are administered by the Bureau of Religious Affairs, which is staffed by hard-core Communists with little patience for religious needs or activities. With an increase in local travelers, foreign visitors, and Overseas Chinese – who were essential in the religious revival after 1980 – Daoist institutions also came to be supervised by the Department of Tourism. Manned by foreign-oriented and more modern officials, the Department is interested mainly in revenue and the smooth entertainment of large crowds. It, too, has no concern with religious activities or the creation of a spiritual atmosphere.

The effect of this multiple administration is twofold. On the one hand, the two agencies tend to squabble over money, and if one gets more from a temple activity than the other, they alert the police and accuse monks of nefarious activities. On the other hand, they channel state and tourist funds toward restoration and expansion, so that many Daoist sanctuaries now have a revived and energized look, are open to the public, and offer a wide variety of Daoist resources (books, charms, herbs, teas, martial training).

There is great regional variation in the degree of support and cooperation between these agencies and Daoist institutions. In some areas (Sichuan, Hubei), Daoists are made very welcome and religious activities and festivals are supported with enthusiasm. In others (Shaanxi, Shandong, Hunan), the politicians are wary of all religious organizations and a restrictive mode prevails.

Important centers

The most important Daoist centers are on mountains. The five sacred mountains of traditional China all have Daoist institutions: Mount Tai in the east (1545m, near Confucius's birthplace in Qufu), Hua in the west (2200m, near Xi'an), Heng in the north (2017m), Nanyue (Hengshan) in the south (1290m, near Changsha), and Mount Song in the center (1440m, near Luoyang; south of Shaolin monastery). Most of these mountains have multiple peaks and include large-scale temples at the bottom as well as numerous hermitages and monasteries perched on mountain tops and built into cliffs.

In addition, there are several important Daoist mountains. They are Mount Longhu, the headquarters of the Celestial Masters in Shanxi; the Zhongnan mountains (west of Xi'an) with Louguan, where Laozi allegedly transmitted the *Daode jing*; Mount Qingcheng in Sichuan (northwest of Chengdu), where Zhang Daoling founded the

Celestial Masters; Mount Mao near Nanjing, the location of the Highest Clarity revelations; Mount Lao in Shandong (near Qingdao), where the Complete Perfection school developed; and Mount Wudang in Hubei (near Wuhan), the state-sponsored sanctuary of the Dark Warrior and main Daoist martial arts academy.

In terms of inner city temples, the most prominent is the White Cloud Temple in Beijing, headquarters of the CDA and a major training center; another White Cloud Temple is found in Shanghai, which also houses the popular City God temple now run by Daoists. Beyond the eastern seaboard, there are: the Black Sheep Temple (Qingyang gong) in Chengdu (Sichuan), where Laozi supposedly met Yin Xi before they emigrated to the west; the Eight Immortals Temple (Baxian an) in Xi'an, the headquarters of the local association; and the Temple of Mystery and Wonder (Xuanmiao guan) in Suzhou, a flourishing institution in the downtown shopping district.

The Complete Perfection school has another important temple in Ruichong (Shaanxi), the alleged birthplace of the immortal Lü Dongbin. Moved due to dam construction to Longquan village in 1959, the Palace of Eternal Happiness (Yongle gong) is the site of exquisite murals from the thirteenth century and a major ritual center.

Daoist lives

Within this overall framework there are five reasons why someone would pursue a Daoist career. The most common is to take refuge from the vicissitudes of civilian life. Statistics show that hardly any Daoists have advanced education, and most have barely made it to a high-school diploma. They often come from low-class families with no resources or from communities with no job opportunities. In some cases, their marriage has turned sour or they have a health issue, and they simply do not know where else to turn.

With little religious motivation and less understanding of the tradition, they just want to be comfortable and enjoy their state stipend. They do their duty manning the entrance gate or selling souvenirs, but most of the time they play games, watch TV, chat, or otherwise hang out.

The comfort-seekers make up about 80 percent of all Daoists. The remaining 20 percent divide into two groups: approximately 16 percent who wish to do community service or advance in the administration, and maybe 4 percent who are in Daoism for spiritual cultivation or business profit.

Community service

A Daoist career lends itself easily to community service, either on the local level, where small temples play an increasingly important role in satisfying the religious needs of the people, or on the national level, where well-trained (and properly indoctrinated) representatives are needed to run central institutions, Daoist associations, and relevant state agencies.

Local temples have revived continuously since the 1980s. First, priests and monks were allowed to return from their lay occupations as farmers, carpenters, or vendors, and buildings were reassigned from their civilian uses. Then funds were raised for the materials and workers necessary to refurbish the places, add new wings, and create new statues and ritual implements. As time went on and private ownership became possible again, the temples were also given back their land holdings so that they became self-sufficient. Many temples rent out their lands for planting or to be built on, thus ensuring a private income in addition to the state stipends.

As religious restrictions lessened, communities in many places recovered their ritual needs – although often ancestral tablets and ritual manuals had been burned during the Cultural Revolution and are lost forever. Today, all major life transitions (birth, marriage, retirement, death) are marked by religious ceremonies, Daoists taking a large portion of this market. In addition, the old practices of purification, exorcism, healing, and blessings (for houses, cars, and businesses) as well as the production of talismans, amulets, charms, and other gewgaws are flourishing greatly. The numbers of local priests and monks – with the Celestial Masters dominating the southeast (Fujian) area – have increased drastically and the popularity of personal and community rituals is on the rise.

On a more official level, Daoist community service can also take the form of administrative work in one or the other state-sponsored institution, from the local Daoist association through the large training monasteries to government agencies. Daoists on this level have to be ordained centrally and cannot just hold one or the other local lineage. They are accordingly better educated and there is a much higher degree of standardization in doctrine and practices. The tendency is for an increased demand toward such centralization and, as more training seminaries are founded around the country, there will be more officially sponsored religious education.

Hermit life

Another Daoist lifestyle choice is being a hermit outside institutional structures. Daoists have traditionally supported life away from society, and to the present day there are hermits in far-off mountain reaches as well as in the inner cities. Mountain hermits tend to subsist on a minimum of food and drink, often gathering nuts or herbs that they eat and sell for basic necessities such as flour and cooking oil. Almost all had to descend during the Cultural Revolution, take on employment, and even get married. There is only one case reported where a hermit, interviewed by Bill Porter in the early 1990s, upon the question of how he fared under Mao Zedong, said: "Mao who?"

Most mountain hermits choose the isolation intentionally, but there are also situations where a particularly unruly monk, who does not conform to state-imposed discipline, is banished to a distant cliff. Left out of the tourist loop and thus deprived of income, he becomes a spiritual seeker by default. Other hermits do not even retire to the mountains but live in the cities, where they do minimum work to keep themselves alive and otherwise engage in Daoist cultivation. An example is a former vice-abbot of a famous mountain monastery. In 2006, he got tired of continuous politicking and left the official hierarchy for a withdrawn existence in the cities. There he is all but unknown and can live in splendid isolation.

All hermits share the goal of attaining personal realization through Daoist cultivation – unlike martial arts, an activity hardly ever found in monastic institutions today. They are ordained as lineage holders and specialize in specific methods, be they dietary, breathing, exercise, meditation, or a combination of these. Unless they take on disciples who spread the word of their accomplishments, they remain hidden, and there is no way of telling how common this phenomenon is in China today.

Daoism as business

A completely different Daoist lifestyle has emerged recently with the growth of a free-market economy and the rise of newly rich business executives who are in desperate need of stress release and body pampering. This is the path of Daoism as business or the establishment of Daoist spas.

An example is the Intertwined Dragon Temple (Shaolong guan) in the southwestern metropolis of Chongqing. A vast complex of various buildings, nicely refurbished in traditional style, it contains not only worship, lecture, and meditation halls, but also extensive areas dedicated to massages, physical treatments, medical diagnoses, herbal prescriptions, and exercise. It has modern hotel facilities for visitors, spacious rooms and up-to-date dining areas, a computer lab to stay in touch with business affairs, hot tubs and pools to languish in after working out, as well as all sorts of other amenities associated with pricey retreats.

Its infomercial, shown by Abbot Li Jun at the end of the Third International Conference on Daoism in 2006, presents the monastery entirely as a center for the unique acquisition of Daoist secrets of long life, following the ancient model of the Yellow Emperor who, about 5,000 years ago, concocted his cinnabar elixir on this very mountain. Its monks appear as model healers, serving as grand masters of qigong and performing acrobatic moves of taiji quan and other martial arts. They offer a new version of Daoist service by teaching the newly wealthy and accordingly stressed-out class of upscale Chinese businessmen how to relax and keep themselves fit.

A Beijing spa

Similar spas are springing up all over the country, some even placed in the gym section of modern high-rise apartments. An example is the Daoist Long Life Center in the Blue Iris Garden (Qingzhi yuan) condo complex in Beijing. Run by Wang Chengya, a Beijing University graduate and White Cloud ordinand, the Center occupies several floors of the community building. Arranged according to fengshui principles, its rooms are extremely well furnished and tastefully decorated with Daoist art.

Clients are first taken to two intake rooms to have themselves evaluated for physical ailments and astrological predispositions. They then receive a treatment plan, which includes dietary suggestions, herbal concoctions, special teas as well as herbal baths, massages, facials, qigong, and healing exercises. The Center employs an extensive staff and has a high rate of success, treating senior party cadres, the prime minister, and increasing numbers of foreigners.

Its founder, who owns twenty-nine companies including herbal nurseries, publishing businesses, and other resorts, is himself a Daoist scholar and teaches its theory and methods at reputable academies. His work shows how Daoism can develop and what an impact it can have when taken on by gifted, enterprising individuals who are not fleeing society and have no need to resort to hyperbole of any kind.

Ritual activities

As Daoism makes further inroads into various levels of Chinese society and serves wider needs of the community, its ritual activities increase. In addition to private rites and village events, Daoists also perform large-scale ceremonies, known as Grand Offering (*dajiao*). Traditionally held once every sixty years to coincide with the sixty-year cycle, they are venues to renew the world and society, pray for peace and stability, and enhance community cohesion.

A Grand Offering is an elaborate event that can last from three days to several weeks. It involves the establishment of temporary altar facilities, the participation of several Daoist troupes, the invitation of major deities, and continued ritual services with full community participation. Historically the successor of the medieval purgation (*zhai*), the first Grand Offering was held in 759 to pray for peace and stability after the devastation of the An Lushan rebellion. In the Song dynasty, the Offering became the main venue of public Daoist ritual, and various detailed descriptions survive from the eleventh and thirteenth centuries.

No major Daoist rites were held in China from 1947 to 1993, when a first Grand Offering took place at the White Cloud Temple in Beijing. This was followed by a ceremony on Mount Min in Shanxi in 2001. In addition, offerings were held in Taiwan in 1980 (Gaoxiong), 1984 (Tainan), and 1998 (Taipei, at the Lü Dongbin

Figure 11.2 A temporary altar at the Grand Jiao

temple). The most recent was a Grand Offering to the Highest Heaven (*luotian dajiao*) held in Hong Kong in November, 2007.

The Hong Kong offering

The specific purpose of this Offering, which lasted for eleven days, was to pray for world peace, the harmony of yin and yang, and the cessation of all disasters, as well as to give thanks for ten years of mainland rule over Hong Kong and forty years of successful activities of the Hong Kong Taoist Association.

The ceremony was sponsored by various Daoist organizations in Hong Kong and was accompanied by a lecture series, an international conference, an art exhibition, a martial arts competition as well as several concerts and book publications. It took place at the Yuen-Yuen Institute, a Daoist center in Tsuen Wan in the southwest part of the New Territories. The Institute, which has both resident and visitor facilities and can easily accommodate large crowds for vegetarian meals, has ample space behind its main halls.

Situated auspiciously on a north–south axis, protected in the back by gorgeous mountains and overlooking both city and ocean, the sacred space was filled with six temporary halls plus an imposing triple gate for the ceremony. The timing

Figure 11.3 The officiant at the Grand Jiao

was auspicious as well: activities began on the fourth of the tenth lunar month (November 13), the day of the traditional La Festival, and ended on the fifteenth (November 24), the full moon day which was also the day of Lower Prime Festival, the last of the Three Primes of the ancient Daoist calendar.

Over 400 Daoists, many of them women and including numerous lay disciples, participated in continuous ritual activities for those eleven days, with the exception of the eleventh (November 20), which was considered unlucky. They came in groups of various sizes, representing Daoist institutions and bringing their various forms of Daoist ritual and incantation to the meeting. Groups came from Hong Kong (18), mainland China (14), Singapore (3), Taiwan (1), Macao (1), and Hawai'i (1).

Daoist gods

The Offering was dedicated to the Highest Heaven and involved the presence of numerous Daoist deities, representing the entire pantheon. They were arranged in six halls. The Three Pure Ones, central to the main heavens, schools, and scriptures, were placed in the main sanctuary at the far end of the sacred compound. It was the site for the most important rites, in which all different groups participated.

To its right was a hall to the Jade Emperor, a popular deity adopted into the pantheon who is in charge of the celestial administration. Usually he is assisted by the Ruler of Fates, who manages the records of life and death; and the King of Hell, who supervises all activities in the underworld prisons. To the left of the main sanctuary was the hall to stellar deities: Sun, Moon, Northern Dipper, Pole Star, Purple Tenuity, and other heavenly bodies that furnish residences for immortals and govern the rhythms of the world.

Next were two halls for divinities associated with specific schools. On the right was the Celestial Masters Hall with a special altar for Zhang Daoling. Opposite was a hall dedicated to Lü Dongbin, the Eight Immortals, as well as the founder of Complete Perfection, Wang Chongyang, and his main disciples, the Seven Perfected. Last, but certainly not least, and facing the main sanctuary was a hall dedicated to the Numinous Officials, a host of 1,200 celestial administrators arranged in a hierarchical system, commonly designated by the ranks of immortal, perfected, and sage.

Popular gods adopted into Daoism were not given a special hall. To conclude this survey of the pantheon, they include deities with a special portfolio and divide into two major groups: general protectors, such as the God of Wealth (Guandi), the City God (Chenghuang), the Goddess of Mercy (Guanyin), and the Goddess of Wayfarers (Mazu); as well as healing deities, including the Yellow Emperor, the King of Medicines (Sun Simiao), the Goddess of the Morning Clouds (Bixia yuanjun), and the Lady Who Brings Children (Songzi niangniang).

Ornamentation

Each hall at the Grand Offering centered on an altar, featuring an image as well as the official seal of the residing deity together with various tablets and ritual implements. Colorfully veiled in red and yellow curtains of soft gauze, they created the feeling of a gradually deepening cave. In front of the hall was a table, ornately decked out with offerings of flowers, fruit, and incense, as well as a large incense burner where community participants would place joss sticks at specified intervals.

Each hall also was furnished with tables and folding chairs for the participants to sit and do their chanting. On the left of the main sanctuary was room for the musical troupe, consisting of about ten players of percussion, string, and wind instruments. The entire area was wired for sound and large speakers created a massive presence of music and chanting.

In addition, the main area was widely covered with multi-colored flags, banners, and sacred lamps. The flags represented various levels of the cosmos by showing the symbols of the five sacred mountains, the four heraldic animals, and the twenty-eight lunar stations. The banners were printed with the mystic talismans of various groups of Daoist heavens, including the Three Clarities. The lamps again showed the holy signs of the twenty-eight lunar mansions, representing the order of time in the universe.

Ritual activities

The Grand Offering usually involves an initial opening of the altar area and formal invitation of the participating deities – visualized in their splendid garb by the officiating priest. It then proceeds through several cycles of scripture recitation, repentance ceremonies, and audiences with the gods (that include the submission of official presentations, memorials, petitions, and mandates) to conclude with the sending-off of the deities.

The Hong Kong ceremony, since it was carried by large numbers of different kinds of Daoists, featured many variations of these rites, so that on any given day there would be repentance services and audiences in several halls. Both the initial invitation and final send-off as well as the big offering to Highest Heaven were held at the main sanctuary and involved participants from all groups, as did the huge concluding banquet that celebrated the successful blessing of the cosmos.

Figure 11.4 Ceremonial procession at the Grand Jiao

The qigong connection

Qigong is a system of slow body movements in coordination with deep breathing and mental guiding of body energies that releases tension, effects healing, and contributes to overall well-being. Adapting it from traditional Daoist and medical exercises, the Communist Party gave it its modern name and set out to transform it, cleansing it from all ancient cosmology and "superstitions" and making it compatible with Western science. Over the five decades of its existence, qigong has spread and changed, affecting both the Chinese people and Daoism in various ways.

History

In its first decade (until 1964), it served as the main vehicle of health maintenance for Party cadres and was predominantly practiced in a medical setting, both in specialized qigong clinics and general hospitals. During the Cultural Revolution it was banned, clinics and hospital wards were closed, and practitioners went underground. In the1970s, when practitioners "came out of the mountains," qigong became a popular movement, encouraging self-healing by ordinary people in parks – the kind of practice best known in the West. In the 1980s, the government set up various national organizations to control the rapidly expanding scene while the main focus of the practices shifted to the acquisition of extraordinary powers, like clairvoyance, telepathy, psychokinesis, distance healing, and so on.

The craze for these powers slowed down in the 1990s, when several masters were arrested for fraud and many feats were unveiled as quackery. While the state issued more stringent regulations, demanding that qigong leaders be certified doctors or therapists, millions of followers found themselves at a loss of who to trust. This vacuum was filled by new groups that made ethics a fundamental part of the practice. To all intents and purposes new religions, they claimed to lead their followers to transcendent salvation.

This in turn resulted in the emergence of Falungong, a messianic cult centered on the founder Li Hongzhi who was set to rid the world of demons and prepare a generation of purified and highly empowered followers for the new world to come. To this end, he controlled people's lives and minds, prohibiting the reading of anything except his books and the practice of healing other than through his practices. He was also opposed to mixed marriages, women's autonomy, and various other modern features. His group was outlawed and has been actively persecuted since 1999. The fall-out from this is that qigong in China has shrunk considerably and is no longer practiced in public. Exercise in parks tends to focus on taijiquan which is officially sanctioned as a sport (soon to be part of the Olympics), Western-style aerobics, or ballroom dancing. Also, yoga is making great headway in China, seen entirely as a physical workout and to the exclusion of all spirituality or religious context.

Daoist response

Daoist temples, adapting to the physical fitness market, sponsor exercise practice for lay followers and encourage it among its residents. Some of them have also developed specific styles so that, in addition to Wudang martial arts, there are now systems related to various holy places, such as the "Mount Emei Sage Style" qigong form in twenty-four movements that will open energy channels and enhance personal healing abilities. In addition, they have adopted bodily well-being as part of Daoist doctrine, integrating it with the traditional emphasis on moderation and longevity techniques.

An example of this is found in a small pamphlet from Mount Qingcheng (Sichuan), entitled *Daojiao yangsheng quanxiao geyan* (Pertinent Words on Daoist Long Life and Filial Piety). Written in an easygoing, popular style and rhythmic verses that are easy to remember, it covers various activities and aspects of daily living. It begins:

> Work the body and live long;
> Enjoy your pleasures and cut life short.
> Rest in quietude to nurture spirit;
> Move with vigor to exercise the body.
> If you can rest and move in equal measure,
> You can extend your destined years.
> And if you really want health,
> Then practice every day.

It then recommends that one should do exercise of some sort or the other

> Practice self-massage.
> Study fist or sword,
> Kick a ball,
> Or go for a walk,
> Maybe bathe in sunlight –
> But never cease your efforts.

In addition, the text stresses the need for a healthy diet, limiting the intake of fat, sugar, and salt while eating much greenery and vegetables. "It's O.K. to drink a little wine, but tea is better – and don't smoke!" Also, not unlike traditional longevity texts, it recommends that one never fill the stomach and take walks after a meal. "And when you eat," it says, "start with a nice, hot soup, then even in old age you won't be tired." The only more religious note in this otherwise entirely health-centered booklet is an encouragement to "accumulate merit" by doing good deeds and behaving ethically. But again, it is not morality for its own sake. Instead, it will aid the attainment of long life by keeping one's conscience clean and one's mind pure.

Key points you need to know

- Daoism today is subject to political interference. It was suppressed until the early 1980s and has since made a major comeback, but it is still administered through various governement agencies, including the Chinese Daoist Association with many branches, the Bureau of Religious Affairs, and the Department of Tourism.
- Ordained Daoists are either disciples of individual masters whose lineage they continue or trained in large state-sponsored institutions that also require courses in Marxism. Most join the religion to escape from civilian life and take it easy. Some are dedicated to do community service, filling the rising ritual needs of the population or working for government agencies. Few, but influential members are hermits or set themselves up in business, mainly utilizing Daoist health practices.
- Communal Daoists engage in rituals, both personal and village-based. They also, every few years sponsor a Grand Offering, which serves to renew the world and strengthen peace. An example of such a rite held in Hong Kong in 2007 shows the grand scale of the ritual, the cooperation of numerous Daoist groups, the continuation of the tradition, and the cultural impact of Daoist practice.
- Individual Daoists may also practice health exercises which in China are now known as qigong – a Communist supported, cleansed version of traditional practices. Matching the dominant emphasis on physical training, they incorporate health advice into their modernized doctrines.

Discussion questions

1. How are religious organizations run in the West? Are temple/church leaders elected? What kind of councils, committees, management offices do they have? How are they funded? How does tourism enter the picture?
2. Are there any large-scale rituals comparable to the Grand Offering in other countries or religions? What kind? Do members of other religions come together in joint ceremonies even though they belong to different sects?
3. Look up qigong on the Web and examine some forms. How is it different from yoga? What are some claims people make about its effects? What is its appeal?

Further reading

Herrou, Adeline. 2005. *La vie entre soi: Les moines taoïstes aujurd'hui en Chine*. Nanterre: Société Ethnographique.

Katz, Paul R. 2000. *Images of the Immortal: The Cult of Lü Dongbin at the Palace of Eternal Joy.* Honolulu, HI: University of Hawai'i Press.

Lagerwey, John. 1987. *Taoist Ritual in Chinese Society and History.* New York: Macmillan.

Ownby, David. 2007. *Falun Gong and China's Future.* New York: Oxford University Press.

Palmer, David. 2007. *Qigong Fever: Body, Science and Utopia in China.* New York: Columbia University Press.

Pas, Julian F., ed. 1989. *The Turning of the Tide: Religion in China Today.* Hong Kong: Oxford University Press.

Porter, Bill. 1993. *The Road to Heaven: Encounters with Chinese Hermits.* San Francisco, CA: Mercury House.

Wang, Yi'e. 2006. *Daoism in China: An Introduction.* Warren, CT: Floating World Editions.

12 *Western adaptations*

In this chapter

In the course of its long history, Daoism has been transmitted and adapted variously beyond China. Deeply embedded in Chinese language and culture, its ritual and communal practices have generally been less adaptable, but *Daode jing* thought, tales of immortals, and the various longevity and meditation techniques have found eager audiences. Especially Daoist thought and long life practices have spread in several East Asian countries, notably Korea, Japan, and Vietnam.

In the West, too, the best known and most widespread aspect is Daoist thought; many concepts and maxims of the *Daode jing* have made their way into American and European culture. Much less well known and embedded in a different social milieu is the transmission of Daoist temples and ritual structures. Many remain within the framework of Chinese immigrants, but some organizations also attract Western devotees.

Most recent is the Western adaptation of Daoist-inspired health practices and meditations. Following in the wake of increased health awareness and the popularity of yoga and Buddhist meditation, Daoist associations, centers, and masters are becoming popular. However, not all of them are, properly speaking, Daoist; rather, they often focus on qigong and taiji quan.

Main topics covered

- Transmission in East Asia
- Western apperception
- Temples and communities
- Health practices

Transmission in East Asia

In comparison to other religions, Daoism is a hybrid. Most religions tend to be either ethnic or universal. That is to say, an ethnic religion is embedded in a certain culture to the point where one has to be born into a specific country or ethnic community or else adopt the culture to a large extent (e.g. Hinduism, Shintō, Judaism). A universal religion, on the other hand, is freely chosen by the individual and has core principles independent of local culture. As a result, it moves easily from country to country, changing somewhat in the process but still retaining its essence (e.g. Buddhism, Christianity, Islam).

Daoism does not fall into either of these categories but has aspects of both. Its rituals, with formal petitions in classical Chinese presented in imperial-style audiences to various gods – many of whom, especially in modern Daoism – are either socially or locally anchored in China, are more on the ethnic side and do not lend themselves easily to transmission. Its philosophy, notably the thought of the *Daode jing*, and its practices, especially longevity techniques and energy-based meditations, have no such limitations. They can be translated into many different languages, are independent of local connections, and – most importantly – have a strong appeal to people all over the world. As a result, there is relatively little ritual Daoism in countries beyond China but a pervasive influence and growing culture of Daoist thought and health practices.

Korea, Japan, and Vietnam

The three East Asian countries with the most Daoist influence are Korea, Japan, and Vietnam. All three had a close relationship with the Chinese imperial court: Vietnam was part of the Chinese empire for over 1,000 years; Korea served as a vassal state by sending regular tributes and emissaries, and Japan adopted large segments of Chinese political organization and culture, especially in the Heian era (Tang dynasty). All three, moreover, made classical Chinese their official language, modified and slowly replaced as independent alphabets were created – *hinagana* in Japan in the 800s, *hangul* in Korea in the 1400s, and the Western alphabet in Vietnam under French occupation in the nineteenth century.

Ideas and immortals

As a result of these close ties, the *Daode jing* was transmitted early and has formed an important part of the countries' culture to the present day. Its sayings are well known, its thought has influenced political and economic thinking, and its concepts pervade the culture – as much as the traditional cosmology of yin-yang and the five phases. Similarly the stories of the *Zhuangzi* and tales of immortals have inspired the people's imagination, and there are famous hermits and magical masters in all three countries.

Thus, both Korea and Japan claim to be the original location of the paradise mountains of Penglai. They have various places of this name, some even with temples dedicated to the Chinese admiral who was supposed to discover them for the First Emperor. Both countries have also developed their own brand of Daoist mountain asceticism, best known from the Japanese tradition of Shugendō, which integrates the Buddhist goal of enlightenment, Shintō beliefs in sacred mountains, and Daoist magical and ritual practices (spells, incantations, talismans, charts, fasting, exercises, and various exorcistic rites of empowerment.) Shugendō is still quite common today; it is also a key factor in Agon-shū, one of the new new religions of Japan, which was founded in 1984.

Official practice

In a more official vein, the East Asian countries adopted various Daoist institutions and rituals, especially as they developed under the Tang. There was thus a certain degree of Daoist influence on the Japanese Tennō system, while Korean rulers engaged in various performances of offerings for the sake of the state and established Daoist-based state temples, and Vietnamese kings followed Daoist state-religion models. In all cases, this adaptation involved the integration of Daoist cosmology and ordination patterns; it also brought the worship of Daoist gods such as the Queen Mother of the West, the Northern Dipper, and the Lord of Mount Tai.

Aristocrats, moreover, eagerly took to the practice of holding a vigil on the night of the fifty-seventh day of the sixty-year cycle to prevent the Three Worms – who live in the body as emissaries of the celestial administration – from ascending to heaven and making their (potentially damaging) report. Named *gengshen* or in Japanese *kōshin* after the day of their ascent, the practice involves purification exercises and a vigil, based on the assumption that the worms, like souls, can only leave the body if and when the person is asleep.

Aristocrats enjoyed this practice very much, holding extensive vegetarian feasts in conjunction with community activities and prayers to a protective deity in charge of helping believers. A tantric god known as the Bluefaced Vajrapani (Shōmen kongō), this deity was added to the practice under Buddhist influence in the Tang dynasty. Although meant to be a time of confession and repentance, the Kōshin vigil thus became a major social event in medieval East Asia. Today it is quite unknown in China, but still observed in conjunction with health fairs for seniors at certain Buddhist temples in Japan.

New developments

Since the seventeenth century, Daoism has been part of forming new religions in East Asia. It brought a strong culture of internal alchemy to Korea, and the practice of honoring and following morality books to both Korea and Japan. Partly carried by immigrants, partly encouraged by the adoption of Neo-Confucianism as state doctrine in both countries, new Daoist texts arrived, were studied and interpreted, and became part of a developing tradition.

Often linked with the transmission of Chinese medical materials, Daoism also provided access to ways of self-cultivation and personal improvement, and in this role has inspired the founding of certain new religions, especially in Korea. These included the Donghak (Eastern Doctrine) religion (now called Chōndo kyo or Teaching of Heavenly Principles), founded by Choi Jaewu in 1860, and the Jūngsan kyo (Teaching of Jūngsan), founded by Kang Ilsun in 1901. They both make ample use of Daoist talismans and ecstatic excursions, worship gods of the Daoist pantheon, and name immortality as their key spiritual goal.

In Vietnam, too, a new religion called Caodai arose under Daoist influence. Founded in 1921 by Ngo Minh Chien after a revelation from the creator god Caodai – the High Tower and heart of the universe. It integrates all major world religions through the notion of Caodai's dispensation to the Buddha, Laozi, Confucius, Moses, Jesus, Mohammed, and finally Ngo. In practice it combines the virtues and social consciousness of Confucianism, the precepts and vegetarianism of Buddhism, and the rituals and talismans of Daoism, with an organization patterned on the Catholic Church and guided by a central leader known as "pope." Caodai has undergone a varied fate through the twentieth century; it is still active today, especially in southern Vietnam.

Western apperception

Just as different aspects of Daoism have attracted different audiences in East Asia over the millennia, so the modern transmission of the religion to the West matches a variety of interests and works in multiple social contexts. Most generally one can say that philosophical or literati Daoism was attractive first of all to missionaries and later to the intellectual elite. It offered a different way of looking at the world, proposed new principles of life, and encouraged a change of attitude toward the world. Today it is seen as opening a balance to the American (and Western) tendencies toward uncontrolled growth, environmental exploitation, corporate greed, and political corruption. Small is beautiful, and most happiness can be found in a simple life.

Organized Daoism with its priestly hierarchy, religious scriptures, and devotional practices, on the other hand, fosters a sense of connection to the gods, community integration, as well as ritual services of protection, purification, blessings, and exorcism. It came to the West with Chinese immigrants and in close connection with Chinese popular religion and has remained for the most part an ethnically based organization, housed in inner-city temples and supported by local residents.

Longevity Daoism, with its exercises, meditations, diets, and fengshui, has only been available in the West for a few decades. It appeals to well-situated, health-conscious people who are concerned with personal well-being, business success, and environmental protection. They often come to the practices for health reasons – be it recovery after an accident, weakness due to chronic disease, increased signs of aging, or the wish to reduce body stress exerted by contact sports, hard martial arts, or power yoga. Typically practitioners begin by looking for merely physical benefits, but then develop a sense of *qi* flowing in the body and gain an empowerment of a completely different sort. While many stop there, some move on to inquire more deeply into the conceptual and historical background of the practices and thus encounter Daoism. From there, some go on to advanced training in internal alchemy and more spiritual techniques whose ultimate goal is complete health leading to immortality.

Daoist thought

Daoist thought in the West is represented first and foremost in the *Daode jing*, the best-known representative of Daoism wherever it appears. In the West, it attracted first attention through a translation into Latin by Jesuit missionaries, presented to the British Royal Society in 1788. This rendition hoped to show that the mysteries of the Christian faith were known to the ancient Chinese, matching Dao with God, like logos conveying the triple sense of supreme being, reason, and word.

The first English translation by James Legge (1831–1905) appeared in 1891. It, too, attempted to impose Christian theology onto the Chinese text. This changed in the course of the twentieth century, so that by the end of World War II a number of translations and interpretations had appeared that attempted to read the text in its own right and do justice to Chinese thinking. By now, there are over 300 English translations of the text and its concepts have made major inroads into Western societies. The dominant mode of apperception is individual and personal; people appreciate the philosophy as it helps them to change their own thinking and their way of being in the world. Unlike in China, where the text has always also had a strong public dimension, there are very few political concerns associated with the *Daode jing* in the West.

Key notions

Popular *Daode jing* ideas tend to involve four distinct areas of application: the Western tendency toward action and progress; the importance of reducing stress; the reversal of some common cultural and ethical values; and concerns for the environment and social harmony.

Balancing the Western push for increased consumption, the need to always have more, always get new things, and always acquire bigger objects, is the essential idea of the text to "know when it is enough." This means that there is a level of material wealth and internal satisfaction that requires one to go along with the present and let go of advancement and progress. Having reached this point, an increase in consumption, a rise in position, or a multiplication of wealth will add nothing further to one's community status or internal well-being. On the contrary, it will create complications and various kinds of difficulties that are entirely unnecessary and make one feel worse, not better. This latter concept in the *Daode jing* is expressed as the "continuous alternation of yin and yang." Understanding the world as moving in an ongoing flow of rise and fall, increase and decline, people can make wise decisions. Too much growth will result in reduction; a period of calmness and apparent stagnation is the beginning of a new surge of energy. There cannot always be nothing but growth; nature requires moves in all directions, up and down, rise and decline, come and go.

Nonaction

The preferred attitude to take, then, is "nonaction," a way of being that allows the flow of nature to move at its own speed and in its own way. This can be applied to relationships, parenting, careers, businesses, and much more. In parenting, for example, it is wise to allow children to make their own discoveries, develop their dominant talents, and grow at their own rate. There is no point in pushing them to do things they are ill equipped for or are not ready to tackle. Businesses, too, have a dynamic of their own, matching the tendencies of the market and moving along with the needs of the populace. There is little one can do if the circumstances are simply not right.

On the other hand, the *Daode jing* asserts that "by doing nothing, there is nothing that is not done." This means that, instead of being constantly active and on the move, trying to control and manage everything, one steps back and lets things unfold naturally. Matching one's activities to the dominant patterns of the time, all will work out for the best – and with a great deal more pleasure and less stress. A reduction in personal tension is also the target of another famous *Daode jing* saying: "A thousand-mile journey starts with the first step." This guides people to be patient and make small efforts toward big goals. Rather than trying to do everything at once, one should move in small steps, keeping a clearly defined but limited goal purposefully in mind. Thus, for example, in writing a long paper or a book, one sets a goal to complete three or four pages on one specific aspect at one time, then moves on to the next.

Personal values

While action should be in accordance with the flow of things and in an attitude of patience and nonaction, the *Daode jing* also encourages certain key values. For example, it extols "weakness and softness," indicating that strength often does not prevail but creates more problems than it solves. Cultivating a value of gentleness and kindness, a laid-back relaxation, or an inner sense of fluidity will often be more satisfying and create better success, both with people and with situations, than exhibiting strength and using force – a philosophy that is put into concrete practice in the soft martial arts, such as taiji quan.

Another value in the *Daode jing* is truthfulness or reliability. It says: "True words are not beautiful; beautiful words are not true," emphasizing that one should always be honest and clear in what one says and not be taken in by the marvelous claims of some orators. Another Chinese proverb that expresses a similar idea is: "Dogs aren't good if they're good at barking." In other words, look to the quality of the person, not to his or her outward expression, and make sure you yourself express inner sincerity in word and deed.

A similar concept with a slightly different twist is expressed in the text's emphasis on seeing to the value of emptiness or what is not there: "Thirty spokes make a wheel, but it is the empty center that makes it work." This, as other sayings that speak of the bowl and the bellows, whose empty inner space makes them useful, indicate that one should look beyond the obvious and realize the value of what is not there. This goes for people as much as for spaces, utensils, and business dealings. The person who is quiet and restful often has more to offer than the party lion; a room can be so much more inviting if it is not filled to overflowing; a swimming pool or a tennis court are only effective if they are essentially empty.

Social impact

The person in the *Daode jing* who exemplifies these attitudes and values is the sage, ideally the ruler, but any individual who follows the principles of the text. Such a person, moreover, will not remain in a vacuum but his or her good values will have a lasting impact on society, creating a sense of stability and harmony wherever he or she goes.

This impact is never on a grand scale and does not involve political parties or elections. Rather, it begins with the transformation of small communities or social units that develop a model of simple living and show the importance of applying nonaction and using resources responsibly. Eventually the process leads to the realization of "naturalness," an overall balance in society and nature. This aspect of the Daoist teaching, moreover, connects most actively to modern ecology and has often been related to visions of environmental harmony and the protection of all species. Although nature in ancient China was seen more of a threat (with its wild animals and unpredictable weather patterns) than as being threatened, the concept of naturalness ties in closely with the overall attitude of live and let live, of harmony within oneself and with the world at large.

Temples and communities

The earliest presence of Daoist priests in the West occurred in the mid-nineteenth century in connection with the Gold Rush (1848–1855), when numerous Chinese emigrated to work on the great American railroad. They established communities and built local temples, some of which were staffed by Daoists and a few of which still remain in northern California.

Today, Chinese-based Daoist communities still have temples in major cities, such as New York, San Francisco, Los Angeles, and Toronto. In addition, there are also several ritual organizations run by ordained Westerners who attract a more ethnically diverse clientele. And, last but not least, there are efforts to create Chinese-style Daoist associations in various Western countries with the purpose of teaching a Daoist lifestyle and ritual practices.

Chinese communities

There are three Daoist temples in San Francisco: Quong Ming, Chi Sin, and Ching Chung Taoist and Buddhist Associations, founded in 1967, 1976, and 1978, respectively. They are all offshoots of Hong Kong organizations that follow the Longmen branch of Complete Perfection and actively "harmonize the three teachings:" they combine Confucian ethics with Buddhist meditation, Daoist practices, and popular rituals, such as ancestor worship. Specifically Daoist activities include veneration of Lü Dongbin and the practice of spirit-writing. They have a few hundred members each and cater primarily to the local immigrant community, for whom they perform practical services, such as weddings and funerals.

A similar organization is also found in New York City: the American Buddhist and Taoist Association, founded in 1979 by Hsien Yuen from Taiwan. Its temples have altars to both Buddhist and Daoist deities; they perform rituals and community services of various kinds. The congregation is small and consists mostly of Chinese-Americans.

Another set of Daoist temples is found in Toronto, Denver, and Tallahassee. They are run by Fung Loy Kok (Penglai Pavilion), founded in 1968 by Moy Linshin and Mui Mingte as a branch of the Yuen-Yuen Institute in Hong Kong. Claiming lineage to a sect based on Mount Hua, they established the Toronto shrine in 1981, followed by many others, including also centers in New Zealand and Australia. They have around 10,000 followers worldwide. Like its parent organization dedicated to the harmonization of the three teachings, these temples are different from other Chinese-based shrines in that they also teach taiji quan and qigong through an organization called the Taoist Tai Chi Society, thereby increasing their popularity and attracting a wider variety of members.

Western temples

Four Daoist temple organizations in the United States are run by Westerners: the Center of Traditional Taoist Studies by Alexei Anatole in Weston, Mass. (1970s); the Taoist Sanctuary by Kenneth Dickerson (Khigh Dhiegh) in Los Angeles (1970s); Orthodox Daoism of America (now Da Yuan Circle) by Charles Belyea (now Liu Ming) in Oakland, Calif. (1986); and the Abode of the Eternal Tao by Solala Towler in Eugene, Oregon (1993). They all have in common that they combine traditional ritual services with *Daode jing* and *Yijing* philosophy as well as with various health practices, such as breathing, diet, meditation, qigong, and soft martial arts.

Alexei Anatole is originally from Russia, where he studied with a Chinese martial arts master for twenty years and later received formal ordination as a Daoist priest. In the 1970s, he emigrated to the United States and established his temple in a suburban villa near Boston. Since 1994, it has also a formal association with the White Cloud Temple in Beijing. Anatole's teachings being rather exclusive, his community is small and consists mostly of Westerners who come every Saturday for joint practice and ritual services. The facility has a three-tiered layout, with an altar dedicated to a wide Daoist pantheon at the top, a reading and study room in the middle, and a martial arts studio at the bottom. He emphasizes the need to properly understand the *Daode jing*, on which he has written a commentary, as well as train physically to keep the *qi* moving harmoniously while yet also showing the proper ritual devotion.

A very similar combination appears in the Taoist Sanctuary in Los Angeles, one of the first Daoist organizations to receive official status as a "church." It was founded in the 1970s by Kenneth Dickerson (1910–1991), an American of Near Eastern descent who played Oriental villains in Hollywood movies, and Share Lew (b. 1918), an ordained Daoist and martial arts master from Guangdong. Now called the Taoist Institute, it has transformed into a martial arts and qigong center and focuses largely on health practices.

Further organizations

Orthodox Daoism of America, too, encourages a combination of practices and has been recognized as a church. It is different, though, in that its founder Charles Belyea, after training for many years in Tibetan Buddhism, claims to have received the transmission of Celestial Masters ritual from the Liu family in Taiwan in the late

1970s. He accordingly changed his name to Liu Ming and set up various small temples in northern California plus a branch in Seattle. Doubts about the authenticity of his ordination created a schism in his community, and he moved his center to Oakland in 2003. His community is small and consists entirely of Western adepts.

Solala Towler came to the practice of Daoism through health problems. He trained in several forms of qigong that helped his condition while immersing himself in the thought of the *Daode jing*. Continuing to grow as a Daoist, he opened a shrine dedicated to the Three Pure Ones, Lü Dongbin, and other deities in Eugene in 1993. There he offers ritual services as well as classes in meditation and health practices. He also publishes the quarterly journal *The Empty Vessel*, the only non-scholarly Western publication solely dedicated to Daoism.

The overall tendency among these Daoist communities is to begin with a ritual transmission from a Chinese lineage, then develop specifically Western forms of administration and practice. Those that hope to attract Westerners, moreover, tend to add martial arts and health practices to their curriculum. For the most part, the numbers are small, but some (such as Fung Loy Kok) have succeeded in creating a worldwide organization and are spreading rapidly.

Daoist associations

In imitation of the Chinese Daoist Association, several Western organizations have sprung up that aim to represent the different forms and models of Daoism. In the United States, a first effort was made in 2000 by Brock Silvers, an initiated Daoist who supports Daoism in all its forms and is also the head of the Taoist Restoration Society which provides funds for temple repair in China. The United States Taoist Association was conceived as a web-based organization in the hope to increase global awareness of the religion and provide networking and information. Never getting off the ground, it was succeeded by the American Daoist Association in 2004, which is still in its formative phase.

In contrast, the British Taoist Association is well established. Formed in 1996 by a group of four ordained Englishmen and with active help from Chinese masters, it represents various strands of Daoist teachings. Its major center sponsors weekend seminars on a variety of Daoist-related topics as well as retreats in qigong, Daoist exercises, and internal alchemy. Maintaining close contacts with its Chinese parent organization, the Eight Immortals Temple in Xi'an, the Association is officially recognized by the Chinese Daoist Association and supports temple restoration and other projects in China. It hopes to maintain an active exchange with Chinese practitioners and to spread Daoist thought and lifestyle in Britain.

Health practices

Chinese health practices and martial arts began to make serious inroads in the West in the late 1960s, after the 1965 repeal of the Asian Exclusion Act (established in the 1920s) opened American immigration to large numbers of Asians. As a result martial arts masters, Chinese medical doctors, fengshui practitioners, and other health-related professionals entered the country. When qigong began to boom in China in the 1970s, qigong masters arrived in the West; in the 1980s, moreover, the first serious Daoists – specialists of internal alchemy – began to gather followers and establish formal centers.

Today the scene of Chinese and/or Daoist health practices is highly complex and increasingly popular. It can be divided according to four types of teachers and practices, with the underlying commonality that the original masters were Chinese but current teachers tend to be Westerners, and followers come from all social strata and ethnic backgrounds.

Kinds of practitioners

First and most common are martial artists, taiji quan masters, and qigong healers who are concerned strictly with health issues and physical improvements. Like acupuncturists and practitioners of Chinese massage (Anmo, Tuina), they work within the framework of traditional yin-yang cosmology but make no claim to anything Daoist in their teachings. Well-known masters here include Roger Jahnke, James MacRitchie, Jerry Alan Johnson, and Jeffrey Mayer.

Next are practitioners who are still mainly martial artists and taijiquan masters yet also have some training in meditation (often Buddhist) who call themselves or their centers Daoist. They have come to Daoism from a combination of religious and health concerns and make every effort to represent the tradition in a Western setting. Stuart Olson, Paul Gallagher, Stephen Chang, Jerry Shuey, and Al Chung-liang Huang are examples of this kind.

A third group of teachers is similarly trained in physical cultivation and meditation, but they also have undergone Daoist initiation. They undertake medical cultivation and meditation with ritual overtones and retain a strong link with the Chinese tradition. Here we have Ken Cohen, Michael Rinaldini, Harrison Moretz, Scott Rodell, and B. K. Frantzis.

Finally, there are several serious adepts of internal alchemy who have training in physical cultivation and meditation but who have also advanced to more sophisticated levels of Daoist practice and whose goal goes beyond healing and reaches for transcendence and immortality. The most important groups here are Integral Way and Healing Dao.

Daoist living

All these practitioners, many of whom are members of the National Qigong Association (NQA), have in common that they teach a way of yin-yang living in the contemporary world, a lifestyle that focuses on the smooth flow of *qi* and includes various self-cultivation methods. They typically arrange their living space and furniture to optimize energy patterns with the help of fengshui and subscribe to a *qi*-friendly diet that pays attention to the seasons and consists largely of whole foods, organic vegetables, and hormone-free meat. They supplement this diet with herbs and minerals and, if they find themselves out of balance, consult Chinese health professionals for more specific herbal prescriptions, massages, acupuncture, and external qigong – the infusion of *qi* into a patient's body by a trained master.

In addition, they may also practice physical cultivation, such as the breathing method of the Six Healing Sounds, the exercise systems of *daoyin* and qigong, as exemplified in the Five Animal Frolics, and engage in meditation that focuses on the circulation of *qi* through the energy channels of the body (especially the central vessels of the torso in the Microcosmic Orbit) or on storing and enhancing the energy of the five organs (by sending good wishes to their organs and visualizing colored *qi* in them in a practice called the Inner Smile). A minority will in addition engage in ritual or devotional practices, relating to the deities and performing daily prayers.

The goal of the practice – and what attracts many Westerners to it – is to create a balance of different aspects of life, allowing *qi* to flow smoothly through work, family, friends, and solitary time without favoring one above all else. They also hope to develop a strong and healthy body so they can enjoy life and live long; and they encourage success, understood as good relationships, enjoyable work, and the creation of wealth.

Modern alchemy

Two groups go further in their ideal of opening paths to immortality in addition to health, wealth, and success. They are Integral Way and Healing Dao: established by Chinese-trained masters, they are today worldwide organizations with numerous certified instructors and thousands of members.

Integral Way was founded by Ni Hua-ching from Wenzhou, a coastal city in Zhejiang province. After training as a physician of traditional Chinese medicine, he moved to Taiwan in 1949, where he continued his medical practice and began to study Daoism. In 1976, two students of the Taoist Sanctuary brought Ni to California. They installed him in a house in Malibu, where he opened a shrine called the Eternal Breath of Tao and began teaching classes in a venue he named College of Tao. Over the years, his organizations have multiplied: his acupuncture clinic is known as the Union of Tao and Man; he founded Yosan University of Traditional Chinese Medicine; and he created the Integral Way for supported practice.

Ni began publishing books in English in 1979, and today, with the help of his students who work as volunteer editors, designers, and publishers, he has some sixty self-published books in print. He lives in semi-retirement, and his various ventures are headed by his sons, Maoshing and Daoshing. They enjoy wide popularity and include advanced training in internal alchemy.

Healing Dao is the other major Daoist training venue in the West. It operates in a more strictly Daoist mode and without any medical and acupuncture connection. It was founded by Mantak Chia (b. 1944), the son of a Chinese family in Thailand. Recognized early for his spiritual potential, he began Buddhist meditation at age six. During his teens, he went to live in Hong Kong, where he learned taiji quan, aikido, and kundalini yoga. There he met the Daoist master Yi Eng (One Cloud), who taught him internal alchemy. Achieving expertise in these methods, he decided to integrate them with Western thinking to enhance health, reduce stress, and open higher spiritual awareness.

In 1978, Chia established a first Western foothold in Huntington, NY; in 1983, he opened a center in New York City. Today he resides in northern Thailand but travels widely to give lectures and workshops. His main disciple is Michael Winn, who runs the Healing Dao University in North Carolina and supports local centers that can be found in all metropolitan area, such as the Healing Tao Institute run by Jampa Stewart in Austin, and the White Cloud Institute under directed by Caryn Diel in Santa Fe.

Stages of progress

Modern adaptations of internal alchemy see the unfolding of spirituality in three levels:

1. create healing energy, strengthen and calm the body;
2. change negative emotions into strong, positive energy;
3. develop creative and spiritual practices.

As outlined by Healing Dao in particular, on the first level practitioners engage in qigong and taijiquan, learning to consciously contract and relax their muscles to gain maximum flexibility and control. This serves to open the body and strengthen the *qi*-flow, greatly enhancing health and well-being. On the second level, they move into several meditations that clear negative emotions and enhance connection to the Dao. Practices include the Six Healing Sounds, the Microcosmic Orbit, and the Inner Smile.

From here they proceed through the recovery of *qi* from sexual energies to different levels of fusing the five phases back to their origin. As they master the redirection of internal, cosmic energies, they achieve the transformation of the self into a divine child. They thereby create an inner sense of oneness with Dao, an empowerment within the body that transcends the limitations of physical existence.

Key points you need to know

- Daoism divides into three major kinds: philosophical speculation, ritual and communal devotion, and health practices. All three have been transmitted beyond China and are making inroads in the West today, the philosophical and health aspects more so than ritual.
- In East Asia, Daoist traces are found in Korea, Japan, and Vietnam. People in these countries venerate the *Daode jing* and practice forms of Chinese medicine and Daoist cultivation. They have also integrated Daoist ritual and had state-sponsored Daoist institutions for a period in history.
- In the West, the *Daode jing* is widely known and people gain benefits from its concepts of nonaction, patterned change, softness, relaxation, and naturalness. Its thought is seen less in a political context than for personal balance and harmony which it achieves by counteracting certain dominant tendencies of the modern world.
- Ritual Daoist practice appears mainly in Chinese immigrant communities and is found in major cities, such as San Francisco and New York, but there are also some temples that integrate forms of cultivation and invite an ethnically diverse membership.
- Daoist health practices, finally, are often indistinguishable from generic martial arts, taiji quan, and qigong. They use the practices in a more spiritual and religious context, adding meditation and ritual, as well as – in the case of Integral Way and Healing Dao – subtler transformations through internal alchemy.

Discussion questions

1. What characteristics make a religion prone to being transmitted from culture to culture? What characteristic make such transmission impossible? Name three each and apply them to religions you know.
2. Find a translation of the *Daode jing* and read some parts of the text. Are there sayings that resonate with you? If so, why? How can you apply the text's maxims to your life?
3. Find a Taoist center or temple on the internet and examine its background, teachings, and practices. Do its offerings appeal to you? Would you go there for training? If so, why? Or, why not?

Further reading

Clarke, J. J. 2000. *The Tao of the West: Western Transformation of Taoist Thought*. New York: Routledge.

Hardy, Julia. 1998. "Influential Western Interpretations of the *Tao-te-ching*." In *Lao-tzu and the Tao-te-ching*, edited by Livia Kohn and Michael LaFargue, 165–88. Albany, NY: State University of New York Press.

Jung, Jae-Seo. 2000. "Daoism in Korea." In *Daoism Handbook*, edited by Livia Kohn, 792–820. Leiden: E. Brill.

Komjathy, Louis. 2004. "Tracing the Contours of Daoism in North America." *Nova Religio* 8.2: 5–27.

Masuo, Shin'ichiro. 2000. "Daoism in Japan." In *Daoism Handbook*, edited by Livia Kohn, 821–42. Leiden: E. Brill.

Siegler, Eliah. 2001. "The Tao of America: The History and Practice of Taoism in the US and Canada." Ph.D. diss., University of California, Santa Barbara.

Winn, Michael. 2006. "Transforming Sexual Energy with Water-and-Fire Alchemy." In *Daoist Body Cultivation*, edited by Livia Kohn, 151–78. Magdalena, NM: Three Pines Press.

Part IV

Reflections

13 *The nature and study of Daoism*

In this chapter

Daoism is hard to classify in standard terms: it has both ethnic and universal characteristics, embraces both cyclical and linear models, and engages with nature both through alignment and transcendence. It is, moreover, closely connected to various other aspects of Chinese culture, so that its study has tended to linger on the margins of sinological awareness.

As a field of its own, Daoist Studies began in the 1930s; it centered in Japan and France until the 1980s. Currently the field is rapidly expanding, and awareness of Daoism as a world religion is beginning to spread. Scholarly focus shifted first from the reading, dating, and analysis of texts to the study of history, biography, and the cosmology of specific schools. More recently it has moved on to include the critical examination of Daoist practices, such as ritual and self-cultivation. Only little effort has yet been made to study Daoist religious philosophy, political involvement, literature, art, music, and regional diversity. However, various activities, such as international conferences, workshops, websites, and dedicated journals, are moving the study along with great acumen.

Main topics covered

- Key characteristics
- Evolution of study
- Current trends
- Activities and resources

Key characteristics

In comparison with other religions, Daoism is difficult to pinpoint. It is neither clearly an ethnic nor a universal religion, but combines elements of both. It fits to a certain degree into the mold of ancient cosmologies that see the world as cyclical and create ritual and other patterns to match the ebb and flow of the seasons. Yet it also has a distinctly linear outlook in its vision of Great Peace and the complete overcoming of the human condition in an ideal world.

The same tension between cyclical and linear also applies to its relationship to nature: for the most part Daoist practices serve to create greater harmony with nature, better health in the individual, increased communication with the gods. But then there is also its ultimate goal of immortality, which clearly means to transcend all natural constrictions and live in an utterly nonhuman manner: eating *qi* instead of food, flying through the air instead of walking, communing with spirits instead of people, serving as officials in the celestial administration instead of the local yamen, and living forever instead of undergoing death, rebirth, and ancestral veneration.

Cultural connections

While all this makes it difficult to classify Daoism in a comparative framework, the picture is made more complex by the fact that the religion is also deeply embedded in Chinese culture, and often the boundaries between Daoism and other cultural aspects of China are blurred. The question "What is Daoism?" has plagued religion scholars and sinologists alike, and there is no easy answer. The boundaries between Daoism and mainstream thought, traditional cosmology, Chinese medicine, Buddhism, and popular religion are vague at best.

For example, even in its very early stages, the Daoist school of thought was closely related to other forms of Chinese philosophy, the term *dao* being used by all to refer to the underlying patterns of the cosmos and ideal way of governing. Throughout its history, moreover, the religion has never lost its connection to the Confucian mainstream, extolling Confucian virtues, integrating Confucian ethical principles, and often working closely with Confucians in the government of the empire. The same holds true for classical Chinese cosmology. Daoism actively participates in Chinese culture through the system of yin-yang and the five phases, a wide use of the *Yijing*, the traditional calendar, forms of divination (astrology, physiognomy), and various ways of manipulating *qi* (fengshui, music, exercises). Although often called "Daoist," there is nothing uniquely Daoist about any of these.

Similarly blurry boundaries exist between Daoist practice and Chinese medicine, Daoist and Buddhist forms of meditation and worldview, and between Daoist worship and popular cults. Daoism has, throughout its history, continued to adapt to the changing times by integrating new and varied forms of practice and visions of the universe. It has never stopped doing so, and the increasing popularity of Daoist health spas today testifies to this ongoing process of adaptation and transformation. While this explains the apparently amorphous nature of the religion and the wide variety of its concepts and practices, it also makes it even more difficult to answer the question: What is Daoism?

Unique aspects

Despite all these, however, there are a few things that make Daoism unique and delimit it clearly vis-à-vis other religions and various aspects of Chinese culture. Three are most important: the concept of Dao as the underlying power that creates and supports everything in the best possible way and to which one can relate through intuition and by cultivating nonaction; the understanding of multiple layers of heaven, occupied by pure, cosmic deities and transcendent bureaucrats, in their turn aided by human priests who become their equals through ritual transformation; and the firm conviction that the *qi*-based human body-mind can be transmuted into an immortal spirit entity through the systematic and persistent application of longevity techniques and advanced meditations.

Daoists thus differ from Confucians in that – without denying their value – they do not see social relationships and ethical rules as central nodes of life. They expand on traditional cosmology by proposing additional levels of heaven that are closer to the purity of creation and house uniquely Daoist gods. They work with the fundamental methods of Chinese medicine yet take them to new heights by applying them to transmutation above and beyond healing and long life.

In addition, they add a dimension to popular religion by enabling their priests to become otherworld officials who engage in bureaucratic interactions with the divine, often winning law suits against spirits and successfully delivering people from the depths of hell. And they are clearly distinct from Buddhists not only because their monks keep their hair and maintain relations to their native families while their nuns and priestesses are treated as equals, but also because they do not seek release from rebirth in the complete cessation of nirvana but find ultimate perfection in a permanent spirit existence in the heavens above.

Periodization

This being so, Daoism underwent a series of distinct stages of development. Three are most obvious: an ancient or classical phase that includes the philosophers and extends through the Han dynasty; a medieval or formative phase that sees the emergence of the major schools and their integration in the systematic hierarchy of the Tang; and a modern or popular phase characterized by the emergence of martial culture, the integration of popular gods, and the harmonization of the three teachings.

Each of these can be further subdivided into two sections each, delimiting the Warring States philosophers from the integrative cosmology, mythology, and medicine of the Han; the emergence of the separate schools through various revelations during the Six Dynasties from the integration and political application of Daoism in the unified empire of the Tang; and the open market and multiple facets of Song religion from the tight imperial restrictions and increasing local centers in the Ming and Qing.

To all this, moreover, a seventh stage should be added that marks Daoism today with its adaptation of modernity, relation to qigong, and spread to the West.

Evolution of study

Daoist Studies began in the 1930s after the Daoist canon, whose woodblocks had barely survived the centuries stored away in monastic basements, had been reprinted in Shanghai in 1923–1925. Japan and France, present in China as colonial powers, were the two countries that purchased copies of this newly available treasure trove, and it was there that the academic study of Daoism first emerged, with few Chinese scholars taking an active interest.

Key figures

The pioneers of Daoist Studies were Henri Maspero in France, Yoshioka Yoshitoyo in Japan, and Chen Jingyuan in China; their works are still classics in the field. The next generation of scholars furnished the grand old men of Daoist Studies, whose institutions and students are shaping it to the present day. They were Maxime Kaltenmark in France, Ōfuchi Ninji and Fukui Kōjun in Japan, and (more recently) Qing Xitai in China.

The students of Maxime Kaltenmark, trained in the 1960s and 1970s, in turn, became the teachers of senior Western scholars today: Anna Seidel, Michel Strickmann, Isabelle Robinet, Catherine Despeux, Farzeen Baldrian-Hussein, and – most importantly, his successor – Kristofer Schipper. Another great source of Daoist scholars was the training offered by Edward Schafer at the University of California at Berkeley, who can be considered the grandfather of American Daoist Studies. Since then, students and scholars have multiplied, and there are numerous institutions worldwide that offer academic training in the field.

Spreading the study

Partly due to the work of these inspiring scholars and partly because of the 1960s Taiwan reprint of the Daoist canon in a reduced edition (which made it both affordable and movable), the study of Daoism began to spread in the 1970s. While France and Japan have remained great centers, there are now also serious Daoist scholars in other European countries (Great Britain, Germany, Holland, Denmark, Italy) as well as in the United States, Canada, and Australia. In addition, after the end of the Cultural Revolution and with the increased religious revival in mainland China, the field has picked up momentum in the religion's homeland.

In Japan, the main research organization is the Japanese Society for Daoist Research (Nihon Dōkyō Gakkai) with its journal *Tōhō shūkyō* (Eastern Religions).

Both Tokyo and Kyoto, as well as various regional cities, have universities that offer courses in the field and train young scholars – often in close cooperation with Chinese and Western institutions. In France, two research and two teaching institutions promote Daoist Studies: the Centre National d'Recherche Scientifique, a major research center in Paris; the Ecole Française d'Extrême-Orient with representatives in Japan, Hong Kong, China, and Taiwan; the Ecole Pratique des Hautes Etudes, located at the Sorbonne and the academic home of Kaltenmark and Schipper; and the Collège de France with the Institut des Hautes Etudes Chinoises that produces an extensive publication series including many important works on Daoism.

As the field grew, leading scholars from these two countries were responsible for organizing three international conferences, which took place in Bellagio (Italy) in 1968, Tateshina (Japan) in 1973, and Unterägeri (Switzerland) in 1979, and also included participants from various other countries. French and Japanese scholars are moreover responsible for the compilation of a number of important indexes and concordances to the Daoist canon and various individual texts, materials that are essential in opening access to key sources. The most important of these reference works is *The Daoist Canon*, edited by Kristofer Schipper and Franciscus Verellen (2004), a comprehensive guide to texts in the *Daozang* and the result of a major international cooperative project that was begun in the 1970s with funding from the European Union.

Areas of exploration

The overarching tendency of the early generations of scholars, in the 1940s–1960s, was to focus on textual issues. Which texts belonged to what school? What were their dates? How were they related to each other? Had they survived intact or were they composites including later additions? Who were their authors? And what were the circumstances of, and motivations for, their compilation?

All these were essential questions in an initial effort to come to terms with the approximately 1,500 texts of the Daoist canon plus its various supplements as well as manuscripts found at Dunhuang, a large variety of stele inscriptions, and texts contained in non-Daoist collections. Guided by Japanese scholars who excelled at this kind of philological groundwork, this effort led to a fairly clear understanding of the major schools, texts, and protagonists of the religion. It centered particularly on the formative phase in the middle ages, between the Han and Tang dynasties, leaving the study of modern Daoism to later generations.

Following the fundamental identification and analysis of texts, plus the establishment of a basic vocabulary of technical terms, in the 1970s–1980s, scholars turned their attention to the understanding of Daoist history. Who exactly was active in what school under what circumstances and for what reasons? How did Daoist schools, concepts, and practices relate to events in Chinese history? What were their cultural and political connections to mainstream patterns? Beyond the fundamental coming-to-grips with the tradition, a key concern at this stage was also to overcome the inherent prejudice among classical sinologists. Their dominant attitude was that Daoism was a subject to be taken up after retirement and that its study had little to offer for the understanding of mainstream Chinese politics, literature, and philosophy.

Since the 1990s, while the exploration of both texts and history – especially also of modern Daoism since the Song – has continued unabatedly, the focus has shifted to also include the study of Daoist practices. There is now much material, both ethnographic and historical, available on Daoist ritual. The various techniques of self-cultivation and meditation have received a great deal of attention. For example, internal alchemy, all but unknown a few years ago, is now being explored in its many modifications, differences between schools becoming better known and special practices for women being understood in more detail.

Current trends

The current tendency these days, after exploring the basics of the tradition, is to create comprehensive surveys, integrated histories, and encyclopedic collections. These works greatly support the spread of Daoist knowledge among academics of other fields and the general populace. They also serve as textbooks in college classes and allow interested students to access relevant information with relative ease. In addition, there is a trend toward the intensified exploration of new areas of study, including the relation of Daoism to other aspects of Chinese culture, such as politics and the arts. This trend, too, opens the examination and presentation of the tradition to a wider audience – notably scholars and the public interested in a deeper understanding of China, its history and culture.

Another widening effect is achieved through the increased dialogue with contemporary practitioners, both in China and the West. More and more young scholars are undertaking field work in China, not only studying priests, monks, nuns, and Daoist business men, but also learning from them. The same holds true for students of Daoism in the West. Where scholars until the 1990s tended to ignore Daoist practitioners – who were, admittedly, often self-styled and focused mainly on Chinese medicine or the *Daode jing* – the twenty-first century has seen an active and ongoing exchange between scholars and practitioners that is growing at a rapid rate.

Last, but not least, Daoist scholars are actively engaged in various academic associations, opening an engagement with scholars of Chinese culture and of other religions. They work hard not only to have their voice heard in relevant venues such as a journal of their own, but also to create independent sections in important scholarly societies such as the American Academy of Religion. As a result, Daoist Studies is emerging from being merely one aspect of Chinese religions into a field of its own, and academics who study and teach other religions or comparative topics such as, for example, the role of women or the nature of ritual, now have access to clearly presented information and accordingly can bring Daoism into the discussion of religion in general.

Comprehensive surveys

Following the model of Japanese and Chinese scholars, Western academics have recently made the effort to present integrated and comprehensive surveys of the Daoist religion. The earliest work of this kind was the three-volume *Dōkyō*, a collection of systematically arranged articles edited by a group of Japanese scholars under the leadership of Fukui Kōjun and published in 1983. It was followed, in 1994, by two comprehensive Japanese dictionaries, one arranged again in thematic format, featuring relevant articles, the other itemizing a huge number of topics. All three publications, moreover, were richly furnished with colorful illustrations and priced for the general market. They contributed greatly to the spread of Daoist awareness in Japan.

Around the same time, Chinese scholars began to present systematic histories of Daoism, notably those by Qing Xitai (1988) and Ren Jiyu (1990), as well as three major dictionaries (1994). Edited by Wu Feng, Li Yangzheng, and Hu Fuchen respectively, they are each several thousand pages long and build on the cooperation of numerous local Daoist associations and hundreds of scholars. They present descriptions of Daoist scriptures, personages, organizations, and practices; collect information from many different localities and summarize issues of current scholarship; and provide bibliographies of Daoist Studies as well as systematic chronologies.

Western dictionaries

In the West, the first publication of this kind was the *Daoism Handbook*, edited by Livia Kohn (2000). Arranged chronologically and thematically, it comprises articles by thirty scholars from various countries (including Germany, Italy, France, Australia, China, Japan, and Korea) and covers not only the major schools and periods but also thematic issues such as women, divination, talismans, art, music, and sacred mountains, as well as Daoism in Korea and Japan. A seminal effort that continues to inspire scholars and followers, it has since been reprinted in a two-volume paperback version.

Along the same lines, but arranged according to individual items rather than articles, is the *Encyclopedia of Taoism*, another intense work of international cooperation under the leadership of Fabrizio Pregadio (2005). More than any other work it allows easy access to detailed information on specific texts, people, temples, and concepts, and has been lauded as a model of the presentation of complex and often intractable data.

Histories

As for systematic presentations of Daoism, an early effort was made by Holmes Welch in his *Taoism: The Parting of the Way* (1965). Still very sketchy, this short volume outlines the main contours of Daoist history and for the first time made Westerners aware that there is more to Daoism than the *Daode jing*. A more powerful work is Isabelle Robinet's *Histoire du taoïsme: Dès origins au XIVe siècle* (1991), which came out in English under the title *Taoism: Growth of a Religion* (1997). A well founded chronological survey, it became the standard for Daoist histories in the 1990s. However, as the French title suggests, it outlines the religion only to the fourteenth century, matching available research at the time and leaving out all modern developments.

This changed in the twenty-first century, when three books appeared in English that each presented Daoism in a different way and from a different perspective. Livia Kohn's *Daoism and Chinese Culture* (2001) is a chronological survey of Daoist history from the beginnings to the present day that takes into account events in Chinese history and strives to create connections with developments and key features of Chinese culture. James Miller's *Daoism: a Short Introduction* (2003) is a thematically rather than chronologically arranged work that presents the tradition through its ideas and practices which it places in both historical and contemporary contexts. Russell Kirkland's *Taoism: The Enduring Tradition* (2004) is neither a historical survey nor a thematic presentation but a critical evaluation of what scholars know and do not know about Daoism. The work serves to correct innumerable preconceptions and argues for a different perspective on the religion. Rather than fundamental information on the religion, it provides a different way of looking at it.

New areas of study

Several areas of Daoist Studies that have received only little attention so far are increasingly on a priority list for exploration among young scholars. They include first of all the connection of Daoism to the arts: literature, music, painting, calligraphy, ceramics, and so on. All too often these aspects are neglected, and Daoist works are not recognized as such. For example, when Stephen Little put together the exhibition "Taoism and the Arts of China" in Chicago and San francisco in 2000, he discovered many Daoist art works that had been wrongly classified as Buddhist or simply set aside as "unknown," lingering in the basements of reputable institutions. Similarly, scholars are only beginning to glimpse the impact of Daoist-minded emperors on the symbolism and execution of paintings and calligraphy, as well as the evolution of musical patterns due to Daoist ritual.

Another desirable research goal is the better understanding of Daoist political thought and activities. We know of the Daoist theocracy in the Northern Wei, the use the Tang emperor Xuanzong made of the religion in governing his empire, and of the Daoist infatuation of Song Huizong and the Jiajing emperor of the Ming. However, there is no comprehensive understanding of how Daoists view politics and how they have related to the political elite and to government over the millennia.

Further subjects

A third unexplored area is Daoist philosophy – not the *Daode jing* which is almost too well-known by now, but Daoist religious thought as presented by intellectuals who were also ordained priests and deeply embedded in ritual, devotion, and cosmology. Especially in the Six Dynasties and the Tang, numerous works were written under Buddhist influence that have hardly been examined yet. Advanced practitioners of internal alchemy have created profound treatises on cosmology and philosophy that remain untranslated and for the most part unread. And, of course, there are all those later thinkers harmonizing the three teachings, whose particular take on Daoism yet remains to be studied.

Fourth and finally, scholars are beginning to pay attention to the regional diversity of the religion and its adoption by ethnic minorities in China. Again, a few facts are known, such as that the Yao, a tribe in southwest China and northeastern Thailand converted to the Celestial Masters in the middle ages and still runs its society along Daoist lines, with libationers as officials and the Three Primes as key festival days. However, there is much more than that, and Daoism has exerted various levels of influence on minorities while developing with vast regional differences. These can be explored historically; they are also increasingly the subject of ethnographic investigations, which also shed light on social mobility and structural factors in the practice of religion.

Practitioners

The practical side of the religion, its actual activation in the daily life of dedicated followers, was neglected as an academic resource for the longest time. This had to do with the fact that all religious institutions were shut down under Chinese Communism and that very few serious masters offered courses and training programs in the West. In the past twenty years, this has changed considerably, and we now have a strong presence of Daoist practitioners both in China and in the West.

In China, academic studies of actual Daoist practice include the ethnographic analysis of Daoist temples, the documentation of ritual activities and festivals, and the conscientious recording of the current status and modern history of both individual masters and complex institutions. In the West, they involve an increasing number of cooperative ventures, such as joint conferences, scholar-practitioner workshops, and practitioners' reports at meetings and in journals. The old prejudice that pure

Daoism could only be found in its original country (and there only before World War II) is giving way to an increasing awareness that authentic masters and well-trained teachers are spreading methods of qigong, taiji quan, and Daoist meditation which not only make increasing inroads among the general populace, but are having a strong impact on health awareness and spiritual aspirations in the modern world.

Activities and resources

Daoist scholars match the increasing strength of their field and are active in a variety of venues. They have a strong presence in several key academic associations, publish their own journal, websites, and databases and, more and more often, convene specialized workshops and international conferences.

Academic associations

There are three major academic associations in the U.S. that provide a venue for Daoist Studies: the Society for the Study of Chinese Religions (SSCR) with its *Journal of Chinese Religions*; the Association for Asian Studies (AAS), which publishes the *Journal of Asian Studies*; and the American Academy of Religions (AAR), which has its own organ, the *Journal of the American Academy of Religion*. The latter two have large-scale annual meetings that draw thousands of scholars from Religious or Asian Studies; at each, Daoist scholars furnish several panels and present new explorations. They also actively participate in regional conventions of these two organizations as well as in SSCR meetings, usually held in conjunction with the other annual meetings of the two larger associations. In the AAR, in particular, Daoist Studies has just been elevated from "consultation" to "group" status, which means its representatives can now offer two independent panels at each annual meeting. The journals of all these organizations, moreover, time and again carry important contributions to the field.

Publications

A uniquely Daoist academic journal, called *Taoist Resources*, was first founded in 1988, upon the initiative of two self-styled Daoist nuns who contacted a number of Chinese religion scholars with only secondary interests in Daoism. When the nuns found themselves overwhelmed by the task, the journal passed on to the editorship of Stephen R. Bokenkamp at the University of Indiana, where it prospered in twice annual issues for ten years. In 1997, however, a decision was made to absorb it into the *Journal of Chinese Religions*, published by the SSCR.

Another effort at establishing an independent Daoist forum is underway. It involves the creation of two new journals: *Daoism: Religion, History and Society* is currently being launched. A bilingual academic venue in English and Chinese, it is published jointly by the Chinese University of Hong Kong and the Ecole Française d'Extrême-Orient. At the same time, the *Journal of Daoist Studies,* facilitated by Livia Kohn, Russell Kirkland, Ronnie Littlejohn is published by Three Pines Press. Hoping to bridge the divide between academics and practitioners, it divides into three sections: academic articles, forum on contemporary practice, and news of the field. The first issue (2008) contains five papers that raise some of the issues at the forefront of the field, such as Daoist philosophy in a religious context, a deeper understanding of inner alchemy, and relating the thought of the *Zhuangzi* to contemporary psychology. The section on contemporary practice has several reports on Chinese temples, training facilities, and ritual activities as well as presentations by American Daoists on their education, methods, and concerns. The journal *Daoism: Religion, History and Society* is being launched in Fall 2008, jointly published by the CUHK Centre for the Studies of Daoist Culture and EFEO.

Websites

In addition, various online databases present important materials for the study of Daoism. They include a directory of scholars, students, syllabi, publications, and events at www.daoiststudies.org (James Miller, Queen's University); an extensive database of Daoist artworks (Poul Anderson, Hawai'i); a growing textual collection as part if the Chinese Religions Initiative (Fabrizio Pregadio, Stanford); an overview of textual and organizational resources on the Daoism Information Page (Gene Thursby, University of Florida); as well as articles and information on Daoist Studies at www.daoistcenter.org (Louis Komjathy, Pacific Lutheran University).

There are, moreover, several new foundations that hope to attract wealthy sponsors to enhance the academic study and practical dissemination of Daoism. They include the Daoist Foundation, with its goal of "preserving and transmitting traditional Daoist culture" (www.daoistfoundation.org); as well as Legacy of Dao, "dedicated to spreading ancient Daoist wisdom in the modern world" and "making ancient Daoist knowledge and practices available to everyone" (www.legacyofdao. org). Both organizations, once funded, will offer scholarships to help with the creation of translations of Daoist texts, encourage the increased production of video documentations and practice DVDs, and sponsor conferences and workshops.

International conferences

The three international conferences sponsored by French and Japanese scholars in the 1960s and 1970s did not result in a sustained multi-national effort. The next event of this sort was a small workshop at Toyo University in Tokyo in 1995, when a group of Japanese scholars invited seven Americans to discuss recent explorations in the field. This was followed by a reciprocal invitation of Japanese academics to America in 1998; they convened a three-day workshop at the Breckinridge Center of Brunswick University in Maine. Both events resulted in publications, edited by Yamada Toshiaki and Fukui Fumimasa (1998) as well as ones by Livia Kohn and Harold Roth (2002).

Most important in the evolution of Daoist conferences was the 2002 initiative by Qing Xitai, the doyen of Daoist Studies in China. He asked Liu Xun, a specialist of modern Daoist history who grew up in Wuhan and graduated from the University of Southern California, to establish a venue for Chinese Daoist scholars to meet and interact with Western academics to enhance the international expansion of the field. Liu Xun, in turn, asked Livia Kohn to help him with the organization.

This led to the first large-scale International Conference on Daoist Studies, "Daoism and the Contemporary World," held in June, 2003 at Boston University in cooperation with the Fairbank Center of Harvard University. Unlike all earlier events, this was open to the general public, attracted large numbers of practitioners, and also addressed an interested general audience, such as people involved in Chinese medicine and the martial arts. Funding had been secured to invite a substantial group of scholars from China; however, they could not participate in the end because of the outbreak of SARS that year. Still, the meeting was highly successful and attracted over 150 participants.

The one Chinese scholar who managed to come was Zhang Qin from Sichuan University, who was so enthused about the meeting that he invited everyone to his home for the following year. The second conference accordingly took place in 2004 in Chengdu City and on Mount Qingcheng in Sichuan. This was followed by a third event, held on an island in a Bavarian lake under the sponsorship of the University of Munich and the German Medical Society for Qigong Yangsheng. The fourth conference took place in Hong Kong in 2007. Organized by the Hong Kong Taoist Association and the Yuen-Yuen Institute, it was held in conjunction with a Grand Offering to All Heavens, allowing participants to actively engage with contemporary Daoist ritual. Participation has continued to increase and there is a strong sense of a growing international community of Daoist Studies.

No meeting is planned for 2008. After this, the event is planned to occur every year on the first weekend in June. In 2009, it will be held on Mount Wudang in Hubei; in 2010, it will be at Loyola Marchmount University in Los Angeles. A specific website informs of new ventures and provides access to conference papers (www.daoistconference.org).

Workshops

In addition to these large international efforts, there have also been quite a number of smaller workshops on Daoist Studies, usually focused on one or the other specific theme. Important events include the conference on "Daoism and Ecology" (Harvard University, 1998); the symposium on "Daoism and the Arts of China" (Art Institute of Chicago, 2000); the dialogue of scholars and practitioners under the heading "Daoist Cultivation: Traditional Models and Contemporary Practices" (Vashon Island, 2001); the workshop on "Tantra and Daoism: The Globalization of Religion and Its Experience" (Boston University, 2002); the conference on "Daoism in the Modern World" (Harvard University, Harvard 2005); the symposium on "The School of Complete Perfection Today" (UC Berkeley, 2006), and the workshop on "Internal Alchemy: Energetic Transformations for Vitality and Transcendence" (New Mexico, 2007). Similar events continue to be organized, such as the meeting on the translation and interpretation of texts on women's alchemy (Los Angeles, 2008) and a general Daoism symposium at the University of British Columbia (Vancouver, 2008). Up-to-date information appears in the *Journal of Daoist Studies* and on www.daoiststudies.org.

Taking all these developments together, there is a widespread effort to enhance and increase the development of Daoist Studies. Coupled with a growing presence of Daoist-related practices among the larger populace, this is bound to lead to a greater awareness, wider knowledge, improved presentation, and higher relevance of Daoism in the modern world.

Key points you need to know

- Daoism is in many ways a hybrid religion that defies established categories and developed in close relationship with other aspects of Chinese culture and religion. Its unique characteristics include the creative force of Dao, multiple heavens, and the potential of human transformation toward immortality.
- Daoist Studies began in the 1930s and, until the 1970s, was centered in France and Japan. Scholars from these countries organized three international conferences and were responsible for groundbreaking studies and the compilation of essential research aids.
- In the course of its development, the focus of the field shifted from the philological exploration of the texts through history, schools, and biographies to the examination of ritual and self-cultivation practices. Areas such as art, music, literature, politics, religious philosophy, and local divergences are still largely unexplored.
- Only very recently have comprehensive histories and encyclopedias of Daoism appeared. Similarly, Daoist Studies has only been recognized as a separate entity in the American Academy of Religion in 2007 and has only had its own journals since 2008. However, there are growing numbers of

relevant internet sites and databases, and new foundations have sprung up that hope to attract funding for the dissemination of Daoist wisdom and practices.

● The most important factor in the creation of an international community of scholars is a series of conferences, held every year in June in various countries and attracting around 200 participants. Small workshops, moreover, serve to enhance cooperation among scholars and create forums for productive exchange.

Discussion questions

1. Make a list of religions you are familiar with and examine them in terms of ethnic versus universal, linear versus cyclical, medical versus spiritual, communal versus hermit, ritual versus self-cultivation. What typical patterns emerge? What are some areas to examine with respect to the key characteristics?
2. In the study of religion, which aspects do you consider most important and most interesting? What do you think is most important in the study of Daoism at this point? Which subject would you most like to learn more about? And should this be a book, audio, video, or online presentation?
3. Go to the internet and look up Daoist studies, centers, and foundations. What are some points all these organizations have in common? What are their goals? Do you think they are effective?

Further reading

Ding, Huang. 2000. "The Study of Daoism in China Today." In *Daoism Handbook*, edited by Livia Kohn, 765–91. Leiden: E. Brill.

Kirkland, J. Russell. 1997. "The Historical Contours of Taoism in China: Thoughts on Issues of Classification and Terminology." *Journal of Chinese Religions* 25: 57–82.

Kohn, Livia, and Harold D. Roth, eds. 2002. *Daoist Identity: History, Lineage, and Ritual*. Honolulu, HI: University of Hawai'i Press.

Leung, Man-Kam. 1991. "The Study of Religious Taoism in the People's Republic of China (1949–1990): A Bibliographical Survey." *Journal of Chinese Religions* 19: 113–26.

Sakai, Tadao, and Tetsuro Noguchi. 1979. "Taoist Studies in Japan." In *Facets of Taoism*, edited by Holmes Welch and Anna Seidel, 269–88. New Haven, CT: Yale University Press.

Schipper, Kristofer, and Franciscus Verellen, eds. 2004. *The Taoist Canon: A Historical Companion to the Daozang*. 3 vols. Chicago, IL: University of Chicago Press.

Seidel, Anna. 1990. "Chronicle of Taoist Studies in the West 1950–1990." *Cahiers d'Extrême-Asie* 5: 223–347.

Sivin, Nathan. 1978. "On the Word 'Taoist' as a Source of Perplexity." *History of Religions* 17: 303–30.

Strickmann, Michel. 1982. "The Tao among the Yao." In *Rekishi ni okeru minshū to bunka*, edited by Sakai Tadao kinen kai, 23–30. Tokyo: Kokusho kankōkai.

Yamada Toshiaki, and Tanaka Fumio, eds. 1998. *Dōkyō no rekishi to bunka*. Tokyo: Hirakawa.

Appendix 1
Chronology of Daoist history

B.C.E.

Till tenth century	Shang oracle-bone divination, ancestor worship, bronze vessels, shamanic roots
Till sixth century	Zhou belief in Heaven as natural balance
	Yijing, divination manual working with trigrams and hexagrams
	Shujing, chronicle of ancient history and cosmology
Fifth century	Life of Laozi (legendary)
	Life of Confucius (552–479), philosopher, founder of Confucianism
	Life of Mozi (c. 479–438), philosopher of the Mohist school
Fourth century	*Daode jing*, central text of ancient Daoism
	Neiye, chapter of *Guanzi*, on inward training
	Life of Zhuangzi (c. 370–290), philosopher
	Life of Zou Yan (c. 350–270), cosmologists, systematized five phases
	Life of Qu Yuan (340–278), shaman and poet, author of *Chuci*
Third century	Life of Xunzi (c. 300–230), Confucian and Legalist thinker
	Zhuangzi, text recording Daoist thought of Zhuangzi and other schools (c. 250)
	Reign of First Qin Emperor (221–210), builds Great Wall, Terracotta Army; searches isles of immortals
	Liji, book that codifies Zhou-dynasty ritual
Second century	*Chuci*, collection of shamanic songs from south China (c. 200)
	Zhangjia shan manuscripts (186), including *Yinshu* on exercises

Mawangdui manuscripts (168), including *Daode jing*, *Daoyin tu*, and *Quegu shiqi* on health techniques

Huainanzi (145), philosophical compendium sponsored by Prince Liu An

Life of Sima Xiangru (179–117), author of poem on the Great Man

Life of Dong Zhongshu (179–103), codifier of five phases system

Emperor Wu (140–86), employer of magical technicians

Shiji (104), first formal historical record

First century   *Liexian zhuan* (c. 70), collection of immortals' tales

Life of Heshang gong, commentator on the *Daode jing*

C.E.

First century   first record of Buddhism (50)

Life of Cao Cao (155–220), warlord who conquered the Celestial Masters

Second century   Celestial Masters, aka Orthodox Unity school (142)

Way of Great Peace (145)

Life of Ge Xuan (164–244), magical practitioner

Laozi bianhua jing (180)

Taiping rebellion (184)

Third century   Life of Zhang Lu (fl. 215), leader of Celestial Masters

Xiang'er zhu, Celestial Masters commentary to the *Daode jing*

Zhougui jing, Celestial Masters collection of spells against demons

Life of Wang Bi (226–49), *Daode jing* commentator

Life of Guo Xiang (252–312) *Zhuangzi* commentator

Life of Ruan Ji (210–263), author of poem on the Great Man

Life of Liu Ling (d. 265), author of "The Virtue of Wine"

Life of Wei Huacun (251–334), libationer and revealing deity

Discovery of *Sanhuang wen* by Bo He (292)

Life of Hua Tuo, physician and creator of Five Animals Frolic

Fourth century   *Huahu jing* (c. 300), text on Laozi converting western barbarians

Chisongzi zhongjie jing, text on Daoist ethics and behavior

Yangsheng yaoji, compendium on longevity techniques

Life of Ge Hong (283–343), alchemist and author of the
 Baopuzi
Life of Xu Mai (b. 301) and Xu Mi (303–373), founders of
 Highest Clarity
Life of Yang Xi (b. 330), medium for Highest Clarity
Highest Clarity revelations (364–70)
Life of Xu Huangmin (361–429), distributor of Highest
 Clarity texts
Huangting jing, Highest Clarity meditation scripture
Life of Ge Chaofu (fl. 390), founder of Numinous Treasure
Numinous Treasure school (390s)
Wufu xu, text on Numinous Treasure myth, dietary
 practices, and talismans

Fifth century NORTH:
Life of Kumārajīva (d. 418), head of Buddhist translation
Life of Kou Qianzhi (365–448), leader of Daoist theocracy
Life of Cui Hao (d. 551), prime minister of the theocracy
Life of Yin Tong, descendent of Yin Xi and founder of
 Louguan
Louguan, first Daoist monastery (*c.* 470),
Life of Wang Daoyi (447–510), Louguan leader
Xisheng jing, mystical text from Louguan (*c.* 480)
SOUTH:
Santian neijie jing (420), Celestial Masters cosmology and
 history
Laojun shuo yibai bashi jie, Celestial Masters code of 180
 precepts
Siji mingke, description of Daoist celestial administration
Life of Lu Xiujing (406–477), Daoist master and compiler
 of catalogs
Three Caverns system of textual classification (437)
Daode zhenjing xujue, ritual commentary to the *Daode jing*
Daoyin jing, comprehensive account of exercise practices

Sixth century NORTH:
Court debates on Buddhism versus Daoism (520; 570)
Life of Wei Jie (497–569), Louguan Daoist and debater
Xiaodao lun (570), anti-Daoist polemic
Wushang biyao (574), Daoist encyclopedia
Beginning of Chan (Zen) Buddhism

SOUTH:

Life of Tao Hongjing (456–536), collector and editor of
    Highest Clarity manuscripts

Zhen'gao (500), main collection by Tao Hongjing

Badi jing, text of the Three Sovereigns School

Seventh century	*Yinyuan jing* (*c.* 600) on deeds and karmic effects
	Sandong zhunang, Daoist encyclopedia (680s)
	Sun Simiao (582–683) Daoist, physician, alchemist
	Sheyang lun, long life treatise by Sun Simiao
Eighth century	Ordination of Tang princesses (711)
	Reign of Xuanzong (712–756), supporter of Daoism as state religion
	Life of Sima Chengzhen (647–735)
	Fuqi jingyi lun, outline of Daoist long life and *qi* practices, by Sima Chengzhen
	Zuowang lun, outline of Daoist "sitting in oblivion," by Sima Chengzhen
	Heavenly Treasure find supports dynasty (741);
	An Lushan rebellion (755)
Ninth century	Life of Du Guangting (850–933), court Daoist and compiler of records
	Life of Linji (d. 866), Chan master who used Daoist concepts
	Life of Lü Dongbin (legendary), key figure among the Eight Immortals
Tenth century	Arising of martial deities and ritual masters; growth of Thunder Rites
	Life of Tan Zixiao (fl. 935), founder of Heavenly Heart
	Life of Chen Tuan (d. 989), creator of precursor of Great Ultimate diagram
	Life of Rao Dongtian (fl. 994), codifier of Heavenly Heart scriptures
Eleventh century	Dunhuang caves closed (*c.* 1008)
	Dark Warrior adopted as state protector of the Song
	Yunji qiqian (1023), Daoist encyclopedia
	Development of internal alchemy as main form of Daoist meditation
	Neo-Confucianism established as mainstream Chinese thought
	Taiji tu, formal chart of the Great Ultimate

Twelfth century	Reign of Huizong (1101–1125), Daoist adept and exiled immortal
	Life of Lin Lingsu (1076–1120), founder of Divine Empyrean school, adviser to Huizong
	Life of Yang Xizhen (1101–1124), founder of Youthful Incipience school
	SOUTH:
	Life of Ning Benli (1101–1181), creator of new ritual synthesis
	Life of Zhang Boduan (d. 1182) and Bai Yuchan (c. 1194–1227), leaders of internal alchemy
	NORTH:
	Life of Wang Chongyang (1112–1170), founder of Complete Perfection school
	Life of Ma Danyang (1123–1183), first disciple of Wang Chongyang
	Life of Sun Buer (1119–1182), only female among the Seven Perfected
Thirteenth century	NORTH:
	Qiu Chuji (1148–1227) of the Seven Perfected meets Chinggis Khan (1219)
	Xiyou ji (1220s), record of Qiu's travels
	Murals at Temple of Eternal Happiness depict Daoist gods (1252)
	Persecution of Daoism (1281)
Fourteenth century	Reign of Taizu (1368–1399), establishes system of control
	City God, Mazu, Wenchang, and other popular gods adopted into Daoist pantheon
Fifteenth century	Yongle Reign (1403–1425), sponsors compilation of Daoist canon
	Life of Zhang Sanfeng (legendary)
	Dark Warrior center on Mount Wudang expanded
	Life of Zhang Yuqing (1364–1427), editor of Daoist canon (1445)
	Daoist canon (1445)
	Life of Wang Dao (1487–1547), philosopher of the three teachings
Sixteenth century	Life of Zhan Ruoshui (1466–1560), Wang Yangming (1517–1579), and Lin Zhaoen (1517–1598), Neo-Confucian thinkers integrating Daoist concepts

Reign of Jiaqing Emperor (1522–1566), Daoist adept and
   sponsor of the arts
Qizhen shizhuan, novel about the Seven Perfected
Xiyou ji, novel about the exploits of the Monkey King
Life of Wu Chengen (d. 1582), author of the *Xiyou ji*
Dongyou ji, novel about the travails of the Eight Immortals
Life of Wu Yuantai (fl. 1566), author of the *Dongyou ji*
Fengshen yanyi, novel about the Zhou conquest of the Shang
Life of Lu Xixing (c. 1520–1601) and Xu Zhonglin (d.
   1566), authors of the *Fengshen yanyi*
Chifeng sui (1578), collection of Daoist exercise practices

Seventeenth century *Xu daozang*, the first supplement to the canon (1607)
Beiyou ji, novel about the Dark Warrior
Life of Yu Xiangtou (fl. 1588–1609), author of the *Beiyou ji*
Roupu tuan, pornographic novel with Daoist themes
Life of Li Yu (1611–1680), author of the *Roupu tuan*
Life of Chen Wangting (fl. 1630s), creator of taijiquan
Life of Wang Changyue (d. 1680), abbot Baiyun guan and
   codifier of Complete Perfection ordination

Eighteenth century Life of JIang Yuanting (1722–1819), complior of the
   Daozang jinghua.
Life of Min Yide (1758–1836), 11th Longmen patriarch and
   author *Taiyi jinhua zongzhi* (secret of the golden flower)
   on internal alchemy (1775).
First Western translation of the *Daode jing*, intoLatin
   (1788).

Nineteenth century *Daozang jiyao*, canonical supplement (1820)
Life of Li Xiyue (1806–1856), who channeled Zhang
   Sanfeng's autobiography
Life of Chen Zhangxing (1771–1853), creator of Chen-style
   taijiquan
Life of Yang Luchan (1799–1872), creator of Yang-style
   taijiquan
Founding of Donghak, Korean new religion (1860)
Life of James Legge (1831–1905), English translator of
   Daode jing (1891)
Life of Ding Fubao (1874–1952), complier of the *Daode jing*
Neijing tu (1889), visual depiction of internal alchemy
   practice

Twentieth century

Founding of Jŭngsan kyo, Korean new religion (1901)

Dunhuang caves discovered (1905)

Daozang jinghua lu, collection of new Daoist texts(1922)

Daoist canon reprinted in Shanghai (1923–1925)

Founded of Caodai, Vietnamese new religion (1921)

Beginning of Daoist Studies in Japan and France (1930s)

Life of Ni Hua-ching (b. 1938?), founder of Integral Way

Life of Mantak Chia (b. 1944), founder of Healing Dao

CCP approves health methods and coins the name qigong (1947)

Temples nationalized and consolidated into communes (1952)

Founding of Chinese Daoist Association (1956)

Life of Chen Yingning (1880–1969), president of CDA

Statues and religious implements melted for steel during Great Leap Forward (1958)

Destruction of religion during Cultural Revolution (1966–1976)

Hong Kong Taoist Association founded (1964)

Taiwan reprint of the Daoist canon in reduced edition (1960s)

Growth of Daoist Studies, especially in France and Japan (1960s)

Daozang jinghua, Taiwan collection of new Daoist texts (1963)

Fung Loy Kok temple and organization founded in Hong Kong (1968)

Mainland religious revival through Four Modernizations (1978)

Daoist community temples in New York, San Francisco, and Los Angeles (1970s)

Zhuang-Lin xu daozang, Taiwan collection of Daoist ritual texts (1975)

Qigong boom (1980s)

Life of Jiao Guorui and Liang Shifeng, creators of modern Five Animals Frolic

Qigong yangsheng congshu, mainland collection of qigong and long life practices (1980s)

American Daoist Studies begins (1980s)

Fung Loy Kok temple in Toronto (1981)

Mawangdui manuscripts excavated (1983)

First Healing Dao center in America (1983)

Life of Michael Winn (b. 1952), American leader of Healing Dao since 1985

Life of Charles Belyea aka Liu Ming (b. 1947), founder of Orthodox Daoism of America (ODA) in 1986

Life of Li Hongzhi (b. 1954), founder of Falungong in 1992

British Daoist Association founded (1996)

Persecution of Falun gong and various qigong forms (1999)

Twenty-first century   *Daoist Handbook* published (2000)

International conference series initiated (2003)

American Daoist Association founded (2004)

Encyclopedia of Taoism published (2005).

Grand Offering held in Hong Kong (2007).

New journals initiated (2008).

Appendix 2
The Daoist canon

The Daoist canon (*Daozang*) goes back to the early Ming dynasty. It is also called *Zhengtong daozang* (Daoist Canon of the Zhengtong Era) after the reign title of the year (1445) when it was first printed. Commissioned by the Yongle Emperor and executed under his successors by a large staff in the imperial bureaucracy, its collection and editing was the responsibility of Zhang Yuqing (1364–1427), the forty-fourth Celestial Master, and Ren Ziyuan (fl. 1400–1422), the general intendant of Mount Wudang. It was later condensed into the *Daozang jiyao* (Collected Essentials of the Daoist Canon), a collection of 173 texts that was first published under the Jiaqing Emperor of the Qing (1796–1820).

The Three Caverns

The Daoist canon is the central resource for the study of Daoism. It divides materials into Three Caverns and Four Supplements, following categories that first arose in the sixth century under Buddhist influence. That is to say, the Three Caverns originally matched the Three Vehicles to enlightenment: bodhisattva (savior), pratyekabuddha (self cultivator), and sravaka (listener) and represented the teachings of the three major medieval Daoist schools: Highest Clarity, Numinous Treasure, and Three Sovereigns. Each of these, moreover was supplemented by technical and hagiographic materials as well as texts of non-mainstream schools. The overall system is as follows:

Cavern	Chinese	School	Chinese	Supplement	Chinese
Perfection	Dongzhen	Highest Clarity	Shangqing	Great Mystery	Taixuan
Mystery	Dongxuan	Numinous Treasure	Lingbao	Great Peace	Taiping
Spirit	Dongshen	Three Sovereigns	Sanhuang	Great Clarity	Taiqing
				Orthodox Unity	Zhengyi

It is interesting to note that the school of Complete Perfection, of central importance in late imperial and modern Daoist administration, does not feature in this system at all but has its texts in several Caverns. Also, the Celestial Masters, the original and most fundamental of all organized Daoist schools, appears almost as an afterthought as the last of the Four Supplements under their official name "Orthodox Unity." Although essential to Ming dynasty and later Daoism, they were at the bottom of the medieval hierarchy, requiring only basic precepts and ritual knowledge of their priests and eschewing celibacy and monastic living in favor of services to the larger populace.

The twelve classes

Each Cavern and Supplement contains a variety of textual materials that are further itemized into twelve classes adopted from the Buddhist *Tripitaka* and arranged according to content and format. They are:

1 Fundamental Texts	7 Rituals and Observances
2 Divine Talismans	8 Techniques and Methods
3 Secret Instructions	9 Various Arts
4 Numinous Charts	10 Records and Biographies
5 Genealogies and Registers	11 Eulogies and Encomia
6 Precepts and Regulations	12 Lists and Memoranda

Among these, the first four are considered revealed, i.e. transmitted directly from the gods. Fundamental Texts include the holiest scriptures, texts that are believed to reside originally in heaven and only appear on the human plane in approximate translation. Divine Talismans and Numinous Charts are sacred symbols that directly correspond to holy marks in heaven. Nonverbal and graphic in nature, they are more immediately divine than the scriptures but harder to decipher and in need of human explanation, which is why they are not placed first. Secret Instructions, another revealed category, are the oral teachings received from the gods and immortals that are transcribed by human beings, explaining how best to work with the materials of the scriptures.

Classes five through eight contain human guidelines for proper worship and practice. They involve intimate knowledge of the patriarchs and traditional hierarchies; detailed explications of behavioral rules and moral guidelines; instructions on the proper performance of rituals; and manuals for the many techniques of self-cultivation and enhancement of life and spiritual prowess. They are written by human beings based on direct experience with the divine activities and organizations of the Dao. They tend to be school specific and include for example, collections of rules pertaining to specific lineages and traditions, as well as for monastic, priestly, and lay followers. There is no standard set of patriarchs, rules, rituals, or self-cultivation practices that applies to all Daoists.

The last four classes include works that are even further removed from the purity of Dao. They contain records of practices and experiences through the ages, collected either according to type of practice (Various Arts) or based on individual personages (Records and Biographies). In addition, this part of the canon also contains formal praises for masters and patriarchs of old (Eulogies and Encomia) as well as concrete models and instructions for the preparation of the proper ritual and administrative documents (Lists and Memoranda).

Canonical supplements

In the wake of the publication of the canon in 1445, additional materials collected or compiled in the late Ming dynasty were pulled together in the so-called *Xu Daozang* (Supplement to the Daoist Canon). Inspired by his mother, in 1598, Emperor Shenzong commissioned a reprint of the Daoist canon and assigned Zhang Guoxiang (d. 1611), the fiftieth Celestial Master, to produce a supplement, which was added to the collection when it was printed in 1607. The *Supplement* is still part of every reprint of the canon today.

Under the Qing, a further collection appeared in 1834. Entitled *Daozang xubian* (Supplementary Collection of the Daoist Canon), it was compiled by Min Yide (1758–1836), the eleventh patriarch of the Longmen branch of Complete Perfection. The work assembles twenty-three internal alchemy works not found in the Daoist canon and is especially important for its sources on women's alchemy.

In republican China, Ding Fubao (1874–1952) edited the *Daozang jinghua lu* (Record of Essential Blossoms of the Daoist Canon), which was published in Shanghai in 1922. Consisting of 100 titles, many of which come from the original canon, and focusing on internal alchemy and longevity techniques, it also contains biographical notes, doctrinal statements, and ritual texts. Each text is accompanied by a brief abstract and notes on its origin. It is an important collection for the study of Ming and Qing internal alchemy traditions and for materials written in the late nineteenth and early twentieth centuries.

Another important canonical supplement is the *Daozang jinghua* (Essential Blossoms of the Daoist Canon), compiled by Xiao Tianshi, a Taiwan-based physician and scholar, and published in 1963. It contains both texts from earlier collections as well as later and contemporary texts. Also from in Taiwan is the *Zhuang-Lin xu daozang* (Zhuang and Lin [Family] Supplement to the Daoist Canon) published in 1975 on the basis of fieldwork by Michael Saso. Focusing largely on ritual and exorcistic practices, the materials are especially relevant for the study of communal Daoism in contemporary Taiwan.

Further collections

More recently, on the Chinese mainland scholars have created further reduced editions of the Daoist canon and put its texts on CD-ROM to make it more easily available. They also edited a collection of Daoist related stele inscriptions (*Daojia jinshi lue*; 1988) and assembled Daoist texts published outside the canon (*Zangwai daoshu*, 1992 and 1995). The latter contains 991 titles in thirty-six volumes, including texts from earlier collections, works of single authors, and otherwise inaccessible contemporary materials.

In addition, mainland students put together a series of Daoist-related works that focus specifically on health practices. Called *Qigong yangsheng congshu* (Comprehensive Collection on Qigong and Longevity Practices), this has appeared in installments since the 1980s and to date includes fifty-nine texts, most of which are not found in the original canon.

In Japan, finally, scholars have not only compiled various indexes and concordances, but also a photo-reprint of Daoist manuscripts found at Dunhuang. Dunhuang is a small town in the western desert of China that served as a major Buddhist center on the Silk Road from the fifth century through the Tang. Consisting of hundreds of caves in a steep cliff that were richly ornamented and housed precious statues and devotional materials, the center was abandoned in 1008 under the threat of Muslim invaders. It remained hidden by desert sands until 1905, when explorers such as Swen Hedin, Paul Pelliot, and Sir Aurel Stein uncovered it. Although predominantly Buddhist, its library also contained Daoist manuscripts as well as works on medicine, divination, and fengshui. The approximately one hundred Daoist texts found there were collected by Ōfuchi Ninji and published under the title *Tonkō dōkei* (Daoist Manuscripts of Dunhuang) in 1979.

Indexes and discussions

Boltz, Judith M. 1987. *A Survey of Taoist Literature: Tenth to Seventeenth Centuries*, China Research Monograph 32. Berkeley, CA: University of California.

Chen, William Y. 1987. *A Guide to Tao Tsang chi yao*. Stony Brook, NY: Institute for the Advanced Study of World Religions.

Komjathy, Louis. 2002. *Title Index to Daoist Collections*. Cambridge, MA: Three Pines Press.

Ofuchi Ninji. 1979. "The Formation of the Taoist canon." In *Facets of Taoism*, edited by Holmes Welch and Anna Seidel, 253–68. New Haven, CT: Yale University Press.

Schipper, Kristofer M. 1975. *Concordance du Tao Tsang: Titres des ouvrages*. Paris: Publications de l'Ecole Française d'Extrême-Orient.

Schipper, Kristofer, and Franciscus Verellen, eds. 2004. *The Taoist Canon: A Historical Companion to the Daozang.* 3 vols. Chicago: University of Chicago Press.

Thompson, Laurence G. 1985. "Taoism: Classic and Canon." In *The Holy Book in Comparative Perspective*, edited by Frederick M. Denny and Rodney F. Taylor, 204–23. Columbus, SC: University of South Carolina Press.

Weng, Dujian. 1935. *Combined Indices to the Authors and Titles of Books in Two Collections of Taoist Literature*, Harvard-Yenching Sinological Index Series no. 25.. Beijing: Yenching University Library.

Glossary

abstention from grains   Gradual transformation of the body through lightening of food intake, from grains to raw foods to herbs to breath

Agon-shū   New new religion of Japan that includes Daoist spells and rituals

alchemy   Transmutation of base metals into gold and personal transformation into an immortal through conconction and ingestion of an elixir (cinnabar)

American Academy of Religions   Major American research organization supporting Daoist Studies

American Buddhist and Taoist Association   Daoist community temple in New York

Anatole, Alexei   Founder and president of the Center of Traditional Taoist Studies in Weston, Massachusetts

ancestors   Deceased relatives in the male line, usually up to five generations

Anqi Sheng   Ancient immortal who sold herbs, taught the First Emperor, and vanished

Association for Asian Studies   Major American research organization supporting Daoist Studies

Badi jing **(Scripture of the Eight Emperors)**   Key text of the Three Sovereigns school, containing practical instructions on talisman writing

Baopuzi **(Book of the Master Who Embraces Simplicity)**   Ge Hong's compendium on medieval alchemy; outline of recipes and related practices

beating the heavenly drum   Exercise of alerting the body gods of impending practice; creates the sound of drumming by snapping the fingers against the head while covering the ears with the palms

Beiyou ji **(Journey to the North)**   Vernacular late-Ming novel featuring the exploits of the Dark Warrior as he grows from prince to deity over several life times

Belyea, Charles (now Liu Ming)   Founder and leader of Orthodox Daoism in America, in northern California

Black Killer (Heisha)   Tantric, martial deity; assistant to the Dark Warrior; protector of the Song dynasty

Black Sheep Temple (Qingyang gong)   Main Daoist temple in southwest China, location where Laozi allegedly met Yin Xi before their western emigration

Bluefaced Vajrapani (Shōmen kongō)   Tantric god who helps people overcome the Three Worms; added to *gengshen* practices in the Tang dynasty; still popular in Japan

Bo He   Third-century magical practitioner who received the talismans of the Three Sovereigns

Brahma-Heavens   Four heavens right below the Three Clarities, reserved for true believers

British Taoist Association   Organization to facilitiate Daoist learning and practice in the United Kingdom, founded in 1996

bronzes   Ritual vessels used in Shang ancestor worship, highly ornamented and in multiple shapes and forms

Buddhism   Indian religion that made its way into China in the first century and came to flourish greatly from the fifth century onward

Bureau of Daoist Registration   Central Daoist administration in late imperial China

Bureau of Religious Affairs   Official agency in charge of all religious organizations

Butterfly Dream   Dream of Master Zhuang that illustrates the impossiblity to firmly know what is reality and what imagination

Cao Cao   Warlord of the third century who took over Sichuan and controlled the Celestial Masters

Caodai   New Vietnamese religion, combining Daoism with Confucianism and Catholic Christianity; founded in 1921

Cavern of *Qi*   Energy center in the solar plexus area, middle elixir field, core of primordial *qi* in women

Celestial Masters   First organized Daoist community, centered in Sichuan, millenarian outlook, strict discipline, formalized annual rituals, still present today, centered in southeast China and Taiwan

Center of Traditional Taoist Studies   Daoist temple and training center, founded by Alexei Anatole, in Weston, Massachusetts

Centre National d'Recherche Scientifique   Major institution for Daoist research in France

Chan (Zen) Buddhism   Chinese Buddhist school that arose in the sixth century and integrated a great deal of Daoist thought, especially from the *Zhuangzi*

Chen Jingyuan   Pioneer Daoist scholar in China

Chen Wangting (fl. 1630s)   Ming military officer and creator of proto taijiquan

Chen Yingning (1880–1969)   Second president of the Chinese Daoist Association; major Daoist thinker and leader in the twentieth century

Chen Zhangxing (1771–1853)   Descendent of Chen Wangting, creator of taijiquan in Chen style

Chi Sin Taoist and Buddhist Association   Daoist community temple in San Francisco

Chia, Mantak (b. 1944)   Thai-based adept of internal alchemy and founder of Healing Dao

Chifeng sui **(Marrow of the Red Phoenix)**   Late Ming compendium of healing exercises and meditations, such as the Six Healing Sounds

Chinese Daoist Association (CDA)   Official body of Daoist administration in China; headquartered in Beijing, with many regional branches; established in 1956

Ching Chung Taoist Association   Daoist community temple in San Francisco

Chisongzi (Master Redpine)   Major ancient immortal who nourished on liquid jade, had magical powers, and ascended to the immortal world

Chisongzi zhongjie jing **(The Essential Precepts of Master Redpine)**   Fourth-century text on Daoist ethics and the connection of human behavior and cosmic patterns

Choi Jaewu   Founder of Donghak, a new Korean religion

Chuci **(Songs of the South)**   Collection of shamanic songs from the southern state of Chu, dated to around 200 B.C.E.

cinnabar (elixir) fields   Energy centers located in the head, chest, and abdomen; location of pure deities of Dao (Three Ones) and major places of elixir cultivation

cinnabar   Mercury-sulfite, red in color, found along China's rivers that forms the basis of alchemical experimentation; also the word for "elixir"

City God (Chenghuang)   Office of the celestial administration in charge of registering life and death in specific cities; filled by meritorious ancestors; supervised by the Ruler of Fates

Collège de France   Major institution for Daoist research in France

communitas   Organized group of people outside of mainstream society, located in a liminal or "threshold" space

Complete Perfection   Main school of modern Daoism, next to the Celestial Masters; emphasis on monastic discipline and personal cultivation

Confucianism   Dominant philosophy of traditional China that places key emphasis on proper social interaction, hierarchies, virtues, and learning

Confucius –Ancient philosopher (552–479 B.C.E.) who founded Confucianism, edited the *Yijing,* **and codified the Six Classics**

cosmologists   Proto-Daoist school documented in the *Zhuangzi* that combined the thought of the *Daode jing* with yin-yang cosmology and *Yijing* speculation

creation   Evolution of the world from nonbeing in three stages described in the *Daode jing* as the One, the Two, the Three, and the Myriad Beings

Cui Hao (d. 451) Prime minister of the Toba-Wei and leader of the Daoist theocracy

Dao "The Way," central concept of Daoism, a force underlying all creation and manifesting in the world in natural rhythms and cosmic patterns

Daode jing (**Book of Dao and Virtue**) Main text of philosophicial Daoism, dated to around 300 B.C.E., recovered in multiple manuscripts, the subject of numerous commentaries and translations, a work of pervasive influence as well as ritual importance

Daode zhenjing xujue (**Introductory Explanations to the** *Daode jing*) Fifth-century outline of *Daode jing* background and ritual activation

Daoist Foundation American foundation dedicated to the dissemination of Daoist knowledge and practices

Daoist Long Life Center Modern Daoist-based health center in Beijing

Daojiao yangsheng quanxiao geyan (**Pertinent Words on Daoist Long Life and Filial Piety**) Modern Daoist booklet for lay followers, published on Mount Qingcheng in Sichuan

Daoyin jing (**Exercise Classic**) fifth-century compendium on exercise methods

Daoyin tu (**Exercise Chart**) Mawangdui manuscript showing forty-four figures in different forms of physical practice

Dark Warrior (Xuanwu) Deity of the north, symbolized by turtle and snake; martial hero and popular god in modern Daoism; dynastic protector of Song and Ming

demon soldier Medium-level officer among the Celestial Masters

Department of Tourism Official agency in charge of all travelers and local attractions

divination Fortune-telling on the basis of secondary signs, such as the flight of birds, cracks in bones, or lines based on the throw of coins

Divine Empyrean Song school that identified Emperor Huizong as the son of the Jade Emperor

Divine Farmer (Shennong) Mythical ruler, third of the Three Sovereigns, who invented agriculture and developed herbal medicine

Donghak (Eastern Doctrine) New Korean religion, inspired by Daoism; founded in 1860

Dongyou ji (**Journey to the East**) Late Ming novel featuring the Eight Immortals on their journey to perfection

Du Guangting (850–933) Court Daoist of the late Tang who compiled numerous works on Daoist ritual, cosmology, and hagiography

Dunhuang Desert town on the Silk Road in northwest China with extensive cave temples that were closed in 1006 and contained numerous art works and manuscripts

earthly stems Cyclical signs based on the ten-day week of the Shang dynasty

Ecole Française d'Extrême-Orient   Major institution for Daoist research in France

Ecole Pratique des Hautes Etudes Chinoises   Major institution for Daoist research in France

ecstatic excursions   Shamanic-style soul travel to the far reaches of the world, the planets, and the heavens of the immortals; first developed in Highest Clarity

Eight Immortals Temple (Baxian an)   Main Daoist temple in Xi'an

Eight Immortals   Group of eccentric magical figures, including one woman, who rose to prominence in Yuan drama and are still widely worshiped today

Eight Nodes   Calendar division including the solstices, equinoxes, and beginnings of the four seasons

Emperor Huizong (r. 1100–1125)   Song emperor with strong devotion for Daoism; believed himself to be incarnation of a Daoist god

essence   Tangible form of *qi qi* which governs the kidneys, reproductive organs, bones, teeth, brain; clearly manifest in semen and menstrual blood

Falungong (Dharma Wheel Practice)   New religion in the 1990s, featuring Buddhist and Daoist practices in qigong guise

fasting of the mind   Cultivation practice in the *Zhuangzi* by which perception is made subtle and the person connects to Dao

Feng Shui   The art of siting graves, constructing houses, and placing furniture so as to ensure an optimal flow of *qi* and thereby health and good fortune

Fengdu   Realm of the dead in Highest Clarity Daoism

Fengshen yanyi **(Creation of the Gods)**   Popular novel on the divine battles matching the Zhou's take-over of the Shang empire

First Emperor   Qin Shihuang (r. 221–210 B.C.E.), unifier of China and creator of the empire, builder of the Great Wall and the Terracotta Army

Five Animal Frolics   Exercise sequence devised by the physician Hua Tuo and since revised and expanded; includes movements in imitation of the crane, bear, tiger, deer, and monkey

Five Elders   Creator deities of the five directions in Numinous Treasure Daoism

Five Emperors   Mythical figures of Chinese prehistory, creators of culture; developed from local deities in accordance with the five phases system

Five Paths of Rebirth   Realms of reincarnation adopted from Buddhism: gods, humans, animals, hungry ghosts, and hell dwellers

five phases   Entities that symbolize the changing patterns of yin and yang: wood, fire, earth, metal water; correlated either in a productive or control cycle; associated with directions, seasons, colors, bodily organs, musical notes, emotions, senses, and many more; core system of Chinese cosmology

Five Sprouts   Subtle, germinal energies of the five directions that are visualized and absorbed in a method first developed in Highest Clarity

five virtues   Confucian values to be realized by the gentleman, also goal of Daoist practice: benevolence, righteousness, propriety, wisdom, and faith (trust, honesty)

Fu Lu Shou   Three gods symbolizing essential goals of the Chinese: posterity, prosperity, and longevity

Fu Xi   Mythical ruler of antiquity who allegedly discerned the symbols of the *Yijing* from the stars; senior member of the Three Sovereigns

Fukui Kōjun   Grandfather of Daoist Studies in Japan

Fung Loy Kok (Penglai Pavilion)   Modern Daoist temple and practice organization, affiliated with the Yuen-Yuen Institute in Hong Kong; centers worldwide, including Toronto, Denver, and Tallahassee

Fuqi jingyi lun **(On the Essential Meaning of the Absorption of** *Qi***)**   Manual on longevity techniques by Sima Chengzhen

Gan Ji   Founder of the Way of Great Peace, an early Daoist organization, in the second century

Ge Chaofu (fl. 390)   Founder of the Numinous Treasure school

Ge Hong (283–343)   Retired official and would-be alchemist who wrote the main compendium on Chinese alchemy, the *Baopuzi*

Ge Xuan (164–244)   Magical practitioner, great-uncle of Ge Hong, alleged recipient of the Numinous Treasure talismans

gengshen   fifty-seventh day of the sixty-day cycle; night when the Three Worms ascend to heaven to make their report; occasion for nightlong vigil and extensive partying; still popular in Japan

ghosts   The lost dead, people who have died violently or far off who cannot find rest

God of Wealth (Guandi)   Deified warrior of the Three Kingdoms period; featured with red face and long beard; very popular

Goddess of Mercy (Guanyin)   Buddhist deity, adaptation of the bodhisattva Avalokiteśvara; can appear in many guises and is now commonly depicted as female; helps all sincere seekers in whatever predicament

Goddess of the Morning Clouds (Bixia yuanjun)   Daughter of the Lord of Mount Tai, superviser of the ancient realm of the dead; especially dedicated to the welfare of women

Goddess of Wayfarers (Mazu)   Song-dynasty psychic who would save her father and brothers from mishaps at sea; after death worshiped and later canonized; very popular, especially in Taiwan and south China

goodness   Inherent quality of Heaven and Earth that is activated in moral behavior

Grand Network   Highest of the thirty-six heavens

Grand Offering (*jiao***)**   Major Daoist communal rite since the Song dynasty; held at times of change and renewal; lasts three days to several weeks; involves large numbers of Daoists and a serious community effort

Great Clarity Heaven from which alchemical instructions were transmitted to dedicated seekers; school and textual class with focus on alchemy

Great Emperor of Long Life (Changsheng dadi) Divine identity of Emperor Huizong

Great One (Taiyi) Ancient deity in the center of the universe, representing the primordial state at creation as well as the abstract principle of unity with Dao

Great Peace Ideal state of perfect social and cosmic harmony; attained as part of cosmic cycles and by human means; later seen as new divine age to be brought about through cataclysmic changes and with the help of messianic saviors

green dragon Symbolic animal of the east; also name of ingredient in internal alchemy

guarding the One Form of concentrative meditation in Daoism, often associated with visualizing a central deity in the abdomen

guiding *qi* Exercise that involves physically absorbing *qi* through breath and saliva, then mentally guiding it through the body; first described in jade inscription of fourth century B.C.E.

Guo Xiang (252–312) Philosopher of Profound Mystery; major editor and commentator of the *Zhuangzi*

Guodian Hunan city where the oldest manuscript fragments of the *Daode jing* were discovered in 1993

Hall of Light Ritual hall for seasonal sacrifices by the Han emperor; first of the Nine Palaces in the head in Daoist meditation

harmonization of *qi* Celestial Masters sexual rite, part of initiation into higher ranks

harmonization of the three teachings Integration of Confucianism, Buddhism, and Daoism into one system of thought; dominant trend since the Song dynasty

Healing Dao Worldwide organization that teaches Daoist self-cultivation and internal alchemy, founded by Mantak Chia, with a main American center in North Carolina under the leadership of Michael Winn

healing exercises (*daoyin*) Physical stretches accompanied by deep breathing and the mental guiding of *qi* originally part of the medical tradition, later essential in Daoist body cultivation

Heaven and Earth Central agents of the universe that communicate with humanity through natural phenomena; respond to human good and evil

Heaven Central deity of the Zhou dynasty understood as a natural power that constantly matches and interacts with humanity and provides the governing dynasty with the mandate to rule

heavenly branches Cyclical signs based on the Jupiter cycle and matching animals of the Chinese zodiac

Heavenly Heart   Early school of Song Daoism, combining exorcism and talismans with traditional meditation and ritual

Heavenly Worthy of Primordial Beginning   Central deity of the medieval Daoist pantheon

hedonists   Proto-Daoist school documented in the *Zhuangzi* that encourages following one's every whim as an expression of Dao

hells   Lit. "earth prisons," underworld areas where sinners are punished with horrid tortures; later organized into a system of ten

Heng Mountain (2017m)   Sacred peak of the north

Heshang gong   *Daode jing* commentator of the Former Han, connects concepts with body cultivation

hexagrams   Symbols consisting of six broken (yin) and unbroken (yang) lines interpreted in the *Yijing* as to how best to secure good fortune

Highest Clarity   Heaven from which information about the otherworld and instructions on immortality methods were revealed in the 360s; school and textual class with focus on individual realization through chanting, visualization, and ecstatic excursions

Hong Kong Taoist Association   Main Daoist body in Hong Kong; run by lay followers and supportive of the business community; greatly involved in social services

Hsien Yuen   Founder of the American Buddhist and Taoist Association in New York in 1979

Hua Mountain (2200m)   Sacred peak of the west; near Xi'an, major Daoist center and tourist attraction; consisting of five steep and rocky peaks

Hua Tuo   Third-century physician; original deviser of the Five Animal Frolics

Huangting jing **(Yellow Court Scripture)**   fourth-century meditation manual

Hundun   Chaos, potentiality before creation, often symbolized by the gourd; destroyed through boring of seven sensory openings

immortal embryo   Divine entity created through internal alchemy that will leave the body and become the adept's spiritual alter ego

immortals   Daoist celestials or transformed humans who reside in the higher heavens to administer human affairs and transmit sacred teachings, but rarely respond to acts of worship

inherited evil   Concept that explains the suffering and death of small children as retribution for ancestors' sins

inner nature and destiny   Inherent qualities of Dao in each individual: mental and physical condition, one's genetic make-up and social circumstances or opportunities in life

Inner Smile   Meditation method whereby practitioners send good wishes to their organs and visualize colored *qi* in them

Integral Way American organization that teaches Daoist self-cultivation and internal alchemy, founded by Ni Hua-ching, with a main center in Los Angeles

intention Mental focus used in guiding *qi*

internal alchemy (*neidan*) Major form of Daoist meditation since the Song; combination of physical refinement and internal energy work couched in the language of alchemy and the *Yijing*

Intertwined Dragon Temple (Shaolong guan) Modern Daoist temple-cum-spa; located in Chongqing, formerly part of Sichuan province

Jade Emperor (Yuhuang) Divine ruler of the popular pantheon, equivalent of the emperor on earth

Jade Maiden of Highest Mystery Divine representative of the sun who will engage in sexual relations with selected adepts

Jade Maiden of Mystery and Wonder Goddess, created from coagulated *qi*, who gives birth to the celestial Lord Lao

James Legge Protestant missionary; first English translator of the *Daode jing* (1891)

Jiajing Emperor (r. 1522–1566) Late Ming emperor with strong penchant for Daoist belief and practices; identified as incarnation of Thunder God; lived as a recluse in paradise gardens, hoping to recover immortality

Jiao Guorui Deviser of the modern form of the Five Animal Frolics.

jin Suppleness, internal springiness of muscles and tendons that gives power to the practice of taijiquan.

Journal of Daoist Studies Specialized Daoist journal, established 2008

Jūngsan kyo (Teaching of Jūngsan) New Korean religion, inspired by Daoism; founded in 1901

Kaltenmark, Maxime Grandfather of Daoist Studies in France

Kang Ilsun Founder of Jūngsan kyo, a new Korean religion

Kenneth Dickerson (Khigh Dhiegh) Founder, with Share Lew, of the Taoist Sanctuary in Los Angeles

King of Medicines Deified version of the Tang physician and Daoist Sun Simiao

kitchen-feasts Ritual banquets of medieval Daoists

kōshin Japanese name of the fifty-seventh day (*gengshen*) and activities surrounding the vigil for the Three Worms

Kou Qianzhi (365–448) New Celestial Master, recipient of several revelations from Lord Lao, author of the "New Code," and head of the Daoist theocracy

Kumarajiva (d. 418) Senior Buddhist translator whose work was responsible for a great flourishing of Buddhism in China

Kunlun Daoist paradise mountain in the western region, home of the Queen Mother of the West, location of the peaches of immortality; also name of the head in Daoist meditation

Lady Who Brings Children (Songzi niangniang)   Popular goddess in charge of conception, pregnancy, delivery, and children's welfare

Lao Mountain   Holy Daoist mountain in southern Shandong, near Qingdao; location of Complete Perfection center

Laojun shuo yibai bashi jie **(180 Precepts Spoken by Lord Lao)**   Fifth-century code of Celestial Masters precepts and community rules

Laozi bianhua jing **(Scripture of Laozi's Transformations)**   second-century scripture describing Laozi as god of Dao

Laozi   Legendary figure and teacher of Confucius, alleged author of the *Daode jing* who emigrated to the west and was later divinized as Highest Lord Lao

Legacy of Dao   American foundation dedicated to the dissemination of Daoist knowledge and practices

Legalism   Philosophical school founded by Xunzi (*c.* 300–230 B.C.E.) that sees human beings as inherently evil and proposes strict laws and punishments for the creation of social order

Li Hongzhi (b. 1954)   Founder and leader of Falungong, now living in the U.S.

Li Jun –Abbot of Intertwined Dragon Temple

Li Xiyue (1806–1856)   Sichuan Daoist and trance practitioner who channeled the "auto-biography" of the legendary Zhang Sanfeng

Li Yu (1611–1680)   Author of the *Roupu tuan'*

Liang Shifeng   Deviser of the modern form of the Five Animal Frolics.

libationer   Highest ranking official of the Celestial Masters

Liexian zhuan **(Immortals' Biographies)**   Han-dynasty record of ninety immortals

Liji **(Book of Rites)**   Confucian classic of the Zhou dynasty that specifies formalities among individuals and government agencies

Lin Lingsu (1076–1120)   Daoist advisor to Emperor Huizong; transmitter of the school of the Divine Empyrean

Lin Zhaoen (1517–1598)   Neo-Confucian thinker who integrated both Buddhist and Daoist notions into his system

Lingbao wufuxu **(Explanation of the Five Talismans of Numinous Treasure)**   Text in three chapters, from the fourth century, that outlines the mythical lineage of the Numinous Treasure together with several sets of practices

Linji (d. 866)   Chan (Zen) master who incorporated major *Zhuangzi* ideas into his thinking

Liu Ling (d. 265)   Poet who escaped reality with the help of wine and drugs, lauding the "virtue of wine" in continuation of *Zhuangzi* thought

Liu Yongguang (1134–1206)   Song reorganizer of the Numinous Treasure school

Longhu Mountain   Headquarters of the Celestial Masters in Jiangxi

Longmen lineage   Main lineage of Complete Perfection since the Qing dynasty

Lord Lao   Deified Laozi, third god of the Daoist trinity, representative of Three Sovereigns and Celestial Masters schools, instructor and protector of humanity

Lord of Mount Tai   Popular deity of the sacred mountain of the east; supervisor of the ancient realm of the dead

Lord of the Dao   Second divinity of the Daoist trinity, representative of Numinous Treasure and revealer of scriptures

Louguan   Estate in the Zhongnan mountains that became the first Daoist monastery in the fifth century; major religious center today

Lü Dongbin   Most popular figure among the Eight Immortals; revealer of Daoist secrets to Wang Chongyang; deity of Complete Perfection; subject of murals at Palace of Eternal Happiness; frequently appears in seances to support the faithful

Lu Xiujing (406–477)   Leading master of the Celestial Masters and Numinous Treasure who standardized rituals, compiled the first Daoist catalog, and set up a classification system of texts and schools

Lu Xixing (*c.* 1520–1601)   Author of the *Fengshen yanyi*

Lunyu **(Analects)**   The recorded sayings of Confucius, in twenty chapters

Ma Danyang (1123–1183)   First disciple of Wang Chongyang and leader of Complete Perfection; husband of Sun Buer

magical practitioners   Han-dynasty wonder-workers who acquired magical powers as hermits, then served as diviners, doctors, and exorcists

Mandate of Heaven   Empowerment to the ruler given by Heaven, which can be revoked due to mismanagement of affairs

Mao Mountain   Major Daoist center near Nanjing, home of the the Highest Clarity revelations

Maonü (Hairy Lady)   Qin-dynasty court lady who fled into the mountains, ate pine needles, and attained extensive longevity until she was discovered and had to eat normal food

Maspero, Henri   Pioneer Daoist scholar in France

Mawangdui   Hunan town where the oldest complete edition of the *Daode jing* was unearthed in 1973

Microcosmic Orbit   Meditative pathway of *qi* along the Governing and Conception Vessels, moving up the spine, through the head, and down along the front of the body

milfoil   A plant with a long stem, used in *Yijing* divination

millenarianism   Belief that a new world of lasting peace will arise after cataclysmic changes

Ministry of Rites   Imperial ministry in charge of all religious affairs

Mohism   Philosophical school founded by Master Mo (*c.* 479–438 B.C.E.) that proposes universal love and goodness towards all

Moy Linshin and Mui Mingte   Founders of Fung Loy Kok in 1968

Mystery Metropolis   Central divine city in the highest heaven

Nanyue (Heng Mountain, 1290m)   Sacred peak of the south; near Changsha, also seat of training center for Daoist nuns (*kundao*)

National Qigong Association (NQA)   Umbrella organization for practitioners of qigong and Chinese/Daoist self-cultivation

naturalness   **Key concept in the** *Daode jing*, describing the essential nature of Dao, also described as spontaneity

Neijing tu **(Diagram of Interior Passageways)**   A picturesque illustration of the world inside the body dating to the nineteenth century

Neiye **(Inward Training)**   Chapter of the book *Guanzi*, contemporaneous with the *Daode jing*, that details practical mediation and body cultivation methods to attain oneness with Dao

Neo-Confucianism   New revival of Confucian teachings with Buddhist overtones and the inclusion of Daoist practices

Ngo Minh Chien   Founder of Caodai, a new Vietnamese religion

Ni Hua-ching   Chinese acupuncturist and Daoist-trained master from Taiwan who created a healing and spiritual complex in Los Angeles, notably the Integral Way Society

Nihon Dōkyō Gakkai   Japanese Society for Daoist Research

Nine Palaces   Divine residences in the head, entered by mentally moving up through the nose and into the forehead

Ning Benli (1101–1181)   Song codifier of Numinous Treasure rites in combination with exorcistic practices

Niwan   Central of the Nine Palaces in the head; upper elixir field; residence of central deities

nonaction   Key concept in the *Daode jing*, encouraging the letting go of personal or political agendas in favor of following the natural flow

nonbeing   Underlying state of potential creation, key concept in Wang Bi's exegesis of the *Daode jing*

Northern Dipper (Beidou)   Central constellation in the sky, ruler of natural and cosmic cycles

Nü Ji   Immortal lady who attained her powers through sexual practices

Numious Treasure   Daoist school, beginning in 390, that integrates Highest Clarity practice with Han cosmology, Celestial Masters ritual and, in the fifth century, also with Buddhism

Ocean of Qi   Energy center and acupuncture point located in the abdomen below the navel

Ōfuchi Ninji   Grandfather of Daoist Studies in Japan

oracle bones   Carapaces of turtles or shoulder blades of cattle used for divination in the Shang dynasty, covered in notations about the questions asked

oratory   Quiet chamber where sick followers of the Celestial Masters reflected on their sins

ordination Formal transfer of precepts, scriptures, and ritual methods; attainment of a certain rank in the hierarchy of priests

Orthodox Daoism of America Daoist temple and training center, founded by Liu Ming, in northern California

Orthodox Unity Formal appellation of the Celestial Masters

Palace of Eternal Happiness (Yongle gong) Main Complete Perfection temple, dedicated to Lü Dongbin and other patriarchs; in Ruichong (Shaanxi), moved in 1999 to Longquan; famous for its fourteenth-century murals of the Daoist pantheon

Penglai Daoist paradise island in the eastern sea, part of a group of five islands, carried on the backs of supernatural turtles

Pengzu Ancient immortal, believed to have lived for over 800 years

perfected Ideal human in the *Zhuangzi*, who goes along perfectly with the patterns of Dao; also designation of immortal officers in the heavens of Highest Clarity

planchette Wooden tray of sand with writing implement attached, into which the spirits descend during spirit-writing séances

Pole Star (Beiji) Central star in the sky, the foundation of the world, root of yin and yang

primitivists Proto-Daoist school documented in the *Zhuangzi* that eschews all culture and wishes to return to the Stone Age

principle (*li*) Concept of cosmic structure inherent in Dao; the abstract, patterning partner to *qi*, the material base; key concept in Neo-Confucianism

purgation (*zhai*) Religious retreat or festival developed in the Numinous Treasure school that celebrates seasonal change, prays for political stability, or aids in the expiation of sins

qi Vital energy, life force, the material aspect of Dao that makes up all existence; resposible for human life expectancy, health, and good fortune, it appears in two major forms: primordial and postnata, and its flow can be proper or wayward, excessive or deficient

qigong Lit. "Energy Work," a modern adaptation of traditional healing exercises; name coined by the Chinese Communist Party; system cleansed of all spiritual and "superstitious" elements

Qing Xitai Grandfather of Daoist Studies in China

Qingcheng Mountain Holy Daoist mountain in northwestern Sichuan; alleged location of Zhang Daoling's first revelation of the Celestial Masters covenant

Qingjing pai Lineage of Clarity and Stillness founded by Sun Buer; major order of Daoist nuns

Qiu Chuji (1148–1227) Leader of Complete Perfection school; founder of Longmen lineage; patriarch of all Chinese religions as appointed by Chinggis Khan

***Qizhen shizhuan* (Seven Daoist Masters)** Popular novel of the late Ming describing the marvelous exploits of the Seven Perfected of Complete Perfection Daoism

Queen Mother of the West   Ancient mother and nature goddess, in Daoism the representative of the powers of yin and queen of immortals

Quegu shiqi (**Eliminating Grains and Eating** *Qi*)   Mawangdui medical manuscript on the replacement of physical nourishment with *qi*

Quong Ming Taoist and Buddhist Association   Daoism community temple in San Francisco

Red bird   Symbolic animal of the south; often associated with the phoenix

Register   List of divine generals transmitted in formal initiations and worn by followers of the Celestial Masters

Rio Donation (fl. 994)   Codifier of Heavenly Heart scriptures and talismans

Ritual formality   Key concept of Confucianism, expressed on the three levels of interpersonal politeness, institutional correctness, and ritual propriety

Ritual master (*fishy*)   Lay Daoism practitioner who works rites on behalf of the people

River Chart   Sacred map of the universe revealed by a dragon in the Yellow River

Roan Jig (210–263)   Poet who wrote a major work on the Great Man, expressing his frustration and desire to escape the worldly fetters

Rope tuna (**Carnal Prayer Mat**)   Pornographic novel of the early Sing that includes numerous Daoism motifs

Ruler of Fates (Sliming)   Chief of the celestial administration, manager of the books of life and death

Sage   Ideal human in the *Diode jingo*, realizing simplicity and notation, preferably the ruler

Santana nixie jingo (**Inner Explanation of the Three Heavens**)   fifth-century scripture outlining the creation according to the Celestial Masters

Scripture   Sacred Daoism text, originally created from pure Dao, stored in the highest heavens, and revealed to humanity

Seven Perfected   Group of Complete Perfection leaders after the founder Wang Changing; founders of main lineages

Shangri   Highest Ruler, chief ancestor of Shan dynasty

Sheyang lun (**On Preserving and Nourishing [Life]**)   Manual on dietary and *qi* methods by Sun Simiao

Shiji (**Historical Records**)   Earliest systematic Chinese history, dated to 104 B.C.E.

Shingling Longboat data (**Great Rites of Highest Clarity and Numinous Treasure**)   Major compendium of Song rites by Ming Bali

Shiwen (**Ten Questions**)   Mawangdui manuscript on medical and breathing practices

Shoaling   Buddhist Monastery at the foot of the Southern Peak near Buoying; famous as the residence of Bodhidharma, the first patriarch of Zen in China; also famous martial arts center

Shugendō   Japanese ascetic mountain worship; practiced under Buddhist auspices but includes numerous Daoist concepts and techniques

Shujing (**Book of History**)   Confucian classic of the Zhou dynasty that details historical events and principles of government

Shun   Mythical sage ruler, paragon of Confucian virtue, especially filial piety

Siji mingke (**Illustrious Regulations of the Four Ultimates**)   Fifth-century text that spells out details of the celestial administration in Daoism

Silvers, Brock   Founder and director of the Taoist Restoration Society, which helps rebuild temples in China, as well as of the United States Daoist Association, an online network for Daoist practice

Sima Chengzhen (647–735)   Twelfth patriarch of Highest Clarity and prolific writer of works on Daoist practice

Sima Xiangru (179–117 B.C.E.)   Han aristocrat and author of a major poem featuring the Great Man, a combination of emperor, shaman, and perfected

sitting in oblivion   Cultivation practice in the *Zhuangzi* by which perception and intellect are driven out in favor of a state of complete forgetfulness and openness to Dao

six arts   Ways to realize the Confucian ideal through the practice of poetry, calligraphy, numbers, music (lute), archery, and charioteering

Six Classics   The *Books of Changes, Rites, Songs, Music,* and *History,* as well as the *Spring and Autumn Annals*; allegedly edited and standardized by Confucius, they formed the key to official training in traditional China

Six Healing Sounds   Method of exhalation and breath control to enhance the vitality of the inner organs

sixty-year cycle   System of counting years by combining heavenly branches and earthly stems; key to human life cycles and political renewals

Society for the Study of Chinese Religions   Major American research organization supporting Daoist Studies

solar periods   Twenty-four two-week divisions of the year matching weather patterns and the agricultural cycle

Song Mountain (1440m)   Sacred peak of the center; near Luoyang, also seat of Shaolin monastery

souls   Aspects of Heaven and Earth in human beings, divided according to yang and yin into spirit and material souls (*hun, po*)

spirit (*shen*)   Subtle form of *qi* that works mainly through the heart, governing the psychological and spiritual aspects of the person

spirit-writing   Automatic writing of messages from the otherworld while in trance

Summoning for Investigation   Exorcistic ritual to cure diseases with otherworldly means

Sun Buer (1119–1182)   Only female member of the Seven Perfected; leading disciple of Wang Chongyang; founder of Qingjing lineage within Complete Perfection

Sun Simiao (582–683)   Tang physician and alchemist, wrote extensively on Daoist practice

Sun Wukong   The immortal monkey king at the center of the novel *Xiyou ji'*

taboo   Prohibition against certain actions that might cause cosmic disruptions

Tai Mountain (1545m)   Sacred peak of the east; near Confucius's birthplace in Shandong; also seat of the otherworld administration and center of the realm of the dead in Han China

taiji quan   Lit. "Great Ultimate Boxing," a form of unarmed combat executed in gentle movements with emphasis on relaxation and suppleness; developed in the early Qing dynasty (seventeenth century)

Taiji tu **(Chart of the Great Ultimate)**   Song-dynasty depiction of cosmic unfolding

Taiping jing **(Scripture of Great Peace)**   Main text of the Way of Great Peace organization; lost after their rebellion in 184 and reconstituted in the late sixth century

Taiping jing shengjun bizhi **(Secret Instructions of the Holy Lord on the Scripture of Great Peace)**   Tang supplement to the *Taiping jing* that describes the visualization of lights in the body

talismans   Written signs of divine connection; tallies that come in two halves; usually written on special paper with red ink using celestial characters

Tan Zixiao (fl. 935)   Founder of the school of the Heavenly Heart

Tao Hongjing (456–536)   First patriarch of Highest Clarity; master of alchemy and pharmacology; collector of the original Highest Clarity revelations and author of the *Zhen'gao*

Taoist Resources   Specialized Daoist journal, 1988–1997

Taoist Sanctuary (now Taoist Institute)   Daoist temple and training center, founded by Kenneth Dickerson, in Los Angeles

Temple of Mystery and Wonder (Xuanmiao guan)   Main Daoist temple in Suzhou

theocracy   Form of government where religious structures determine political and administrative powers; Daoist management of the Toba-Wei state, 424–451

Three Caverns   Administrative division of Daoist schools, based on a textual classification

Three Primes   Major festivals of the Celestial Masters, on the full moon of the first, seventh, and tenth months

Three Pure Ones (Sanqing)–   Central deities of the main Daoist schools, Highest Clarity, Numinous Treasure, and Three Sovereigns

Three Sovereigns Mythical sage rulers at the beginning of the universe who ruled in harmony and perfection

Three Worlds Levels of worldly existence consisting of twenty-eight heavens, adopted from Buddhism: World of Desire, Form, and Formlessness

Three Worms Supernatural agents living in human beings (head, chest, and lower body) who report misdeeds to the celestial officers once every two month, then return to make people sick or cause misfortune

Thunder Rites (*leifa*) Ritual and exorcism associated with the Department of Thunder, important administration of fate since the Song

***Tianguan sandu* (Three Ways to Go Beyond the Heavenly Pass)** Set of visualization and incantation instructions of Highest Clarity

***Tōhō shūkyō* (Eastern Religions)** Main Japanese journal on Daoist Studies

trigrams Symbols consisting of three broken (yin) and unbroken (yang) lines that signify cosmic directions and dimensions

turtle and snake Symbolic animals of the north; emblem of the Dark Warrior

virtues Five human characteristics to aspire to, first formulated by Confucius: benevolence, righteousness, wisdom, propriety, and honesty

Wang Bi (226–249) Daoist thinker of Profound Learning and major commentator of the *Daode jing*

Wang Changyue (d. 1680) Abbot of the White Cloud Temple and representative of the Longmen lineage who created the integrated ordination hierarchy of Complete Perfection

Wang Chengya Director of the Daoist Long Life Center; Beijing University graduate and White Cloud ordinand

Wang Chongyang (1112–1170) Founder of the school of Complete Perfection, former government official in north China, then eccentric ascetic and religious leader in Shandong

Wang Dao (1487–1547) Neo-Confucian thinker who integrated Daoist notions into his system

Wang Yangming (1517–1579) Neo-Confucian thinker who integrated both Buddhist and Daoist notions into his system

Western Park (Xiyuan) Daoist paradise garden built by the Jiajing Emperor in the 1550s

White Cloud Temple (Baiyun guan) Headquarters of the Complete Perfection school; seat of the Chinese Daoist Association

white tiger Symbolic animal of the west; also name of ingredient in internal alchemy

Winn, Michael (b. 1952) Leader of Healing Dao in America today; president of Healing Dao University in North Carolina

women's internal alchemy (*nüdan*) Internal alchemy designed specifically for women; documented in texts since the eighteenth century

Wormy Rebel (Chiyou)   Enemy and Traitor of the Yellow Emperor; reason for the first war

Wu Chengen (d.1582)   Author of the *Xiyou ji*

Wu Yuantai (fl. 1566)   Author of the *Dongyou ji*

Wudang Mountain   Daoist mountain in northwestern Hubei; main center of worship of the Dark Warrior; famous for its Daoist martial arts

Wuqin wu gongfa tushuo (**Illustrated Explanation of Five Animal Dance Practice**)   17th-century description of the Five Animal Frolics, adapted for women adepts

Xiang'er   Celestial Masters Commentary to the *Daode jing*, ascribed to Zhang Lu, foundation of earliest Daoist precepts

Xixin ming (**On resting the Mind**)   seventh-century Chan document on mind cultivation

Xiyou ji (**Journey to the West**)   Also translated as *Monkey*, famous novel about the monkey king Sun Wukung who accompanies the Buddhist pilgrim Xuanzang on his travels to India; includes numerous Daoist magical scenes and wondrous motifs

Xiyou ji (**Journey to the West**)   Record of Qiu Chuji's travels to meet Chinggis Khan in the 1220s

Xu brothers   Recipients and recorders of the Highest Clarity revelations in the 360s

Xu Huangmin (361–429)   Highest Clarity leader, grandson of the original recipients, who started to transmit the texts to a wider audience

Xu Hui (b. 341)   Highest Clarity leader who inherited the original revelations, then vanished into the mountains

Xu Zhonglin (d. 1566)   Author of the *Fengshen yanyi*

Xuanzang (596–664)   Buddhist pilgrim who traveled to India to obtain authentic sutras

Xuanzhen jingjue (**Scripture of the Mysterious Perfected**)   Technical manual of Highest Clarity, probably of Tang origin, describing sexual relations with deities

Yang Luchan (1799–1872)   Creator of taijiquan in Yang style; disciple of Chen Zhang xing

Yang Xi (b. 330)   Medium and main transmitter of the Highest Clarity revelations

Yang Xizhen (1101–1124)   Founder of the school of Youthful Incipience

Yangsheng yaoji (**Long Life Compendium**)   fourth-century text on longevity techniques

Yao   Mythical sage ruler, paragon of Confucian virtue

Yellow Court   Residence of central deity, in some cases Lord Lao, in the body; located usually in the abdomen (spleen), may also be placed in the head

Yellow Emperor (Huangdi) Major culture hero of ancient China, god of the center, mediator between humans and celestials

Yellow Turbans Name of the followers of the Way of Great Peace as they rose in rebellion in the *jiazi* year of 184

Yi Eng (One Cloud) Hong Kong Daoist master who taught internal alchemy to Mantak Chia and thus is the grandfather of Healing Dao

Yijing **(Book of Changes)**– Zhou-dynasty divination manual that gives advice on how to best follow the course of Heaven

Yin Tong Alleged descendant of Yin Xi who established Louguan in the fifth century

Yin Xi Legendary guardian of the border pass who coerced Laozi into formulating his teachings and writing the *Daode jing*

Yinshu **(Stretch Book)** Manuscript dated to 186 B.C.E. outlining the concrete practice of healing exercises

Yin-Yang Complementary tendencies of nature; originally names of the shady and sunny sides of a hill, then indicating d sets of dynamic movement: up and down, night and day, begin and end, and so on

Yinyuan jing **(Scripture of Karmic Retribution)** Sixth-century scripture detailing the karmic effects of good and bad deeds

Yoshioka Yoshitoyo Pioneer Daoist scholar in Japan

Youthful Incipience (Tongchu) Song school that combined Thunder Rites, exorcism, and Celestial Masters ritual

Yu Xiangtou (fl. 1588–1609) **Author of the** *Beiyou ji*

Yu Mythical sage ruler and founder of the Xia dyansty; master of the great flood; recipient of Numinous Treasure talismans

Yuanshi wulao zhenwen **(Perfect Writings of the Five Ancient Lords of Primordial Beginning)** Primary scripture of Numinous Treasure, dated to the late fourth century

Yue Chongdai First president of the Chinese Daoist Association

Yuen-Yuen Institute Syncretistic institution in Hong Kong that combines Confucian ethics with Buddhist scriptures and Daoist practice; location of a large Grand Offering in 2007; parent organization of Fung Loy Kok

Zangmigong (Tantric Qigong) New religion in the 1990s, featuring Tibetan Buddhist practices in qigong guise

Zhan Ruoshui (1466–1560) Neo-Confucian thinker who integrated Daoist notions into his system

Zhang Daoling Founder of the Celestial Masters, the first organized Daoist community, upon a revelation from Lord Lao in 142

Zhang Lu Third Celestial Master and grandson of Zhang Daoling; submitted to the warlord Cao Cao

***Zhang Sanfeng quanji* (Complete Collection of Zhang Sanfeng)**   The "auto-biography" of the legendary immortal Zhang Sanfeng, channeled to Li Xiyue in nineteenth-century Sichuan

Zhang Sanfeng   Legendary Daoist of the Song or early Ming dynasty who supposedly invented taiji quan; information on his life, works, and teachings came from an "auto-biography," channeled in the nineteenth century

***Zhen'gao* (Declarations of the Perfected)**   Key record of Highest Clarity revelations in twenty chapters, compiled by Tao Hongjing around the year 500

Zhonggong (Central Qigong)   New religion in the 1990s, featuring Buddhist and Daosit practices in qigong guise

Zhongli Quan   Member of the Eight Immortals and teacher of Lü Dongbin; deity of Complete Perfection

***Zhougui jing* (Scripture on Cursing Demons)**   Celestial Masters work on how to banish demons

***Zhuangzi* (Book of Master Zhuang)**   Second major text of ancient Daoism, prose work in thirty-three chapters, ascribed to Zhuang Zhou (c. 370–290 B.C.E.)

zodiac   Twelve animals signifying years, based on the Jupiter cycle, today on charts commonly found in Chinese restaurants

Zou Yan (c. 350–270 B.C.E.)   Cosmological thinker credited with developing the foundations of the five phases system

***Zuowang lun* (On Sitting in Oblivion)**   Outline of Daoist meditation in seven stages by Sima Chengzhen (eighth century)

Index

Introducing Buddhism

Charles S. Prebish and Damien Keown

'An up-to-date textbook for beginners as well as advanced students of Buddhism. Its clear structure helps beginners getting oriented in the complex field of Buddhism, and its respective chapters are rich in detailed information for students who already have some basic knowledge. Instructors and students alike will appreciate its didactic tools. I have used this book in my classes, with great success.'

Oliver Freiberger, University of Texas at Austin

Introducing Buddhism is the ideal resource for all students beginning the study of this fascinating religion. Damien Keown and Charles S. Prebish, two of today's leading Buddhist scholars, explain the key teachings of Buddhism, and trace the historical development and spread of the religion from its beginnings down to the present day. A chapter is devoted to each of the major regions where Buddhism has flourished: India, South East Asia, East Asia and Tibet. In addition to this regional focus, the introduction takes contemporary concerns into account, covering important and relevant topics such as Engaged Buddhism, Buddhist Ethics and Buddhism and the Western World, as well as a chapter devoted to Meditation.

Introducing Buddhism also includes illustrations, lively quotations from original sources, learning goals, summary boxes, questions for discussion, and suggestions for further reading, to aid study and revision.

ISBN10: 0-415-39234-9 (hbk)
ISBN10: 0-415-39235-7 (pbk)

ISBN13: 978-0-415-39234-1 (hbk)
ISBN13: 978-0-415-39235-8 (pbk)

Related titles from Routledge

Introducing Hinduism

Hillary Rodrigues

'A welcome addition to the current range of introductory materials on Hinduism....
Rodrigues' treatment is sympathetic and sensitive, managing to suggest a sense of
both of the breadth and richness of Hindu tradition and of its underlying unity.'
Sushil Mittal, James Madison University, USA

Introducing Hinduism describes the array of beliefs and practices of the majority of
the people of South Asia, particularly those of India and Nepal.

Introducing Hinduism is the ideal starting point for students wishing to undertake
a comprehensive study of this fascinating religion. This lively introduction explores
the complexities of Hinduism, including its social structures, especially its caste
system, its rituals and many scriptures, its vast mythology and varieties of deities
and its religious philosophies. Hillary Rodrigues, an experienced teacher of the
Hindu tradition, emphasises the importance of Hindu rituals and practice, subjects
of particular interest in contemporary scholarship.

Illustrated throughout, the book also includes text boxes, summary charts, a
glossary and a list of further reading to aid students' understanding and revision.

ISBN13: 978-0-415-39268-6 (hbk)
ISBN13: 978-0-415-39269-3 (pbk)

Related titles from Routledge

Religions of South Asia

Edited by Sushil Mittal and Gene R. Thursby

South Asia is home to many of the world's most vibrant religious faiths. It is also one of the most dynamic and historically rich regions on earth, where changing political and social structures have caused religions to interact and hybridize in unique ways. This textbook introduces the contemporary religions of South Asia, from the indigenous religions such as the Hindu, Jain, Buddhist and Sikh traditions, to incoming influences such as Christianity, Judaism and Islam. In ten chapters, it surveys the nine leading belief systems of South Asia and explains their history, practices, values and worldviews. A final chapter helps students relate what they have learnt to religious theory, paving the way for future study.

Entirely written by leading experts, *Religions of South Asia* combines solid scholarship with clear and lively writing to provide students with an accessible and comprehensive introduction. All chapters are specially designed to aid cross-religious comparison, following a standard format covering set topics and issues; the book reveals to students the core principles of each faith, compares it to neighboring traditions, and its particular place in South Asian history and society. It is a perfect resource for all students of South Asia's diverse and fascinating faiths.

ISBN10: 0-415-22390-3 (hbk)
ISBN10: 0-415-22391-1 (pbk)

ISBN13: 978-0-415-22390-4 (hbk)
ISBN13: 978-0-415-22391-1 (pbk)

Available at all good bookshops
For ordering and further information please visit:
www.routledge.com

Related titles from Routledge

Japanese Cinema
Texts and Contexts

Edited by Alastair Phillips and Julian Stringer

Japanese Cinema: Texts and Contexts includes twenty-four articles on key films of Japanese cinema, from the silent era to the present day, providing a comprehensive introduction to Japanese cinema history and Japanese culture and society.

Studying a range of important films, from *Late Spring, Seven Samurai* and *In the Realm of the Senses* to *Godzilla, Hana-Bi* and *Ring*, the collection includes discussion of all the major directors of Japanese cinema including Ozu, Mizoguchi, Kurosawa, Oshima, Suzuki, Kitano and Miyazaki.

Each chapter discusses the film in relation to aesthetic, industrial or critical issues and ends with a complete filmography for each director. The book also includes a full glossary of terms and a comprehensive bibliography of readings on Japanese cinema.

Bringing together leading international scholars and showcasing pioneering new research, this book is essential reading for all students and general readers interested in one of the world's most important film industries.

Contributors: Carole Cavanaugh, Darrell William Davis, Rayna Denison, David Desser, Linda Ehrlich, Freda Freiberg, Aaron Gerow, Alexander Jacoby, D.P. Martinez, Keiko I. McDonald, Joan Mellen, Daisuke Miyao, Mori Toshie, Abé Mark Nornes, Alastair Phillips, Michael Raine, Donald Richie, Catherine Russell, Isolde Standish, Julian Stringer, Mitsuyo Wada-Marciano, Yomota Inuhiko, Mitsuhiro Yoshimoto.

ISBN13: 978-0-415-32847-0 (hbk)
ISBN13: 978-0-415-32848-7 (pbk)